P9-CES-092

HOW PSYCHOTHERAPY REALLY WORKS

Also by Willard Gaylin, M.D.

*Psychodynamic Understanding of Depression:
The Meaning of Despair*

In the Service of Their Country: War Resisters in Prison

Partial Justice: A Study of Bias in Sentencing

Caring

Doing Good: The Limits of Benevolence
(with I. Glasser, S. Marcus, and D. Rothman)

Feelings: Our Vital Signs

The Killing of Bonnie Garland: A Question of Justice

The Rage Within: Anger in Modern Life

Rediscovering Love

*Adam and Eve and Pinocchio: On Being and
Becoming Human*

The Male Ego

*The Perversion of Autonomy:
The Proper Uses of Coercion and Restraints
in a Liberal Society*
(with Bruce Jennings)

HOW PSYCHOTHERAPY REALLY WORKS

*How It Works When It Works
and Why Sometimes It Doesn't*

WILLARD GAYLIN, M.D.

Contemporary Books

Chicago New York San Francisco Lisbon London Madrid Mexico City
Milan New Delhi San Juan Seoul Singapore Sydney Toronto

Library of Congress Cataloging-in-Publication Data

Gaylin, Willard.
    How Psychotherapy Really Works: How it works when it works and why
sometimes / Willard Gaylin.
        p.   cm.
    Prev. published as: Talk is not enough. Boston: Little, Brown, © 2000.
    Includes index.
    ISBN 0-8092-9475-3
    1. Psychodynamic psychotherapy.   I. Title.

RC489.P72 G39   2001
616.89'14—dc21   2001028565

Contemporary Books

A Division of The *McGraw-Hill* Companies

This edition is reprinted by arrangement with Little, Brown and Company (Inc.), New York,
New York. All rights reserved.

Copyright © 2001 by Willard Gaylin, M.D. All rights reserved. Printed in the United States
of America. Except as permitted under the United States Copyright Act of 1976, no part of
this publication may be reproduced or distributed in any form or by any means, or stored
in a database or retrieval system, without the prior written permission of the publisher.

1 2 3 4 5 6 7 8 9 0   LBM/LBM   0 9 8 7 6 5 4 3 2 1

ISBN 0-8092-9475-3

The identity of patients referred to in this book, and certain details about them, have been
modified and/or are presented in composite form.

Acknowledgments
"Lassie! Get Help!!" © The New Yorker Collection 1989. Danny Shanahan from
cartoonbank.com. All rights reserved.
"Ohio," by Leonard Bernstein, Betty Comden, and Adolph Green. © 1953 (renewed)
Chappell & Co. & Polygram International Music Publishing Inc. All rights administered by
Chappell & Co. All rights reserved. Used by permission, Warner Bros. Publications U.S.
Inc., Miami, FL 33014.

This book was set in Sabon
Printed and bound by Lake Book Manufacturing

Cover design by Monica Baziuk
Cover illustration © Photonica/Emily Miller

McGraw-Hill books are available at special quantity discounts to use as premiums and
sales promotions, or for use in corporate training programs. For more information, please
write to the Director of Special Sales, Professional Publishing, McGraw-Hill, Two Penn
Plaza, New York, NY 10121-2298. Or contact your local bookstore.

This book is printed on acid-free paper.

My patients constitute a community of intelligent and engaging individuals who have honored me with their trust, confounded me by their courage, and enlightened me with their wisdom. They have informed my understanding of human nature while enriching my life. It is to them that this book is dedicated.

Contents

HOW PSYCHOTHERAPY REALLY WORKS

Introduction: Getting Help

EVERYBODY seems to be going for help these days. They're going because of depression and despair; for phobias, obsessions, and compulsions; for anxiety and anguish; for migraine headaches, irritable bowels, asthma, and psoriasis; for problems with impotence and sterility; failing marriages and faltering careers; addictions to drugs, alcohol, gambling, sex, food, and shopping (yes, shopping); lack of pleasure and absence of commitment. In other words, for everything from nagging dissatisfactions to profound dysfunctions, and from the chronically general to the most acutely specific.

Who are all these people seeking help? What is driving them? And what happens to them when they do enter treatment? The answer to the last question — what it means to get help through psychotherapy — is the subject of this book.

Although we live in a society that has become psychologically saturated, psychotherapy still seems to have a somewhat clouded image. It has been discovered by the masses only to be abandoned by the taste makers. The "in" magazines of the intellectuals and literati are currently preoccupied with anatomical brain centers for specific emotions, genes for complex behavior, and the chemicals that mediate perceptions. Psychotherapy — the wide range of "talking" therapies — is now, if not quite unfashionable, at least not cutting edge. This is a book about psychotherapy by a man who still passionately believes in it.

Actually, psychological illness has never been accorded the same respect bestowed on physical illnesses. For all our current sophistication, there remains a tenebrous ambiguity that contaminates our attitude about the mentally ill. Public figures with cancer are treated not just as tragic victims, but as heroes — as though being cut down by a malignant disease endows its victim with nobility. There is no equivalent eminence granted even the severely mentally ill. Those cursed with depression or schizophrenia shroud their miseries from public exposure, being only too aware of the faint but ubiquitous scent of opprobrium that seems to accompany any public recognition of their equally tragic illness. As a result mental illness lacks gravitas; it is not taken as seriously.

This situation may have been compounded by two quite different developments in the mental health field in the twentieth century. The first is the expanding definition of mental sickness. We have moved a long way from the original prototypes — the "madmen" and the "lunatics" of the nineteenth century. They were not treated well, but they were taken seriously. These were grotesque and scary creatures. They were the lurking presences in *Jane Eyre, Dr. Jekyll and Mr. Hyde,* and *The Woman in White.* They were patently different from "normal" people like you and me.

By the 1950s the patients who crowded the psychoanalyst's office *were* like you and me. Their distress was not always visible and did not take grotesque forms. The heroine of Moss Hart's *Lady in the Dark* seems charming and amusing, dallying with her "neurosis" in the manner of a nineteenth-century gentlewoman suffering from the vapors. Psychotherapy began to be seen as trivial or self-indulgent, something for bored, rich Park Avenue ladies to do in their spare time.

The second factor that has served to trivialize neurotic problems is the precipitous decline in the reputation of psychoanalysis over the past forty years. Psychoanalysis, born at the close of the nineteenth century, is the most formal and rigid form of psychotherapy. It demands four-times-a-week attendance for years, and thus is not financially accessible to many. But psychoanalysis was the prototype from which so many of the talking therapies derived, and a confusion between psychoanalysis and other forms of talking therapy has always existed.

Psychoanalysis *was* oversold in its heyday following World War II, and the psychoanalysts were arrogant. In certain circles, particularly in the arts, psychoanalysis became the "in" thing. Everybody — at least everybody who was anybody — seemed to be doing it, and the cohort of psychoanalytic patients in creative circles became insufferable in their public discussions about their therapies. The world of Woody Allen has never played well in the heartland of America. But I was in psychoanalytic practice during those forty years, and my patients were not the clichéd narcissists of the Allen movies. They were decent people who were suffering, and as their therapist I shared their suffering. Nonetheless, psychoanalysis seemed pretentious, promising much more than it could deliver. People became disillusioned and, worse, bored by the whole process. And it was time consuming. And it was expensive.

Once the hegemony of psychoanalytic therapy was shattered, quirkier, trendier, slicker treatments emerged (EST and other forms of cathartic weekend cures), only further confusing the issue as to what psychotherapy was really all about.

Worthless and shoddy treatments in physical medicine eventually tend to be exposed. The patients don't get better; they may even die. With psychotherapy who knows who gets better? How is it defined? The fragmentation of therapies has led to an almost total chaos in the processes of selecting a therapist, understanding what to expect of therapy, and evaluating the quality of one's therapy. More and more people are seeking therapy in the wrong places, from the wrong people, for the wrong reasons, and with the wrong expectations.

The purpose of this book is to demystify psychotherapy, to examine the complex and often perplexing interactions between therapist and patient that produce significant changes in the patient's behavior and perceptions. How does therapy really work? How can mere talk change behavior? In order to answer these questions there must be some discussion of the nature of mental illness and the limits of therapy: who ought to seek therapy and who ought not, criteria for successful treatment, and so forth. But these topics will be introduced only when they directly bear on the basic discussion defined by this book's title.

Confusion about the nature of psychotherapy exists in the minds of its purveyors as well as its consumers. What exactly is it? Who can benefit from it? How is it done? How does it work? Who should do it — a physician-psychiatrist, a psychologist, a social worker, a minister, friend, guru, self-help author? The doubts and anxieties of prospective patients have only been confounded by the arrogance and certitude of various schools and practitioners all peddling their own version of revealed truth.

Over the years it has become apparent that psychotherapy often seems to work equally well independent of the conflicting schools of therapy and the theories under which they are presumably operating — Freudians, neo-Freudians, Jungians, Adlerians, gestalt therapists, interpersonal therapists, cognitive therapists. How can this be? Something common, and truly therapeutic, must underlie these seemingly contradictory theoretical frameworks.

To find the common elements, we must turn to Freud. The popularity of the current "trash Freud" movement notwithstanding, Freud lives on. While Sigmund Freud had little understanding of the true causes of mental illness, his understanding of human motivation was, and is, unparalleled. Almost all talk therapy utilizes Freudian concepts, whether this debt is acknowledged or not. Therefore, common elements can be found in seemingly diverse therapies.

I will not be including in my definition of psychotherapy such current practices as reflexology, crystalography, zone therapy, the Alexander method, massage, acupuncture, howling and hugging, nor magnetic fields. Nor will I be discussing other more respectable alternatives to psychotherapy, such as operant conditioning, yoga, twelve-step programs, and prayer. I will focus on therapies that involve a professional and his patient seeking understanding and change through a special form of communication — what I have described earlier as the talking therapies. Some major points that will be covered in detail are:

- *Catharsis.* What is the value of talk? It was once thought that talking about a traumatic past event would relieve the pressure. Well, it is not true. If it were we could "catharse" by talking to ourselves in front of a bathroom mirror, or by screaming in the woods, for that matter. Yet there is some profound change that does occur when talking to another person about our sins or our symptoms (are these simply different words for the same undesirable behavior?). What, then, is catharsis?

- *Insight.* Does knowledge change behavior? Saint Paul doubted this 2000 years ago: "I do not understand my own actions. For I do not do what I want, but I do the very thing I hate. . . . I can will what is right, but I cannot do it" (Rom. 7:13). One of the great theoreticians of psychoanalysis, Dr. Abram Kardiner, once suggested to me that insight — then considered the primary agent of change — might actually be the *product* of change (a profound insight he never published). The relation between knowledge and conduct will be discussed in detail.

- *Delving into the past.* Does the past matter? In what way? Why do therapists spend so much time on childhood experiences and memories? How reliable are these memories? And is an exploration of them significant in changing future conduct?

- *The therapeutic alliance.* Something quite extraordinary happens during the course of a therapeutic relationship that does not occur in other profound relationships — penitent to priest, child to parent, lover to lover. What defines the therapeutic relationship? What are the necessary conditions for it to be operative? How are the training and the personality of the therapist relevant? Which is more important, training or personality?

- *The corrective emotional experience.* The great Hungarian American psychoanalyst Franz Alexander coined this term to describe a form of conditioning that goes on during therapy whereby the therapist, by refusing to conform to his patient's bias as to how he is "always" treated by others —

rejected, unloved, humiliated, disrespected — forces the patient to question the very generalizations that shape his life. The fundamental relationship of this to conditioning must be understood.

- *Approval, acceptance, and forgiveness.* These unrefined and unfashionable concepts are seen as being part of the stock-in-trade of such lesser advisers as friends, relatives, or ministers. Nonetheless, they are invariably smuggled into the therapeutic relationship, even though the therapist often advertises his product as "nondirective" and "nonjudgmental." Of course there are dangers when the therapist is too ready to offer support and reassurance. But without something akin to approval and forgiveness, it is unlikely that any therapy would be effective. How do therapists sneak them in? And must they be ashamed of such behavior?

- *Counseling, advice, and the introduction of values.* All three of these practices are presumably eschewed in psychoanalytic treatment. They belong to the world of social workers, counselors, ministers, friends, and family. Most psychoanalysts would see the absence of advice as a defining hallmark that separates psychoanalysis from other, and by their standards lesser, forms of therapy. Nonsense. Psychoanalysis and psychiatry constantly pass judgment on conduct, if only in choosing what to define as either neurotic or healthy. Throughout my discussions it will be made clear that in this regard orthodox psychoanalysis does not differ as much from the more loosely structured psychotherapies as it likes to claim.

- *The disputed role of will.* People suffering from emotional problems were originally stigmatized as weak and lacking in willpower. Recall the infamous reaction of General Patton, who slapped an emotionally traumatized soldier, labeling him a sniveling coward who lacked the courage and will to fight. Psychotherapists have struggled mightily to free neurotic behavior from the stigmatization of being merely an absence of willpower or character. Nonetheless, will and action do play a significant part in the process of getting better. Lying there waiting for change to happen will produce a very long wait indeed. Passivity only induces passivity. Sooner or later the patient must act — the patient, not the doctor — and in the here and now. How does one move a patient from knowledge to action?

• *Magic and mystery.* There is an art to therapy as distinguished from the science of therapy. When the art of therapy is given serious consideration, the personality and style of the therapist inevitably emerge as significant factors in the success of therapy.

The style of this book is central to its purpose. While it will be highly anecdotal — drawing on my more than thirty years of experience as a psychotherapist, psychoanalyst, and teacher — it is designed as a serious and necessary revision of current assumptions about the therapeutic process. Pseudoscientific jargon has inhibited progress in understanding behavior. Too often arcane technical terms are used to add weight to thin arguments. Mindful of George Orwell's admonition in "Politics and the English Language" that "a mass of Latin words falls upon the facts like soft snow, blurring the outlines and covering up all the details," I once asked a class at the Columbia Psychoanalytic Center to "translate" an article in the *Journal of the American Psychoanalytic Association* into everyday English. What emerged was embarrassingly close to *Dick and Jane:* "See Spot. Spot is a dog."

Fancy language must not be used to hide our ignorance. I intend to use everyday language. Simple language and accurate observation were originally the basic tools of psychoanalytic research. They should serve us here. It is time now for some demystification and clarity.

While this book is about the "workings" of psychotherapy — what *really* goes on in that office — to make sense of the process it is necessary first to consider who is going for help and why.

GAINING
KNOWLEDGE

Who Needs Help?

UNTIL THE END of the nineteenth century, few people with emotional disorders went for "help," i.e., professional treatment. They were taken, or more accurately dumped, someplace, that place usually being the insane asylum. These people were not defined as "mentally ill"; something was wrong with their brains or their nerves. The concept of *mental* illness — diseases of the *mind* as distinguished from the *brain* — had yet to evolve.

All illnesses, mental or otherwise, were perceived as dysfunctions whose causes were unknown but variously ascribed to humors, chills, trauma, spontaneous generation, or deterioration of organs from genetic or unknown causes. In other words, some physical disturbance of the anatomy (which by then was well understood) or the functions (which were only beginning to be understood) of the body parts.

The physician looked for a deterioration of structure comparable to what might be observed in any physical entity — a church spire, a bridge, a roof — due to aging or physical trauma. The prototype was heart disease. The heart is an extraordinary pump, with four valves and made of muscle fibers unlike any others in the body. Unlike all other muscle, it never fatigues or cramps from overuse. Thirty-eight million times a year it pumps! When it fails, one can safely assume some physical damage to the pump or its valves has occurred.

Consistent with this model, the insane were expected to have some damage to the brain. But this presented a problem. Abnormalities of the brain were difficult to identify, although the phrenologists tried. We did not (and still don't) understand even the basic anatomy of the brain and its interconnected parts, let alone the modes of operation of such higher activities as memory, cognition, and emotion.

In addition the insane were for years assumed to be different; not really sick but "possessed" by evil spirits — dybbuks, devils, or demons. The metaphoric term "bats in the belfry" had an almost literal meaning. Since the leading cause of psychosis in those days was advanced syphilis, the brain was indeed occupied by little "demons," in this case the spirochete *Treponema pallidum*. But there would be no awareness of this until the birth of modern medicine and the discovery of the germ theory. We had little understanding, for that matter, of the true cause of any disease, mental or physical.

In the latter half of the nineteenth century, all this would change. With a stunning burst of research in the laboratories of France and Germany, the discoveries of such great medical pioneers as Louis Pasteur, Robert Koch, Paul Ehrlich, Ignaz Semmelweis, Wilhelm Wundt, Hermann Helmholtz, and Rudolf Virchow initiated the age of modern medicine. The actual causes of common illnesses could now be scientifically demonstrated in the most rigorous manner, pointing the way to specific, cause-related treatments (although, tragically, seventy-five years would pass between Pasteur's proof of the germ theory in 1862 and the emergence of an effective treatment for bacterial infections with the discovery of the sulfonamides and penicillins). This was not to be the case with mental illness, a concept yet to be discovered.

Modern psychiatry actually emerged from the field of neurology, the study of the structure, function, and abnormalities of the nervous system. The leading center for neurological studies was in Paris, where the brilliant neurologist Jean-Martin Charcot (1825–1893) headed his famous clinic. This pioneer of modern neurology was particularly interested in the study of hysteria. As a disease hysteria does not in any way correlate to such lay usage as overreaction, hyperemotionalism, or a tendency to make scenes in public places. In actuality, the grand hysteria of the nineteenth century was characterized by something quite the opposite, a symptom called *la belle indifference* — the patients displayed profound physical symptoms to which they seemed quite indifferent.

What, then, was hysteria? Hysteria was a physical symptom that did not seem to have traditional physical causes — blindness, deafness, numbness of the hand or foot, and occasionally seizures. Charcot suggested that these were due to some nervous disorder, meaning literally an inflammation of nerves that affected the end organs — the eyes or the ears or the limbs. His theory was still firmly rooted in a physical model.

Sigmund Freud, the founder of psychoanalysis, may rightly be seen as the father of the concept of mental illness, and mental health. He was born in 1856 and received a medical degree from the University of Vienna in 1881. Freud was interested in research medicine, particularly in the field of neurology. He studied with Charcot and took Charcot's theory one giant step further. Freud decided that these nervous disorders — neuroses — were actually caused by psychic distress.

Freud's leap proved monumental. It abandoned the model common to all diseases — physical damage — and further put forward the incredible notion that feelings and ideas could produce illness as readily as toxins and bacteria. Freud postulated a new category of disease. These were clearly defined as *mental* disorders, impairments of function due to psychological processes, not inflammations of organs or neurological decays. Freud created the concept of mental illness as distinguished from brain damage. It was inevitable that we would now look at behavior in a new light and begin to redefine the mentally ill.

The Medicalization of Woe

Prior to Freud psychiatry only recognized what we now call the major psychoses. These patients were irrational and bizarre, different from the rest of us. "Crazy," "lunatic," "insane," were words interchangeably used by layman and physician. Freud began to elaborate an entire new group of illnesses, still not clearly defined as mental illnesses, which he labeled the psychoneuroses, that is, psychological disturbances caused by irritation or inflammation of the nerves. These were mental illnesses characterized by clear-cut symptoms — phobias, obsessions, paranoias, and the like — occurring in a *normal* (not insane) person.

In so doing, Freud destroyed the absolute dichotomy between sane and insane. The symptom neuroses suggested that one need not be totally crazy to demonstrate crazy patterns of behavior. Normal people like his friends and himself could have isolated pieces of behavior that were "crazy."

This began a process that led to an increasing array of mental disorders that, without preconception or intention, paved the way for a continuum from healthy to sick. The on-off light switch had been replaced by a dimmer, or rheostat.

Once the process was started, the elaboration of mental illnesses was rapid, and the distinction between the healthy and the ill was blurred and eventually obliterated.

While Freud was continuing to catalog the whole new species of symptom neuroses, a colleague was formulating a definition of mental illness that involved no symptoms at all! Wilhelm Reich was interested in the structure of character or personality. It occurred to him that one did not have to have bizarre and irrational symptoms to be defined as mentally ill; the very character of the individual could be so damaged as to reduce his capacity for work or pleasure. He affirmed, in psychological terms, Heraclitus's observation that "a man's character is his fate."

Reich's theory was a pioneering piece of work that anticipated the direction of modern psychiatry. Today, particularly in ambulatory or office psychotherapy, the vast majority of patients do not have traditional psychological symptoms; rather, they suffer from what we call "character disorders": they can't succeed at work, they can't fall in love, they can't make permanent attachments, they're afraid of competition, they are overly aggressive or too timid, excessively seductive or painfully shy.

Freud, meantime, had begun to elaborate a general theory of neurosis that could encompass such disparate behaviors as paranoia and compulsiveness, delusion and hysteria. Beyond just explaining diverse mental symptoms, this ambitious theory would lay the foundation for understanding normal character traits, attitudes, cultural beliefs, and the very institutions of society. Freud's general theory would come to be called the libido theory. Here, all mental illness was seen as a function of something gone awry with the developing sexual instinct. In order to define what went wrong, he had to elaborate a "normal" development for human beings. Just as one assumed a normal physical progression of the infant from sitting up to crawling to standing, from infancy to puberty to maturity, so one could assume a traditional normal psychosexual evolution.

By setting a standard scheme of development, Freud allowed for mental illness to be explained in terms of the *absence* of expected normal functioning, as well as in terms of malfunctioning. The patient did not have to demonstrate any aberrancy; he could simply be missing that which we assumed normal people must possess to qualify for a definition of health. Significant omissions became part of the definition of mental illness. The failure to be able to achieve orgasm would be defined as a mental illness, as would the failure to be able to maintain an erection in an adult relationship.

These changing standards expanded the population of the mentally ill far beyond the original group of psychotic patients. By definition the mentally ill now included those with psychoses, symptom neuroses, significant omissions from normal behavior, and character disorders.

The next large group of patients to be added to the population of the mentally ill emerged from the research of physicians concerned with basic physiology and internal medicine rather than psychiatry. Modern medicine began to see links between emotional states and the emergence of physical conditions: hives, neurodermatitis, diarrhea. In addition, emotions were implicated in the onset of what had been formerly seen as purely physical diseases: asthma, ulcerative colitis, migraine headache, peptic ulcer, hypertension. These would come to be called psychosomatic diseases or conditions. Here we had a group of patients who were "mentally" ill, with no mental symptoms; nothing now had to be wrong with your mental functioning for you to be included in the population of the mentally ill.

Some of the early theoreticians of psychosomatic medicine became heady with the opportunity of explaining physical symptoms in terms of psychodynamic causes. They slipped into a disastrous habit of looking for a specific dynamic, or force, for each disease. The silly season arrived and almost sank the ship before the voyage began. I recall reading a psychiatric paper that explained a peptic ulcer as being the "bite of the introjected [swallowed up] mother," whatever that was supposed to mean. More sophisticated researchers began to be aware that mental processes played a part in, but did not have to be the exclusive cause of, psychosomatic diseases. Today we understand how complicated the interplay is between emotion and body functions.

The layman always understood this. The diarrhea that occurred the night before the examination was not seen by the student as some unlucky accident compounding his anxiety about the examination, but rather the product and proof of that anxiety. We knew that we sweated when we were nervous, flushed with embarrassment, often wet our pants with terror or even excitement. But now exact research studies would enable people to understand the mechanisms by which an emotion could provoke a physical reaction. Anger could trigger an increase in hydrochloric acid secretion in the stomach, thus being, if not the sole cause, a contributing factor in a peptic ulcer. We know that specific allergies are due to specific antigens. We can demonstrate this by creating the symptoms in our patients with minute doses of these allergens. We also know that emotions can precipitate the very same allergic responses.

The more sophisticated we become in our knowledge of human physiology, the more we erase the mind-body dichotomy from human medicine. We know that emotions can trigger hormonal releases, changing blood chemistries that act on such end organs as bronchi, lungs, the colon, or the skin to produce symptoms.

This brutally abbreviated "history" of the evolution and expansion of the definition of mental illnesses is presented not for scholarly purposes, but merely to demonstrate why the ranks of the mentally ill have seemed to increase so precipitously. People aren't more neurotic than they once were. Society is not causing the population of the mentally ill to increase. We are changing the definitions.

By narrowing the amount of impairment necessary to define a person as mentally ill, we have broadened the population of the mentally ill. So much so that by the mid-twentieth century, major researchers could do epidemiological studies of the Upper East Side of Manhattan and discover that over 70 percent of the population had evidence and traits of mental distress. Admittedly, the Upper East Side of Manhattan is a peculiar location, but I suspect that these same researchers could have gone into any community and found the same proportion of mental problems.

Psychiatry had now captured 75 percent of the population as a potential constituency. But the net was still not fine enough. What about the 25 percent that eluded our grasp? The mental hygiene movement took care of them.

The mental hygiene movement emerging in midcentury was part of the increased interest in preventive medicine. If we now understood normal psychological development as we understood normal physical development, why should we wait for the deterioration of function or the development of symptoms? Why not act prophylactically, thus guaranteeing healthy development by insuring a proper psychosocial environment?

We had arrived at a point where almost everyone was a little sick and even the healthy could benefit from some psychological guidance. Everything would eventually become a form of mental illness, every failure, even a lack of success — a bad marriage, a disobedient child, antisocial behavior, ennui, mere unhappiness. This being the case, all sorts of problems that formerly might have been directed to ministers, counselors, friends, relatives, correctional officers, teachers, lovers, or parents could now be directed to psychiatrists. If all of these behaviors were a form of sickness, shouldn't they be treated by a doctor? In the beginning it worked just that way. The medicalization of misery led to an expanding population of psychotherapists who were psychiatrists, i.e., doctors.

So now "patients" were consulting with their "doctors," seeking "cures" for "illnesses" — miseries — that were never before perceived of as medical. We had engineered the medicalization of woe.

Consequences of the Medical Model

What had formerly been seen as unhappiness, or a crisis in confidence, or a moral failing was now defined as a clinical condition. Some might say: "What's the difference? Only the *name* of the game has been changed."

Nothing could be further from the truth. With a change of definition comes a change in rules and attitudes. When you go to a psychotherapist for your distress rather than to your minister, you are not simply speaking to a different person about the same problems. You are speaking to a different *professional* with different attitudes about your problems. As a result, your problems will be defined in different ways.

To be "sick" is different from being "bad" or even "unhappy." Compare therapy with the Catholic confessional — with which there is some similarity. Confession in either case can lead to some comfort or relief of distress. But what follows differs dramatically, depending on whether the behavior confided is defined as a sin or a symptom. The penitent goes to his priest confessing something he knows to be "sinful." The priest listens and — in a religion of forgiveness like Christianity — offers penance that absolves the penitent from the consequences of his immoral behavior, or sin. It is clear to both penitent and priest that what the individual has done was wrong, evil, sinful, immoral, name it what you will. The purpose of the confessional is to both condemn the sin and forgive the sinner.

Something much more complex happens in a medical model. The very same behavior is no longer defined as sinful, nor stigmatized. We do not condemn the symptom of a disease. No moral judgments are made about a festering sore or a leaky heart valve. A doctor does not look at your impetigo or your bloody sputum with disgust and condemnation. They are "not your fault." You are the suffering victim of your own symptoms. The doctor's role is to cure the symptoms that are disturbing your life. These symptoms are viewed as independent of your autonomy and therefore are not your responsibility.

To the psychotherapist, as well as to the sophisticated layman, the model of symptoms and disease in mental illness is perceived in the same manner as in physical illness. The drug addict — and all of the behavior that is interpreted as being contingent upon his addiction — is observed neutrally by the psychotherapist, without condemnation, without introduction of ideas of retribution or penance. Drug addicts are to be treated. Similarly, there will be no moral judgments made about the phobic, the obsessive, the hysteric, the kleptomaniac (formerly, "thief"), or the sexual voyeur (formerly, "Peeping Tom").

Being cast in the sick role places one in a different scenario from that of the sinner or criminal. The patient is not responsible for his symptom. It is visited upon him from a hostile environment or from his developmental past. The patient is neither sinner nor criminal, but a victim. He is not to be forgiven, he is to be pitied. He is not to receive penance, but treatment. He is not to receive condemnation and scorn, but succor and sympathy. Whatever we are prepared to define as a symptom of a disease, whether it be exhibitionism, alcoholism, or brutality, will be protected from moral judgment or *criminal culpability* under the medical model. *Theoretically* you are no more blameworthy for the bad temper that caused you to beat your wife than you would be for an epileptic seizure. This already suggests some of the problems that follow when attempting to apply the medical model (suitable to psychotherapy) to the broader world of social living.

The ramifications of the medical model are profound, influencing such diverse areas as the schools, the courts, and the workplace. Moral and legal culpability for many actions for which we would formerly have been held accountable are mitigated when such behavior is seen as the symptom of a disease rather than a willful choice. For our purposes here, it is only important to realize that the therapist, in his dealing with the same piece of behavior that the court or the priest had dealt with previously, will have a different frame of mind, create a different set of conditions, and institute different methods of change.

The Walking Wounded and the Worried Well

While the population of the mentally ill has grown dramatically since Freud's time (by definition, if by no other means), the percentage of that population who seek and receive treatment is still small. And a bizarre situation has evolved. The sickest, the traditional mentally ill, are receiving less attention than the less sick. Psychotherapy in particular has been occupied with treating the *least* disadvantaged. A number of events have conspired to create this anomaly.

A person's decision to go for psychiatric treatment is not determined by his psychological or emotional condition alone. Some of the most profoundly disturbed will never receive help, while others will devote years to treatment for the alleviation of what may be perceived by friends or acquaintances as a relatively minor dysfunction. An individual will seek psychotherapy not only because his mental health requires it, but also because certain social conditions are conducive to his going to a therapist.

A number of factors influence a person's decision to seek treatment: the extent to which a particular emotional illness burdens him socially or financially; the value he places on the function impaired by such illness; the readiness to define his pain (headaches) or disability (the inability to hold down a job) as a psychological problem; the degree of his understanding that emotional illnesses are treatable; the availability of psychotherapy; the availability of money for psychotherapy; the stigma he and his community attach to psychotherapy.

Let me offer some examples. If a sophisticated, urban, young, male advertising executive was suddenly to find himself incapable of maintaining an erection, he would be likely to end up in a psychotherapist's office, even fifty years ago. If a comparable woman was completely frigid, she would, until very recently, be unlikely to seek treatment.

This difference has been dictated by several facts. First, the biological peculiarity of the male genitalia is such that a man has to be aroused to perform. No interest means no action; the pleasure and procreative aspects of sex are linked. In a woman, however, sexual arousal and fecundity are biologically separated. A woman can, despite the total crippling of her sexual pleasure, support intercourse and be capable of procreating.

In addition, a man's impotence is publicly announced to his mate. A woman can dissemble. But more important, her rights to sexual pleasure had not been fully established until very recently. Many women simply did not know what they were missing, and when they did they did not feel the right to claim their pleasurable due. Orgasm was not fully established even in a woman's own mind, let alone in societal judgment, as her right and her norm. Whereas the *absence* of potency threatened the very identity of a man, the *presence* of female sexual passion was often viewed as somewhat inelegant and unladylike. Male and female sexual impotence are both crippling, yet one was much more likely to drive the individual to seek help than the other.

Even now, when the attitudes that contributed to such divergent behavior are changing, it remains true that an educated and sophisticated New York professional woman will be more likely to seek psychotherapy than a small-town or rural housewife. The sophisticated urban woman assumes that lack of orgasm is a medical problem; that it is treatable by psychotherapy; that there are therapists in the community who earn their living treating such conditions. Many unsophisticated women still view sex as a masculine pleasure and a feminine duty.

With neuroses in general, peer attitudes influence people's perspectives and determine their readiness to seek treatment. During the fifties, in certain professions such as acting, psychoanalysis was not only acceptable but de rigueur.

As previously suggested, geography can also be a factor. A white, upper-middle-class New Yorker is more likely to be analyzed than her Laramie or Biloxi counterpart. One reason is that there are more therapists in New York than elsewhere. Their mere availability permits people who are enduring certain problems to think in terms of therapeutic solutions.

The fact is that those who seek psychotherapy these days are not necessarily sicker than those who do not. They are often simply more ambitious, unwilling to settle for less than what they perceive as the fullest and richest life. Similarly, lack of education, social class, and religious bias all cause some people to go through life operating at less than their full potential rather than face what is seen as the indignity of seeking help.

That a person has undergone psychotherapy must not be perceived as an indication of emotional impairment. It may actually indicate reasonableness, courage, and emotional maturity. I have never found my patients to be a sicker population than my circle of friends.

Meanwhile, some perverse and paradoxical cultural effects are emerging in the attention we are paying to differing forms of mental illness. We have divided the population of the noninstitutionalized mentally ill into two divergent, and often politically antagonistic, camps, sometimes labeled the walking wounded and the worried well.

It early had become apparent to Freud and his immediate followers that psychoanalysis was ineffectual with the classically psychotic patients — those suffering from delusions, hallucinations, and major disruptions of lifestyle. Some psychotics were totally incapable of functioning on their own, but others — "compensated" psychotics — were still able to operate in the everyday world. Nonetheless, even this latter group, the so-called walking wounded, were screened out of the psychoanalyst's practice. This was not just because they were unresponsive to psychoanalytic methods, but also because psychoanalysis can be disastrous for them, precipitating acute psychotic breakdowns in schizophrenics who are tentatively holding on to their sense of reality.

Early treatment for severe psychoses consisted of rest, confinement, care, time, and nurture. In recent times we have seen the blessed emergence of psychotropic drugs. Antipsychotic drugs have revolutionized the treatment of the severely mentally ill. Many of these patients could still benefit from the support and counsel of a therapist, but, alas, they will often avoid therapy once their primary symptoms have been alleviated through drugs. In addition, such supportive treatment of psychotic patients is less dynamic, and therefore less exciting and challenging for most therapists. Chronic illness is "less fun" for physicians than acute illness. Curing is more exciting than caring. Both these factors — the patient's avoidance and the therapist's indifference — contribute to therapeutic neglect of this population.

The discrepancy in who gets psychotherapy has become illuminated in the battle of the bucks. In these days when budgets for health care are lean, with mental illness the particular stepchild, there is real danger that the sickest people, the traditional mentally ill — the walking wounded — are getting shortchanged.

Whether it is fair or not, those suffering from neuroses or simple maladjustments — the worried well — form the majority of patients in psychotherapy. The term does them an injustice. They are not well, and they are more than worried. They are suffering. These are, at any rate, the people who constitute the population that seeks ongoing psychotherapy (the "talking cures"), and these are the people that I will deal with in this book.

The Nondirective Interview

WHEN AN uninitiated patient first walks into a therapist's office, it becomes apparent that this is going to be a different experience — unlike medical treatment, physiotherapy, or rehabilitative therapy. No diagnostic equipment is visible; no nurses or technicians are scurrying around; there are no laboratories, no examining table, no equipment whatsoever. There may not even be a receptionist. More likely the patient has been forewarned by the therapist that she must enter an empty waiting room, and when her appointment time arrives, she will be received by the therapist himself.

Most singular and unexpected, in addition to having the place to herself, there will be no waiting in the waiting room! The analytic session begins and ends precisely on time. If it does not, one is in the hands of an idiosyncratic therapist. The failing may not be disastrous, but it should always be cautionary. The consultation room, when its doors are closed, will be insulated from sound from all other rooms — no half-walls here — and it is more likely to look like a small sitting room than a typical office. It will sometimes not even have a desk. Invariably it will have a couple of comfortable chairs, and almost always, when you are dealing with a psychoanalytic therapist, a couch.

Yet diagnostic and therapeutic equipment are all there. They are present in the persona and the skills of the therapist. Diagnosis and treatment will all take place through verbal communication between patient and therapist, occasionally supplemented by drugs.

Getting Started

If the therapist is a clinical psychologist, he may choose to begin with a battery of psychological tests. This is particularly true when dealing with children. But for the most part this is the exception and not the rule. When people think of psychotherapy, they think of talking cures. This is the great legacy of Freud and his collaborators from their work on hysteria. What is most amazing is that after one hundred years the basic principles of what ought to be done, what must be done, to effect improvement in the patient's condition have changed relatively little.

A revealing index of the historic change in attitudes about the techniques of psychotherapy may be gleaned by examining the changed decor of the psychotherapist's office. Photographs of Freud's study where he treated patients are revealing of the taste and personality of the man. Mementos and memorabilia are everywhere evident. His interest in antiquity is immediately apparent. Freud's office was a warm, cluttered, typically Victorian study. By contrast, when I was in training there were serious admonitions about office decoration, dictated by the perceived necessity of shielding patients from awareness of the personality of the therapist. One of my supervisors cautioned me about pictures, paintings, or telltale personal knickknacks that might excessively expose the patient to the conditions of my life or the nature of my personal interests.

There were even debates about whether diplomas and certificates of training should be on the walls, since they would reveal biographical data about the therapist. Some supervisors insisted that even if questioned about training one should not answer. The typical response to such inquiries was to redirect the question back to the patient with a statement like, "Why do you ask?" or "Why do you want to know?" The "anonymity" of the therapist is a benefit in a long-term, psychoanalytically oriented therapy. Presenting the therapist as a neutral and enigmatic figure allows the patient to impose his preconceived biases on the subject of the therapist, thus exposing those biases, a bit the way the interpretations of an amorphous inkblot in the Rorschach test reveal the inner fantasy life of the subject. This is the heart of the process called transference. The transference thus offers clues to the patient's unconscious attitudes about, and expectations from, authority figures.

In the service of the transference, questions about credentials often remain unanswered. This is a clear violation of generally accepted professional ethics and on occasion becomes a rationalization for the inexperienced or incompletely trained therapist to hide inadequacies. A patient has a right to know the qualifications of his therapist. A patient's failure to ask for some verification of training would seem to be worth questioning, for it implies a disrespect for the seriousness of the enterprise. Would the patient have a coronary bypass without confirming the credentials of his surgeon?

The post-Freudian assumption that the therapist must be as neutral a figure as possible was justified as encouraging the emergence of transference fantasies, allowing the patient to construct an image of the therapist that suited his need. There is some merit to this position, but the idea of the therapist as a tabula rasa is ludicrous and unnecessary. First, a great deal of information is always readily at hand. The patient sees the therapist, identifies age, stature, gender, accent, body build, taste, dress, and on and on. If total anonymity were really desirable, we could use technology to shield the patient from the therapist. We could place the therapist behind a one-way mirror and have him use a voice modulator. Or we could conduct therapy via E-mail.

Second, it is neither desirable nor, for that matter, necessary for the therapist to remain a blurred and enigmatic figure. Despite all of the apparent clues, the patient will still insist on seeing the therapist according to his own needs and lights. This is a demonstration of the power of the transference. This very need to distort his perceptions of the therapist will eventually be used by the therapist to enlighten the patient. Examples of this will be presented in the discussion of transference in Chapter 3.

Therapists today are somewhat less obsessive in their insistence on a neutral environment. Still, most of us will avoid provocative paintings — nudes or disturbing surrealist images — that might unsettle some patients, and we all will set serious limits to how forthcoming we will be to the queries of the inquisitive patient.

Most therapists will start with taking a history from the patient, but the method of obtaining this data is a far cry from the typical procedures in most medical offices. We are all used to giving histories to our physicians or their nurses, and we are all familiar with the checklist of questions that dominate the history taking. Often the doctor is not even looking at you while he is going down his list of various systems — respiratory, cardiovascular, skeletal, and so on — asking if you have ever suffered from traditional problems associated with your age and gender. In these days of medical miserliness, more often the patient will be sitting in the waiting room with a checklist, filling it out on his own.

The doctor will also traditionally take a family history and, again, what he is interested in is a record of diseases, this time those that may have genetic influence. Diabetes, seizures, cardiovascular disease — the list is increasing as we are more prepared to accept genetic directives.

The psychotherapist is also likely to take a history. But the history taking is visualized as the opening phase of the therapeutic process; therefore, the way the history is taken establishes directions and attitudes that will dominate the therapy throughout. The knowledgeable therapist draws no sharp distinctions between diagnosis and therapy. Therapy begins with the first contact with the patient, and the rules of engagement are set early.

The Longest Way Round as the Shortest Way Home

The psychoanalytic interview has been described as being nondirective, i.e., the direction of the interview is not explicit and its order and form seem to be dictated by the patient rather than the therapist. This psychoanalytic model pervades most forms of psychotherapy. Having said that, we must go on to say it was never literally true. Ultimately the interview is always "directed" by the therapist, although she will be guided by the prevailing emotions and interests of her patient. A patient who is not forced to follow a rigid and predesigned interrogatory format will inevitably, if elliptically, lead his therapist to the proper therapeutic course. The "ramblings" of a patient unconstrained by a fixed menu of questions inevitably provide the most direct path to the patient's problems.

The therapist is likely to start her history with a purposely casual, vague, ambiguous, and nonexplicit statement, such as, "Tell me about yourself," or "Please tell me why you are here," or "How can I help you?" The very subject that the patient chooses in starting, whether he is direct or elliptical, taciturn or prolix, tells us stuff as important as historical data. The nondirective approach allows for early self-presentation of style, character, personality, emotional range, and relatedness. Even when dealing with the same symptoms, for example those of depression, how the patient reveals these symptoms is informative. A blunt announcement of despair and pain from the patient signals a different person from one who taciturnly says, "What's the use," or from one who says, "My wife thought it would be a good idea." Even though all three patients may be suffering from acute depression, these variations in how the patient describes his problems will be of enormous help to the therapist in discerning the individual beneath the neurosis. Psychiatrists cannot afford the luxury or indulgence of treating diseases. We are forced to treat patients.

To many patients the therapeutic interview seems a discursive and uneconomic approach. Questions and answers always seem so much more direct, so much more informational, and many patients will want the therapist to ask them some questions. The therapist is trained to resist such requests. While questions and answers may seem more direct and informative, they have significant limitations. A questionnaire not only defines that which is included but also vast amounts of material that will be excluded.

This is the problem with psychological surveys. To think one knows the appropriate questions to ask is to assume too much. Still another problem with questions and answers relates to how one should value the answers. Are they truthful or deceptive? What does the answer to a question really tell you? When one questions someone as to personal feelings, the answer one gets is most likely to be what the patient thinks he should feel, what he would like to feel, what he thinks is prestigious to feel, and only incidentally what he really feels.

Sociologists dealing with large populations are dependent on sampling techniques. But the sophisticated ones have long since been disillusioned by direct questions and answers. While not necessarily trained in psychoanalytic interviewing, they have other methods. Direct observation of specific behavior correlates much more reliably in certain circumstances than does the answer to a question. For example, a measurement of the number of times a man makes a trip from his desk to the bathroom, the water cooler, the coffee shop on the ground floor; the number of accidents he has had; the number of illnesses he has; the number of personal telephone calls he makes — all of these will be far more reliable indicators of his interest in his work than his answer to the question "Are you interested in your work?"

Any group of typical Americans when directly polled as to what is most important in their selection of an automobile, safety, styling, or power, will automatically list safety. This is the sensible answer. This is what one ought to believe. But a

Detroit motor executive, in all his wisdom, becomes rich by producing unsafe, flashy, and powerful automobiles, knowing that the status value of these autos, the psychological sense of empowerment they give, is more important to the individual consumer than he is likely to admit.

In newspaper polls the vast majority of people will indicate that whether a candidate for public office is black or white, Jew or Christian, affects their voting "not at all." But party leaders know better. Indeed we all know better. In the area of opinions and beliefs, the reliability of questions and answers is so poor that few social scientists still credit the specific answers given. In areas where polling is valuable, questions are planted that indicate the degree of insight or honesty of the person being polled.

Of course the psychotherapist needs data. With a nondirective approach, and time, the patient will eventually get around to telling all the facts you might have elicited by questions — his age, his siblings, his life history. But in his way of telling, the order of telling, his emotion in telling, he will indicate to the therapist much more than just the facts. If he should omit a significant area — never mentions his mother while describing every other member of the family down to his cousins — you are always free to question him. Besides, you have as a bonus the significance of the omission itself. You would probably not ask him directly about his mother, but ask the more interesting question, "How come after two sessions of describing almost everybody in your life you never once mentioned your mother?" The value of this approach becomes immediately apparent: since everything is selected by the interviewee, everything will expose something about him. Over a hundred years ago, Freud had the critical insight that only when one stops asking questions is the truth likely to emerge. Only when the therapist stops talking can the patient have his say.

This does not mean that a therapist will never ask questions. I ask them frequently. But when I ask a question it is not generally in search of data. The questions that I ask during the middle and late phases of therapy are the sort that could be misinterpreted as rhetorical questions, but they are never that. I am likely to say, "Why are you so angry?" This does not mean, "Don't be so angry," or "Stop making a big deal out of something inconsequential," as it would when asked in the same way by most other people. I try to make my manner of asking the questions such as to preclude a judgmental tone. But since the very nature of the questions suggests criticism, they are often misinterpreted. And so I have resorted to the rather inelegant tactic of putting it up front. I tell my patients that I tend to ask questions that may sound rhetorical and therefore critical, but, I assure them, I never ask a rhetorical question. When I ask, "Why are you getting so angry?" it must be seen as a literal inquiry.

When a patient responds with rage over a trivial event that would elicit mild annoyance from most others, I know that the anger only appears disproportionate. I understand that there are intermediate, usually unconscious and metaphoric, allusions that are elicited by the "trivial" event that make it a profound threat to the patient. When I ask the patient why he is so angry, I know that he has no idea why. Why the question, then? The purpose of the question is to direct the patient to think about the anger, to thus implicitly acknowledge its excess, and to try to recover some of the unconscious feelings that make him feel so threatened by something that others would treat as a minor offense.

Clues to the Inner Self

The various sources of information available to the therapist in the course of an open-ended interview are so numerous that they could consume all the pages of this book. For purposes of introduction, though, I will mention here briefly the most significant and broadest informational sources, allowing the more detailed points to be observed as they emerge in the subsequent chapters.

First, there is the verbalized material of the session. The expressed facts and opinions, the content. But as has been suggested, verbalization reveals more than just data, more than just content. By emphasis, association, and expression, tacit feelings and opinions about the subject being discussed are revealed.

Suppose a therapist specifically asks a patient to tell him about his father. One first response might be, "My father . . ." followed by a long pause. So far he has ostensibly told you nothing at all. But the tone in which he says it, the expression on his face, the shaking of the head, the gesturing, and the emphasis offer a considerable amount of information before we actually know this father's name, his occupation, and whether he is living or dead. "My father . . ." with a long, long, long pause is an introduction to an entirely different subject than, "My father is a successful broker with . . ."

Independent of the content, the various qualities of the verbalization will reveal much about the patient and his relationship to the subject of his discourse. The vocabulary, the tone, and the expression of pride and awe are different from those of scorn and contumely. One almost inevitably sees a change in body language, voice quality, vocabulary, and emotion when a patient moves from a less emotionally charged subject to a more threatening subject like his relationship with a parent.

The verbalizations also indicate an enormous amount about the narrator, independent of the subject he is discussing. They tell us his command of language; the extent of his vocabulary; the richness of his metaphors and descriptions; often his class and region; his tendency toward hyperbole or understatement; his frankness or constraint; his expansiveness or reserve; his guile or his innocence; his capacity for trust or his paranoia. Also we will have a read on his communicative style. We all know people from whom words pour like water from a faucet. And we also know people who measure words like pennies pried from the change purse of a miser.

The therapist utilizes all aspects of verbal communications — the voice quality; the nature of the speaking (hesitant, whining, seductive); the degree of fluency; the degree of spontaneity; the breadth of vocabulary; the nature of the vocabulary (florid, sparse, portentous, sardonic); not to mention the purposes of speech (is it used to intimidate or ingratiate, to threaten or beguile?). And we pay special attention to stammers, tics, hesitations, slips of the tongue, and significant omissions.

What the therapist *hears* — that is, what he makes out of what is told him — will be different from what a friend or minister might make of the same presentation. The therapist is listening with a special orientation, a special view of human development and conduct, that will color the meaning of the facts presented.

This discussion barely begins to tap the potential uses of verbal communications in the course of therapy. Talk is, however, only one of the means of communication between therapist and patient.

The emotions speak profoundly to the therapist: we are interested in the range of emotions that a patient is capable of experiencing, and his degree of comfort or readiness to express each emotion. The two are not always the same. There are patients who are only too ready to express anger but would be humiliated by expressing tenderness, appreciation, gratitude, or affection.

The quality of the dominant emotion is important — whether a patient seems driven by fear, rage, or guilt. The real depth of emotionality is critical. Often the diagnosis of schizophrenia is first detected by the shallowness of the emotional range of a patient in a situation in which one expects profound feelings. This flat affect is characteristic of the personality of an individual with the capacity for schizophrenic deterioration. The absence of emotion when profound emotion is only too appropriate has always had major diagnostic relevance. *La belle indifference* — the aplomb — with which a patient faced her sudden blindness was considered a major touchstone in the diagnosis of hysteria in the late nineteenth century.

Also significant is whether the patient sees his emotions as a strength to be used or a weakness to be controlled. The most manipulative of all emotions is "feeling hurt," at least in terms of those who love you. It is practically designed to induce guilt. Tears can represent shame and humiliation, but they also can be a manipulative maneuver.

Certainly we are interested in whether a patient is aware of his own emotionality. I remember once discussing a book that I intended to entitle *Angry All the Time*. An editor objected to this title, stating that it was hyperbole — that no one was angry all the time. I agreed but nonetheless thought the expression was one that would resonate with most people. It captured the mood of crowded city streets and highways. Nonetheless the editor persisted, insisting that she did not know angry people, and that she herself rarely experienced anger. This was an astonishing statement — not just because it contradicted my own subjective impression of her but because of her general reputation. Highly respected and revered though she was, she was almost inevitably described as "brilliant and prickly." It didn't take psychoanalytic skills to recognize her need to deny her own considerable store of anger.

As the therapist will register the quality, degree, and depth of emotionality of the patient, so too will he register his own emotional responses to the patient. While he must mask his emotions to protect the purposes of the therapy, this does not mean he does not have them. I always asked my students in supervision at the psychoanalytic clinic whether they "liked" a specific patient whom they were treating. Students were often offended by the subjectivity of the word "like." Nonetheless their answers invariably said something not only about the nature of the patient, but also about themselves. For instance, some people, and therapists are people, are threatened by aggressiveness. I myself have always been attracted to the quick and the smart, even if they are smart-assed. I tend to have more difficulty with the passive patient.

I never treat a patient I don't like. But that is a luxury of my current status. In the early days of desperate poverty, I would treat almost anyone referred to me. Surprisingly, the sympathy one feels for a suffering fellow human being usually engenders a sense of identification and affection. But not always. I remember a patient who in his initial interview described a lifelong habit of picking up stray cats and dogs and torturing them. Obviously this was a piece of "sick" behavior that ought to have been treated by some therapist, but not this one. I referred him to an equally needy colleague. Early empathy and affection are almost always sensed by the patient and supply a much-needed kick to initiate the therapeutic process.

It is also instructive to notice how attuned the patient is to the therapist. Does she include the therapist, or does she ignore him? Is she measuring and weighing the therapist's emotion? How wary is she of him? How trusting?

Another primary focus of any psychoanalytically oriented therapist is the nature of the defenses employed by the patient. Defenses are the devices that an individual characteristically uses in handling her tensions and are described in great detail in Chapter 9. Defenses are crucial to an understanding of the quality of the patient's ego, the nature of her self, the strength of her self-esteem and pride. Defenses are also predictors of ingrained patterns of behavior. They allow the therapist to anticipate the patient's responses in the future, in and out of therapy. When threatened or challenged, does the patient use projection, rationalization, denial, isolation? Does she lie or confess, ingratiate or attack? When dealing with defenses, it is not just the selection of the defense but the breadth of the repertoire of defenses that is illuminating. We are always happier to see a variety of defenses employed. And we tend to find some defenses healthier than others. A patient who consistently uses projection — the attribution to others of emotions arising within herself — and only projection, is going to have problems accepting her own responsibility in her current state of unhappiness.

In nontherapeutic situations (and nondirective interviewing is more and more frequently used in hiring and admissions interviews), the interviewer will test the defensive structure by intentionally placing the subject under a certain amount of stress, hence the term "stress interview." This is unnecessary and unwise in psychotherapy, where there is always more anxiety and stress than one needs. The mere silence of the therapist and his insistence that the patient must take the initiative in leading the discussion, must fill the hour with her associations, is stressful enough. But in a hiring or admitting interview, the stress interview can be a profound and enlightening instrument.

At the crudest level, this could be done by baiting the interviewee to see how much it takes to make him angry. How does he handle his anger? Will he expose it to himself or the interviewer? Will he be frightened of it? Guilty? Ashamed? This approach has achieved some cachet in recent times, particularly in employment interviews. I find it manipulative and unnecessary. Generally speaking, the less artificial the method for producing stress the better. It seems somewhat inelegant and offensive for an interviewer to be the one to introduce a note of hostility into the interview. Almost inevitably, the interviewee will provide sufficient tension to indicate his responses to anxious moments. All that is really required of the interviewer is that she resist the natural temptation to dissipate the tension. This suggests that the interviewer herself ought to be prepared to tolerate a significant level of social discomfort.

I recall interviewing a candidate for admission to the Columbia Psychoanalytic Center many years ago. He was bright, personable, and accomplished. He started the interview intent on impressing me with his knowledge of the analytic literature. He obviously had prepared well. I was not interested in discussing analytic theory. I wanted to get to know him, not to find out how much he knew about psychoanalysis. I believed the latter to be irrelevant. If he were a walking encyclopedia it would have counted little in determining his potential as a therapist. And if he were totally ignorant, well, knowledge — unlike character traits — is something readily acquired by a smart young student. In addition, I wanted to observe him engaged in more spontaneous conversation.

I therefore quickly aborted this discussion by saying, "Let's not talk shop. Why don't you tell me what you do for fun." He was somewhat startled by this, having prepared a presentation of his own that he assumed would show him in his best light. He hesitated and then responded, "Oh, lots of things; the usual things." Again I persisted and asked specifically what. He mentioned that he enjoyed reading, that he was, indeed, an "avid reader."

I responded that I was delighted to hear that, since I too was an avid reader, and I asked him to tell me three books he had read in the last year, outside of the psychoanalytic literature, that he had particularly enjoyed. He became flustered, fidgety, and confused. I simply remained silent, looking at him inquiringly and expectantly with what I hoped was a benign and patient expression on my face. But I did engage him eyeball to eyeball. After a few "Let me think's" and "Why can't I remember's," to which I persistently responded, "Take your time," a definite sense of anxiety emerged. This was not as he had planned the interview. This seemed irrelevant, perhaps inconsequential to him. He began to sweat and to fiddle with a folder he had in his hand. It was, I suspected, a paper he had written and had wished to present to me for admiration and discussion. Then, with the first suggestion of annoyance, he announced that he was afraid nothing specific came to mind that he had read over the past year. I was quiet for a few more moments and finally said, "Well, think about it a little more. It needn't be something that you read this year. Tell me anything that you may have enjoyed in the last *few* years." And I returned to my patient, silent self.

Now he truly seemed disturbed. It was apparent that the last couple of years had involved residency training, in which there would be little time for outside reading unless one were truly an impassioned reader. It was obvious to me that I was dealing with a bright person but not necessarily an intellectual, and certainly not an "avid" (voracious, passionate, insatiable, ravenous) reader.

I think his answer to my question about what he did for fun was a perfunctory one designed to project what he thought I expected in an analytic candidate, rather than a true measure of his current leisure habits. I had no idea what he did for pleasure. He may have done nothing for pleasure. He may have been a pleasureless individual, an anhedonic personality, which would have had some serious portent for a prospective psychoanalytic candidate, although he had supplied me with sufficient emotional indicators to reassure me that that was not the case. He may have watched television, read thrillers, been addicted to junk movies, all of which would have been swell with me. But obviously not with him.

After a few more extremely uncomfortable moments, he braced himself, cleared his throat, and said: *"The Brothers Karamazov."* I was proud of my self-control. The impulse to laugh out loud was almost overwhelming, yet I believe I did not reveal any of this. It was such a stereotypic answer, the one novel that at the time of the interview surely would have been listed at the top — in competition with *War and Peace* — of everyone's list of great novels.

I remained composed and said to him: "Surely someone who has been to the college you have, with the background you have, read *The Brothers Karamazov* prior to the last two years, or are you saying that you *reread* it recently?"

To answer affirmatively to the latter would have required a lie, which could have been detected and readily exposed by my simply asking him details, assuming I was familiar with this popular icon of literature. I myself had first read it (if one can call it that) at age thirteen. How little I got from that reading became only too apparent when I reread the novel for a college course at age eighteen. And how many details I remembered by the time of the interview was open to speculation. Realizing that he was treading on very thin ice indeed, and not wishing to find himself even deeper in a hole, he confessed that he had read it his freshman year in college.

I could sense his frustration and rage. I do not think of myself as sadistic, and I wanted to give him a chance to collect himself before confronting him with his anger. I steered the interview to safer terrain by asking him his opinion of the latest trendy existential psychoanalyst. He proved very articulate. By then the interview was almost over. I always save the last ten minutes of the interview for what is a provocative and informative question, asking the candidate to evaluate the interview.

Just prior to my closing ploy, I made a slight and almost disastrous detour. I wanted to satisfy my curiosity about the candidate's last name. He shared the name with a distinguished, although not preeminent, Eastern European writer. For the sake of anonymity, let's assume the candidate's name was "Henry Babel." I said to him, "You aren't by any chance related to the distinguished Russian writer Isaac Babel, are you?" He responded quickly and proudly: "He was my great-grandfather, although I never knew him." I then asked — out of curiosity, I would have said at the time, but in retrospect I admit there may have been an element of teasing mischief — "How do you like his works?" To my surprise, he literally paled. He stared at me stonily and said: "I've never read any of his stuff." I had pressed him further than I wished, and I was truly sorry. I then brought the interview to a close with my standard ending.

I said, "The interview is almost over, and I thank you for it. We have about ten minutes left, and I'd like to know how *you* felt about the interview."

The moment of truth was at hand. He composed himself for a moment and then looked me in the eye and said, "I thought it was grossly unfair and a waste of time." I asked him to tell me why. He said he was not applying for a job as a comparative literature teacher; that he was applying for analytic school; that unlike the previous interviewer I gave him no opportunity to demonstrate his knowledge of the psychoanalytic literature and theory; and on and on. Then he said I had insisted on frittering away the interview by "catching me up."

He went on for a while, expressing his anger openly and his displeasure with (contempt for?) me in a direct, forthright, and I thought admirably courageous manner. When he was finished, I said I quite disagreed with him. I felt the interview was extremely informative and productive and I had found out a great deal from it. I told him that I was, as he correctly observed, not interested in his knowledge of psychoanalytic theory; that whether he knew a great deal before he came into the analytic school was irrelevant; by the time of his graduation he would have learned much; that given the fact that I only had forty-five minutes to appraise his ability I was more concerned with his character, his ego structure, his defenses, their strength, his capacity to relate to an individual (i.e., myself), his emotional range, his integrity, his character, the way he handled a difficult situation, his responses to stress, and so on.

I said that I was sorry the interview had disappointed him, but that I had found it extraordinarily helpful. Certainly, I said with a smile, at least I know you are capable of expressing anger and confronting authority. Both of those are reassuring.

I liked him. I felt he was a strong, healthy individual, ambitious and smart — if not an avid reader. I recommended him for admission. The reader may be forgiven if he finds me here a bit manipulative and a trifle sadistic. In retrospect, I suspect I was. I knew from the first ten minutes of the interview that he was a likely prospect for admission, and in my attempt to confirm his ego strengths and weaknesses, I may also have been indulging my own propensity, as the eldest of three brothers, to play teasing games. An admission interview is never a game to the candidate, however, and I should have been gentler and more considerate. I like to think that today I would be.

With the patient in therapy, with his transparent need for comfort and approval, stress is produced merely by refusing to supply the normally expected responses to tacit pleas for reassurance. To the patient who is particularly and obviously anxious to please his therapist, all that is necessary to produce stress is the procedure itself, the withholding of approving comment as characterized by the head-nodding, clucking, smiling, and yessing that we all routinely use to indicate "That's all right, I understand."

The nondirective interview allows for the full utilization of those very special tools identified with psychoanalysis and psychoanalytic therapy: dream interpretation, free association, analysis of the transference, and the like.

Psychoanalytic Tools I: Free Association, Transference, and the Couch

3

WHILE PSYCHOANALYSIS in its traditional form represents a minute fraction of the psychotherapy practiced today, the tools that were derived from psychoanalytic theory are pervasive in almost all talking therapies. Like Molière's M. Jourdain, who was astonished and delighted to discover that for over forty years he had been speaking prose without knowing it, most psychotherapists speak Freud whether they know it or not. Freud elaborated a theory of mental illness, a method of treatment for such illness, and a new way of searching for knowledge about, and understanding of, the principles that guide human behavior. Out of all of this emerged a new way of looking at patients.

Nonverbal Clues

Before a patient speaks his first words, mentions his primary complaint, or offers a scintilla of historical data, the therapist has formed a significant and clear impression of him suggested by a host of nonverbal material. How the person is dressed is certainly significant: it can be an indicator of economics; a suggestion of taste; a sign of rigidity or chaos. It also displays attitude, often indicating the seriousness or lack of seriousness of a patient toward the therapy, particularly when combined with a complementary body language. When someone has obviously "dressed up" for the interview, it indicates an attitude different from — not necessarily superior to — that signaled by a teenager who slouches in without taking off his baseball cap (peak backward) or his "shades" and uninvited plops into the first chair he sees — often the wrong chair, far away from the therapist's — and sullenly looks at the floor, avoiding eye contact. One is not "better" than the other. Each reveals the patient and in so doing helps the therapist anticipate the direction that therapy may take.

One of the exercises I routinely performed when teaching interviewing was to have one student interview another in front of the class. The interviewer was told she had a half hour to find out as much about her colleague as she could. And were she to ask if there was some special information I was interested in, or direction I preferred, I invariably responded with a vague, noncommittal answer: "Whatever you think necessary to get to really know or understand him." I asked the rest of the class to observe the interview carefully and told them they were free to take notes.

At the end of the half hour, I would ask the class what they had learned about the *interviewer* as distinguished from the interviewee. The class would often respond in a startled manner, indicating that they thought this was an unfair, even ridiculous question. Yet an hour and a half later, what we could reconstruct about the interviewer — having acquired no specific knowledge about her background, her interests, her tastes — was significant. We would know how involved she was, how engaging or reserved, how maternal; whether she avoided tension when she sensed it emerging from her colleague by protectively changing the subject, or whether she homed in on it; whether certain subjects that would seem to be critical, such as a sexual history, had been avoided. We would sense the range of her emotions and the ease with which she handled *his* emotions. We could observe her body language. We would have seen how she engaged not just the interviewee, but the class. The purpose of this exercise was to impress upon the class the amount of nonverbal data always available to an observant and knowledgeable examiner.

Occasionally, I would assign a Sherlock Holmes story for reinforcement. These stories are delightful parodies of the powers of observation, in which Holmes seems capable of constructing whole life histories largely on the basis of nonverbal clues.

In "The Adventure of the Dancing Men," Holmes interrupts a few hours of silence by asking, "So, Watson . . . you do not propose to invest in South African securities?"

Dr. Watson is incredulous, in a way that parallels a patient's astonishment at information that can be inferred from a dream or a simple projective test like "draw a person." "Accustomed as I was to Holmes's curious faculties, this sudden intrusion into my most intimate thoughts was utterly inexplicable." He insists on an explanation.

Holmes says that when he offers one, Watson will claim it to be "absurdly simple." Before giving his answer he constructs the basic theory that underlies such problem solving, explaining that what seems like magic when one presents the conclusions is simple logic when all the intermediate deductions are at hand.

Holmes then informs Watson that he came to his conclusion by an inspection of the groove between Watson's left forefinger and thumb! When Watson implies there can be no connection, Holmes supplies the missing links:

1. You had chalk between your left finger and thumb when you returned from the club last night. 2. You put chalk there when you play billiards, to steady the cue. 3. You never play billiards except with Thurston. 4. You told me, four weeks ago, that Thurston had an option on some South African property which would expire in a month, and which he desired you to share with him. 5. Your check book is locked in my drawer, and you have not asked for the key. 6. You do not propose to invest your money in this manner.

And how does Watson respond? Well, of course, he answers precisely as Holmes predicted: "How absurdly simple."

The anticipation of that response was the ultimate statement of Holmes's understanding of the logic inherent in conduct as well as words. Holmes's creator, Sir Arthur Conan Doyle (1859–1930), was almost an exact contemporary of Sigmund Freud, and in his way he expressed the same love and respect for analytic reasoning and scientific observation that characterized that age.

Although the therapist may find out a great deal about her patient in this way, she would be well advised to tread gently in this area, as it is the kind of information that is likely to be resented by the patient and rejected out of hand. When a patient walked into Freud's office on her first visit, neglecting to close the door behind her, he instantly interpreted this as an act of aggression and contempt for the procedure and instructed her to go back and shut the door. Freud may have been able to get away with such imperious behavior — it was a different time and culture, and his was the only show in town — but most therapists must be more circumspect, operating on a more delicate scale. What we find out from these indirect clues is generally stored away, categorized in our mind, and used at a more appropriate time. We therapists have time on our side.

Much, perhaps too much, has been written about body language, but it can reveal an extraordinary amount about a patient, even one the therapist knows well. When I moved from one office to another, the location of my chair was changed by perhaps two feet, so that the patient was now that much closer to me than before. In my old office, an awkward space had compelled a distance that seemed to me personally "unfriendly," slightly too far away or detached. Nonetheless, my patients adjusted to it and very few had problems with it.

When I moved to the new office and placed the chairs at an appropriate distance for conversation, none of my current patients complained about that either. However, a former patient who returned after not having seen me for a year found the reduced distance totally discomforting. She literally could not continue with her consultation until she moved the chair back. It was simply too intimate.

Chair behavior is constantly and continually informative. Some patients hide in a corner of the chair. Some capaciously occupy its full breadth. Some lean forward as though preparing to dive into the therapist's lap, while others press their back into the chair or tilt their body at such an angle that eye contact is difficult to manage.

The characteristic body language of a patient supplies an index to measure alterations or changing attitudes over the course of time in the relationship between patient and therapist, and may signal changes in the patient's self-presentation in other relationships as well. As much as the more valued cognitive insights, body language is a reliable indicator of change.

What Freud did in the area of nonverbal deductions, as well as with dreams and fantasies, was to take general observations about human conduct that had previously only been intuitive, or ad hoc, and through careful analysis and codification create a logical method for interpreting such knowledge. His writings on this subject gave therapists a new analytic tool. This is precisely what other investigators in the natural sciences were doing at about the same time.*

One intriguing area of nonverbal communication with which we are all familiar is lateness, a commonplace personality trait. It is an example of an area given legitimacy for interpretation by Freudian theory. We have always been free to make inferences about friends who are chronic latecomers. Most of us are annoyed by the inconvenience they cause us, but our anger is disarmed by their sweet but cavalier greeting, "Sorry I'm late." It took someone like Freud to grant respectability to our anger by pointing out that they are not sorry and, even more important, they are usually not truly *late*. Chronic lateness is a planned event.

Some of my patients are in a sweat of anxiety if they are so much as five minutes late (that in itself may be a problem), while others are totally nonchalant about arriving fifteen

---

*Similar observations of amateur naturalists and philosophers laid the foundations of anthropology, archaeology, comparative philology — all fields that were "created" in the late nineteenth century. The sovereign example is the work of Charles Darwin.

minutes late. One of my patients, however, invariably arrived eight to ten minutes late and always started the interview by saying, "Sorry I'm late."

After the fourth or fifth time, I told the patient that she was not late. She looked at her watch and asked, "What do you mean?" I said, "You obviously *plan* on coming here eight to ten minutes late." She denied it and said she wasn't "good with time." I said that mere chaos, in which bad timekeeping would be the equivalent of bad housekeeping, was something with which I was quite familiar. Not being good with time would mean that some days she would come five minutes late, some twenty minutes late, some days ten minutes early, in a random fashion. She seemed to me, I indicated, extremely competent with time to manage always to arrive precisely eight to ten minutes late.

It was a struggle for her to accept this conclusion. When she did, her lateness at first became more erratic. Finally, she became reasonably punctual, and when she was late, she herself would start those sessions by seeking the reasons for her lateness. This was a clear sign that she accepted the responsibility for the behavior and saw coming late as a symptom, as serving a dynamic purpose.

Unlike a migraine headache, lateness doesn't discommode the patient. As a result, she is unlikely to report it. The therapist must *pursue* evidence of lateness in everyday life when it has been demonstrated in the patient-therapist relationship. A symptom may be viewed as a small hole in a sweater; it is focused, evident, and can be directly approached. A neurotic character trait is like a wild thread woven through a sweater that may not even be apparent to the patient. The therapist must identify it and meticulously tease it out. The passive therapist who is waiting for the patient to bring up examples of such character traits in life is likely to predecease the problem.

Lateness is something that has fascinated me all my professional life. It has multiple, often opposing meanings. In some, lateness is a product of anxiety that forces them to delay activities that they see as fraught with danger. With others it is a matter of status — who waits for whom. And it is the quintessential passive-aggressive mechanism.

This patient brings to mind another, who had been referred to by her friend as "the Admiral." As is often the case, the discussion emerged from the interpretation of a dream image. In the dream she appeared in the uniform of an admiral. She mentioned this to me with an embarrassed laugh, obviously resenting the epithet. She explained that it was the result of a motor trip through France that she and her husband had taken with this friend, a former naval officer, and his wife. He had pointed out something she had never noticed. He said she was always the first one out of the car and the last one to enter it. He compared this with an admiral in a rowboat going to and from shore, where the admiral — befitting his dignity, rank, and station — always entered the rowboat last and always left it first, so that he didn't have the discomfort of sitting in a rowboat for too long, and never, never had to wait for lesser creatures.

She thought this was a rude explanation, and again laughing to cover her embarrassment and anger, she suggested to me how inappropriate and unfair it was. It seemed totally consistent with her behavior to me, and while I was not unkind enough to say so that bluntly, I insisted that she examine the charges seriously.

Such is the way that insight insinuates itself into a therapeutic session. Lateness — one's own lateness, that is — is not something that one could imagine spending time discussing with a priest, teacher, or lawyer. It is the very stuff of therapy. In a masterful essay dating from 1901 (*The Psychopathology of Everyday Life*), Freud gave legitimacy to consideration of such trivial everyday behavior, insisting on its seriousness and viewing it as a scientific index of underlying character and intent.

Time and its uses are profound metaphors, and variations on its usage continue to emerge and to amaze. Only recently a new patient of mine routinely dismissed herself, getting up from the chair, thanking me for the session, and leaving three to five minutes before the end of her allotted time. At first the pattern was not evident, since she anticipated the end of the hour with stunning accuracy. Watching the time is normally the therapist's responsibility. My clock is intentionally placed where it is visible to me and not the patient, whether sitting or lying down. Patients will often say, "Do we have time?" suggesting they do not want to be dismissed in the middle of their account, but this patient was operating like a stopwatch.

After the pattern became apparent, I mentioned it to her. As she got up to leave, I simply asked her why she was leaving early, stating that by my reckoning we still had five minutes left of our hour. She said something to the effect that she didn't want to be unfair and poach on the time of the patient who followed her. Smiling, I indicated to her that I was a pretty good timekeeper. Besides, I pointed out, she was doing this at every session. After the usual circumlocutions, we came to her reluctance to be "dismissed." Of course, this being the end of her hour, she was then — politely — dismissed, although I told her I wanted to hear from her what being "dismissed" meant.

The next hour was a particularly rich one, in terms of historical material. She hated, she said, to overstay any welcome and never allowed herself to be in a position where she was dismissed. This is a woman who has suffered from rejection all her life at the hands of a stone-cold, narcissistic mother and has managed to compound the original hurt by assiduously cultivating the most exploitative group of male and female friends one could imagine. She has always left social engagements early, not wanting to overstay her welcome, not being able to bear the thought that, whatever the engagement — a business meeting or a social luncheon — she might see the other party furtively looking at their watch, indicating boredom. She brought this same behavior into therapy, terrified at the thought that therapy would be yet another in a series of rejections or dismissals. It was not that this patient was unaware of her sensitivity to rejection, but when she was forced to recognize this habitual pattern acted out in so concrete a way, it was particularly enlightening and, I believe, therapeutic.

Freud talked about how much knowledge could be gleaned from slips of the tongue, malapropisms, forgetting, "accidents," lateness. Because of the natural delight in this insight of Freud's, many therapists have a tendency to overvalue this material, to pounce on it as being somehow superior to or more definitive than information gleaned through conversation. Actually it is more troublesome and can be provocative. Patients often resent such interpretation as overreaching, far-fetched, or gimmicky. The patient must make a leap of faith to accept it. As a result, he or she may resent the insight and protect against recognition of the problem when it later emerges more naturally in the context of a relationship. As useful as such information might sometimes be, it is more likely to be of service to the therapist's ego than to the patient's insight. With rare exceptions such data is better reserved to corroborate that which the patient recognizes for himself through the slower mechanisms of speech and analysis.

Free Association

While the world of nonverbal communication is fascinating, most of the communication between the therapist and the individual is verbal and guided by the nondirective techniques suggested in the previous chapter. Free association is an alternative to dialogue or programmed inquiry of any sort. The idea is to encourage the patient to simply lie back and say whatever comes to mind. The purpose is to re-create the quality of random thoughts — the stream of consciousness — that one has lying in bed just before falling asleep, or while staring into space on a long airline flight. The hope is that what will emerge will be something akin to Molly Bloom's soliloquy, the final forty-five pages of James Joyce's *Ulysses*. Alas, it never is. First, it is simply not possible for verbalization to keep up with the rapidity of thoughts. Second, the patient is not only verbalizing, he is doing so in front of an audience. The presence of another person will inevitably intrude into the thought processes, even if the other person is totally silent. But the therapist is rarely totally silent. Remember that while I will continue to use the term "nondirective," for that is the accepted nomenclature for this kind of interview, it is something of a misnomer. In one way or another, the therapist always manages to organize the interview according to his purposes.

A comment by a therapist is often referred to as an intervention, suggesting that it intervenes in (interrupts) the patient's stream of consciousness. Few interventions are actually profound insights or complex interpretations; a therapist is not likely to reveal the "true meaning" of your life with one brilliant statement. Most therapeutic interventions are simple comments. Sometimes the therapist is unaware that he is selecting the direction he prefers the patient to take. Let's say a patient is rattling off a list of subjects: "I don't know where to start today. I had a fight at the office; my mother called; my migraine acted up; I had a fantasy of killing myself just before going to bed . . ." Were the therapist to interrupt and repeat the last part of the list by simply saying, "A fantasy?" that would inevitably be the area in which the patient would continue his associations.

The typical form of intervention for a therapist is a question. If, for example, the patient said he was going for a first job interview and was feeling anxious, the therapist would most likely remain silent. That is a common source of anxiety, and not to feel some performance anxiety here would be more suspect. If, on the other hand, the patient said that he had to have his hair cut after the session and was feeling anxious, the therapist might ask, "Why are you anxious?" As I indicated earlier, this does not mean, "Why in the world are you anxious about a thing like that!" which is what it would mean if a friend made that statement. From the therapist it is not a statement of incredulity but a question of inquiry. The therapist will often ask questions that if asked by anyone else would be seen as rhetorical. She is asking a specific question, looking for a specific answer. She is asking the patient if he knows why he might be anxious about something that commonplace. She is directing the patient to seek the source of his anxiety and by so doing is also marking the inappropriateness of the emotion. It is crucial that the patient realize the therapist is not hectoring him with these questions. I do not know how other therapists handle this. Perhaps they ask no questions. As I earlier stated, I indicate to the patient at the beginning of therapy that I *never* ask rhetorical questions, and I never do.

If the patient answered, "I'm always anxious when I get my hair cut" (or "visit my mother," et cetera), the therapist might repeat her question. "Why do you think that is?" It is the kind of question that forces the patient to examine common modes of behavior that have become patterned, routine, and acceptable to the patient, and therefore go unnoticed and unquestioned. Whenever a therapist asks questions, particularly about emotions — why are you embarrassed, what are you ashamed of, what are you frightened of, why were you angry with your wife, your child, your boss — these questions are directive. Their purpose is to identify the emotion; to point out that it is not the only, or appropriate, emotion for that situation; and to steer the patient's associations down a new path of reasoning.

There will be many forks in the road where the therapist wittingly or unwittingly will nudge the patient to the right or to the left, thus by her very inquiry indicating what she feels is the preferred direction, thereby introducing her values, and directing the "nondirective" interview. This is not meant to suggest that the therapist acts randomly or in an undisciplined way, or that the prudent therapist should not allow the patient to choose the subject and direction of the hour. But the therapist has an agenda, which is to further the progress of the treatment, and must balance the value of patient-selected material against the need to organize the data of the unconscious for the patient.

So if a patient was in the middle of an emotional tirade against the therapist when his previous session ended, the trained therapist would not start the next session by inviting the patient to continue where they had left off, although logic would seem to dictate that course of action. She would allow him to begin the new session in any way he wished; but before that hour was over, she should ask him why he hadn't continued the discussion of the previous session.

The unwillingness of the therapist to direct the session by picking the subject, even one as important as the example just cited, produces supplementary, and useful, information. It will indicate the patient's anxiety about confrontation, his readiness to force closure on a tough issue, and other useful data that will fill out the picture of how the patient relates to another human being and how he handles multiple pressures. Free association fleshes out the characteristic modus operandi of the patient.

A relatively free associative session (which is probably the most exact term for the process that characterizes psychoanalysis particularly) is most useful with a high frequency of sessions. When all psychoanalytic patients came five days a week, the therapist had the leisure to wait out her patient — observing his patterns of avoidance, denial, self-deception — while still having the time to deal with the stuff of his conflicts.

Free association and frequent hours force the patient to get the "easy stuff" out of the way early. He will then get stuck. It is during those moments of "stuckness" that the patient will be driven into himself and his internal world will be exposed. If a patient chooses to fill hours with technical talk about the stock market, and his problems at work as a money manager, and his relative successes and failures, he is often permitted to do so. Eventually he will realize — if only by his therapist's total lack of participation in such discussions — that he is avoiding central issues, and he will begin to look into himself for other things to discuss. When a patient says to me that he doesn't have much on his mind and has very little to say today, I usually assume we are going to have a productive session. In the words of Alexander Portnoy's analyst, Dr. Spielvogel, "Now vee may perhaps to begin. Yes?"

Significant Omissions

Significant omissions are another special form of communication of great value to a therapist. Even a priest will recognize such omissions. When a parishioner is ready to confess to almost every sin in Deuteronomy while ignoring any of his sexual activity, the priest will become suspicious. A therapist is ever watchful for these omissions. They are as important to a therapist as the subjects that are persistently emphasized. I was personally reminded of this when I recently heard from a long-lost and distant cousin. I asked after his parents, was given a report, and then we discussed his siblings. He told me about his married brother and his children; he told me about his divorced brother and his child; and then he asked me about my family. After a few moments, I vaguely recalled his having a sister, and I said, "Don't you have a sister, or am I mistaken?" There was an obvious embarrassed pause and hesitation. He then described his sister's suffering with a severe debilitating psychiatric condition — anorexia — which after many years of remission had recently relapsed, forcing hospitalization. I indicated how sorry I was to hear that. He then said he was not sure that he should have told me. "I don't know if my parents would want the family to know about the problem, but I felt compelled to be honest with you."

I was touched and sorry, and angry with myself for asking about something that was none of my business. This was a distant second cousin, much younger than myself; I should not have placed him in such a dilemma; I should have respected the significance of the omission. I was simply not thinking therapeutically. A social discussion on the phone with a psychoanalyst who happens to be your cousin is more aptly a discussion with your cousin who happens to be an analyst. In a therapeutic session, I would have valued the meaning of the omission while respecting the anxiety that led to it.

Free association and the nondirective approach may now be appreciated as a complicated, rich, multifaceted way of gaining not only the same information that would be articulated in a biography or through a questionnaire, but also material that would simply not emerge into consciousness with most other data-gathering techniques. Through the nondirective interview we gain not only more knowledge of the individual, but a knowledge different from that which will emerge with more traditional interviews.

The Much-Maligned Couch

The poor analytic couch has been the subject of more humor and more ridicule than any other psychoanalytic convention. It is time for it to be demystified. It deserves a little respect. The couch serves a number of purposes:

- It establishes that what is transpiring between these two people, therapist and patient, is different from ordinary conversation and will follow different rules of discourse.
- It allows the patient to minimize the presence of a listener, thus encouraging a free-associative style. The patient is

more likely to drift off into his internal world. Some patients (not all) can induce something approaching the drowsy state that one experiences when lying half awake and half asleep in bed. Something like stream of consciousness can occasionally occur, though never as in fiction.

- It protects the patient. She is free to say many things without having to stare into the eyes of her therapist or even notice the body language of her therapist. It thus makes it easier to express both positive and negative feelings about the therapist.
- It protects the therapist. It allows for a more relaxed therapist. He does not have to control his emotions as rigidly. He need not be concerned about revealing the anxiety that he will often experience, or the pride or disappointment that he may also experience. He can focus all of his attention on his patient.

But each of these particular advantages has a downside. The couch that encourages free association also encourages dissociation. With a patient who has difficulty focusing, who tends to drift off anyway, or with a borderline patient who is not quite clear where reality ends and fantasy begins, the couch can be a disaster. Many therapists have misdiagnosed a borderline schizophrenic patient and put him on the couch, allowing him to dissociate and regress into his own distorted world. With diminished contact with the real world, with no necessity to engage the now invisible therapist, with no check on his fantasy world, a psychotic break can be precipitated. In the early, arrogant days of psychoanalysis, this was a disgracefully common experience.

A couch is also disaster for a passive patient who is only too ready to lie down and free associate for the rest of his life.

Particularly if he has a passive analyst who is ready to join him in a lifetime journey to nowhere.

While the couch protects the analyst, it also allows for abuses. There is nothing more embarrassing to the profession than the frequent accounts of patients who looked up and observed an irresponsible hack of an analyst pursuing various personal activities, from opening mail to reading a newspaper. This ethical lapse is only made more reprehensible when an unscrupulous or embarrassed therapist compounds this misdemeanor into a felony by assigning responsibility for his own unethical behavior to his patient.

A number of patients have reported seeing their therapist asleep during the course of the therapy. Some have had their therapist fall asleep during a face-to-face session! There certainly may be an excusable explanation if this is a singular event. What is inexcusable is for the therapist to say to the patient, "Have you considered that it may be that you are forcing me to fall asleep by avoiding your central problems while being particularly boring?" That is a direct quote from a patient of mine about a previous therapist, who repeatedly fell asleep during therapy. This is unpardonable, and cowardly. Patients are entitled to an alert, conscientious therapist who, like any human being, is allowed to make mistakes. But he must not foist his mistakes on his patient; the patient has enough problems.

One of my patients had a devastating experience with a famous, brilliant pioneer in psychoanalysis prior to coming to me. This was many years ago and was part of a training analysis, that is, the analysis required of a candidate to fulfill his educational goals for graduation as a psychoanalyst. The candidate-patient selected this therapist because he was the premier therapist in the New England region and had written the book on psychoanalytic therapeutic techniques. The candidate became convinced that his therapist was not only blatantly anti-Semitic — which I found difficult to believe, considering the reputation of the analyst and the fact that in those days almost all of his colleagues as well as his patients were likely to be Jewish — but also was simply not listening to him.

I was wrong to be skeptical. The candidate was right on both counts. The analyst's anti-Semitism was later corroborated by others who knew him well. But more important, it was equally well known that he routinely fell asleep during sessions. Actually, with my patient this illustrious pipe-smoking therapist had twice set himself or his chair on fire by dropping his pipe while falling asleep! And all of that — *all* — had been interpreted by the therapist as being the responsibility of the patient! I was later to learn that along with everything else, this training analyst was a notorious alcoholic, which raises questions about the lack of self-disciplining procedures in the analytic schools at that time.

And finally, while the couch encourages full transference fantasies as the therapist recedes into the distance, this is offset by the fact that it will also allow the patient to avoid engaging the therapist. Some patients need engagement, need to be rooted in the attachment to the therapist as a model for, or a bridge to, other attachments in life.

The uses of the couch are inevitably confusing. My friend Bill, whom I used as a reader on an early draft of this book, was bewildered by what he saw as a contradiction between the desire to build a community of two and the exclusion of the presence of the therapist by use of the couch. "Doesn't talking into space mean talking to no one?" he asked.

It had never occurred to me to explain the circuitous process by which the couch builds a stronger community. I acknowledged that free association inevitably does drive the patient further into himself. But without the need to face another, what emerges is the "secrets" one shares with no one: the "shameful" perverse sexual fantasies; the mean-spirited feelings; the personal hygiene problems; all the detritus of unpleasant memories and self-loathing. Not having to engage the therapist — who supports these expressions by remaining silent — encourages the exposure of all that the patient has successfully hidden from public view. Now there is another witness to his ignominy. The therapist has heard all, yet remains unprovoked and unchanged in his alliance with the patient. From this acceptance emerges an attachment that is as fervent as it is unique.

Bill became more confidential during this discussion than he ever had previously. He mentioned that although he had been in therapy, he had never been on the couch. "Speaking personally," he said, "I would think so much of the beauty of therapy derives from the human interaction between patient and therapist, no matter how confined it is by rules and modes of conduct."

This personal exposure encouraged me to do something I usually guard against — cross the bridge between friend and therapist; blur the distinction between social and professional. I said, "You are an articulate and particularly charming person, who unwittingly woos everyone with whom you talk. You know you are engaging, and you feel reassured when you sense the affection you elicit in those about you. I suspect you need this reassurance. For this reason if for no other, were you my patient, I'd probably put you on the couch and see how you fared without these defenses." That was as far as I went — and was farther than I should have gone. To Bill's credit, he laughed in agreement.

Ultimately, whether a patient would be better off sitting up or lying down depends on the judgment of the therapist, who must weigh the advantages offered by the couch over the disadvantages. There is no mystique. A very psychoanalytic dynamic therapy can be done with a patient sitting up, and a very supportive and reassuring therapy can be done with the patient on the couch. Neither is better. Neither is worse. The couch, like everything else, is a tool to facilitate exposure of the patient's feelings and his coming in contact with his internal life.

Transference and Countertransference

In its tightest original definition, "transference" referred to the process whereby emotional responses of the patient to his therapist were clearly replications of significant relationships of his past — his relationship with his mother, his father, his beloved sibling, his hated rival. They were invariably treated as projections, and completely independent of the nature or conduct of the therapist. And of course this does occur. One of my patients consistently skipped his therapeutic sessions when he returned to the pot smoking to which he was addicted, despite my constant insistence that these were precisely the times that would be most useful for me to be seeing him. After all, there is something ludicrous in avoiding your doctor when you are sick. He still would not come when smoking. Weeks would go by when his business affairs were "so hectic" he couldn't leave the office. Translate this to, "I'm back on grass." No amount of insistence, cajoling, or entreating on my part was effective. He was too embarrassed, too ashamed. No reassurance that I was his therapist, not his father, could break through his avoidance, for to him I *was* both his therapist and his father.

Many a time I questioned whether or not to drop him from treatment, but one doesn't drop a patient from treatment because of one's own frustration (that is a problem of countertransference, which I'll get to shortly). Further, these very behaviors were the cornerstones of a lifelong dynamic — the need to please an essentially unpleasable father combined with a lifelong history of withdrawing from life. As a child he would take to bed with various suspect illnesses for months. As an adult he would withdraw into the worst marijuana addiction I had ever encountered. You cannot discharge a patient for persisting in being ill.

Today "transference" is loosely used to include all of the emotional responses a patient has to the therapist, and that is the way I generally will be using the term. The importance of transference interpretations originally rested in part on the underlying assumption that they were independent of the reality of the ongoing relationship with the therapist. This does happen, as I believe with the patient I just described, but the projection is often contaminated by reality. Since no therapist is ever a truly neutral figure, his input, his personality, and his values assuredly affect the relationship. The therapist must know himself well enough to distinguish between what is real — a product of his own personality — and what is truly projection — something attributed to him by the patient's past conditioning.

Still, the patient has a great deal invested in the therapist and will rarely see him as he truly is, but rather as he wants or needs him to be. He will inevitably romanticize him, at least during the opening phases of therapy. The therapist will almost always be perceived as brilliant, insightful, and wise. Since the truly brilliant are as rare in psychotherapy as they are in law or investing, a great deal of idealization is taking place. Not surprisingly, most therapists, being victims of their own vanities, will tend to pay less heed to positive transference. Yet such responses can be highly instructive and are entitled to the same attention as negative transference responses.

Since transference responses are a mix of projections from the past and responses to the therapist as he is, a courageous self-knowledge and honest self-appraisal by the therapist concerning his own personality and behavior are essential. If a patient accuses us of being bored with him, or disapproving, we therapists must have the courage to consider the validity of the patient's observation, rather than attributing it all to transference.

Still, there are whole groups of therapists wedded to the idea that they can be value-free and absolutely neutral, that every feeling expressed toward them will be pure transference, absolute projection. I doubt this occurs. It would be more prudent for the therapist to bravely recognize the true nature of his personality and how he is generally perceived. Then significant deviations from this baseline will be most relevant in understanding the distortions of each specific patient.

It is with fresh delight and amazement that I observe the distortions of me that patients have made over the years, even in cold, hard, objective areas where my own self-deceptions can be eliminated. When I was forty-five I had patients who saw me as twenty years older and others who saw me as ten years younger. I have had patients see me as six inches taller than I am and four inches shorter, as an absent-minded professor and as a dandy. When it comes to personality appraisal, the view has ranged from Charlie Brown to Adolf Hitler. All such obvious deviations are of extraordinary value in focusing the patient on his tendency to distort his perceptions to accommodate his needs and his anxieties.

When the patient finally is prepared to recognize the therapist as he really is, he will begin to realize that the very same distortions that he has imposed on his analyst are inevitably occurring in everyday life, interfering with his proper pursuits of pleasure and performance. If he insists on seeing himself as weaker, less intelligent, and less attractive than his therapist when the evidence for none of this is at hand, he is inevitably doing the same with other authority figures, and most competitors, in his daily life.

Two other invaluable bonuses are offered through the transference. One, it is the only area in which the analyst has firsthand knowledge of the conduct of his patient in relation to another human being (himself). It is the only time when he experiences the patient in action rather than hearing a secondhand account from the patient's biased view. Everything told him by the patient will be as seen through the distorting lens each person reserves for his own behavior, filtered through the selective medium of memory, and screened by the ever-protective ego. The mirror that reflects us to ourselves is as deformed as any grotesque fun house mirror. Of course, the nature of those distortions is instructive to the therapist. I have had patients who have viewed all of their problems as extensions of their "too trusting" nature, when in the course of therapy they have demonstrated just the opposite. "Are you sure our time is up? I thought we started three minutes late." "I think you may have overcharged me last month."

Because of this the transference is also an elegant tool for measuring the patient's self-awareness. When a patient perceives himself, describes himself, and believes himself to be a trusting individual, while consistently behaving in therapy in a guarded and distrustful manner, you have learned something — not just about his capacity to trust another human being, but about his insight into his own behavior. Beyond that it indicates his general capacity for self-deception. The transference becomes a mirror of truth that will reflect the patient's self-deceptions about his own character, forcing him to acknowledge his true self.

The therapist will learn to compensate for the degree and nature of each particular patient's distortions, so that the hysteric's "unbearable" will be translated as "annoying," while the stoic's "distress" will alert one to real "anguish." By knowing whether my patient is one who minimizes his distress or dramatizes it, I can adjust to his particular vocabulary.

Now for the other side of the coin, countertransference, which refers to all of the therapist's personal responses to the patient. As I previously explained, I no longer treat patients I don't like. I have seen patients on consultation to whom I have had a negative personal response, and I have always referred them on. This is a luxury of my later and more successful days. It is difficult to treat someone one truly dislikes.

But "dislike" really covers only one aspect of the point I am trying to make. The anguished patient usually touches the heart of any empathic person, although it is the nature of some neuroses, such as the paranoid personality, to offend everyone. More often than not, compassion for the distress of the patient overcomes whatever antipathy or indifference to personality the therapist may have originally had. If not, some reason should be found for referring the patient on.

The opposite situation is equally relevant, if not more so. We all know that people "charm" or intrigue others in varying degrees. I have friends that other friends, whom I esteem as highly, find obnoxious. Certain people touch and attract me. Over my years as a practicing therapist, I have learned that I am very successful with goofy, self-destructive, intense young men who are their own worst enemy. Is it the older brother in me that makes this so? Is it the aspects of my earlier self that I see in them? Since this is not a study in self-analysis, I will not pursue this area. But it should be pointed out that my being "taken" by these patients does not diminish countertransference problems. If anything, it will increase them. I have little problem with controlling my anger with patients; I rarely experience it. I do have to contain my paternalistic and maternalistic impulses. This represents as difficult a countertransference problem as containing negative feelings.

I have earlier indicated that a patient should not go to a therapist who doesn't "feel right" for him. However, during the course of therapy a patient will inevitably find himself angry, hurt, or disappointed in his therapist. It takes great courage on the part of the patient to expose negative feelings toward the therapist, but their open expression is absolutely essential to successful treatment. Similarly, during the course of therapy the therapist will have some negative emotional responses even to his most cherished patients. Often it will be impatience ("For God's sake, why doesn't he finally take the woman to bed. She has been waiting for this for weeks"). For the most part, these must *not* be explicated.

Therapy is never a truly reciprocal relationship. The therapist must always be cognizant of his own emotional responses to his patient. He must analyze these feelings (to himself) in order to discover as much as he can about why they are being elicited. Through this analysis of the countertransference — the way the patient affects him — he can garner valuable information about the way the patient may be affecting others in his life.

Early in the history of psychoanalysis, transference was recognized as a key instrument for gaining knowledge about the patient. The idea of even admitting the presence of countertransference feelings — let alone using them to further the analysis — is relatively new.

4

Psychoanalytic Tools II: Dreams and Fantasies

D REAMS ARE SPECIAL. They are deserving of a chapter of their own, if only as a testament to the unique role dream interpretation has played in psychotherapy from its very beginnings. The power of dreams in the conduct of psychotherapy is enormous. They cannot be dismissed. Dreams have relevance to current behavior; they illuminate the past; they pinpoint the specific tensions with which a patient is struggling. Dream interpretation is a shortcut to the unconscious life of the patient. Dreams are the X rays, CAT scans, and MRIs of the psychotherapist.

When Freud first added dream interpretation to his repertoire of devices for understanding a patient, he also added salt to the wounds he had already inflicted on the stalwarts of conventional medicine. It was insulting enough to have it suggested that talking could be a therapeutic measure. It was embarrassing to be told that frustrated sexual desires (carried over from childhood, no less) could cause physical symptoms. Now to see added something so unscientific, so unfashionable, as dream interpretation was an affront to logic and science. Dreams were subjective and immeasurable in a time that worshiped evidence, measurement, calibration, laboratory data, and quantification. Phrenology — the "science" of reading character from the shape of the skull — was far more acceptable. At least it dealt with concrete structure and bone, thus relating personality to anatomy, which held a respectable place in the world of medical science. But dream interpretation was the subject of quackery, astrologists, and gypsy fortune-tellers. At least at the dawn of the twentieth century.

Yet in literature the dream had always been recognized as a profound instrument for examining the internal life of the individual and therefore his future fate, since our lives are products of our perception. Think of Shakespeare's dramatic use of dreams and vision. The biblical respect for the power of the dream and its awe of visions are manifest throughout the Old Testament. The great heroes of the Bible — Adam, Abraham, Joseph, Moses, Noah — and all those others who spoke directly to God were men of visions as well as of vision.

To the skeptics, who view dreams and fantasies as pure literary mechanisms, not much can be said here that will be convincing — a reading of what many consider Freud's greatest work, *The Interpretation of Dreams* (1899), might help — but those who are in therapy or have been will surely recognize the power of this medium.

Everyone Does It

Patients dream with different frequencies. Patients with the least troubled sleep seem to dream the least. What happens is that deep sleepers are more apt to forget their dreams. We know from studies of rapid eye movement (REM) that dreaming tends to occur during REM sleep, and we know that everyone has REM sleep and will dream during the course of a night. While there is a marked variability in individual capacity to recall dreams, all patients, with effort, can recall a percentage of their dreams.

Whenever I had a candidate-in-training who told me that his patients didn't dream, I assumed that he himself was wary of dreams, being uncertain of his capacity to interpret them. At the beginning of therapy, I instruct my patients to remember and report their dreams. Since there is little other instruction except the implicit assumptions that they show up for appointments and on time, it makes an impression. When a patient replies, "I never dream," my usual response is, "That's all right. You will." I have never had a patient who could not recall a single dream during the course of a typical week of therapy. If a therapist really wants his patients to report dreams, they will.

There are many categories of dreams, each holding different significance for the patient and indicating different usages for the therapist: simple wish fulfillment dreams, recurrent dreams, frankly sexual (wet) dreams, and nightmares. Patients are particularly captivated by recurring dreams, and these are likely to be reported early, during the history taking. These, however, often have limited use in treatment, since they tend to be stereotypic, the generic dreams that most people experience because they mirror the existential problems we all share with others. They focus on what the patient has in common with mankind rather than on what sets him apart, what is special about him.

Recurrent dreams are most often troubled dreams reflecting the insecurities — the feelings of personal inadequacy — that seem ubiquitous in our culture. Everyone is familiar with them:

- Classic anxiety dreams: being chased by a monster; being in one's bedroom with an intruder at the door; being locked in a closet; being buried alive; being stuck on a high, narrow ledge with no way down.
- Traditional dreams of impotence: being cornered by an attacker, reaching for one's weapon, and finding no weapon there; the tip of one's sword is broken off (a particular masculine dream); the revolver is unloaded or inaccessible; swinging out with all our force, only to find we are underwater and our blows make no impact.
- Frustration dreams: Sisyphean dreams of climbing mountains and finding that there is another peak beyond, and still another beyond that, on to infinity; trying to run and being in a medium like molasses; searching for the key that is always kept in one place but seems to have disappeared.
- Dreams of sexual exposure: nudity in public places; getting caught with one's pants down.
- Dreams of rejection: wallflower and abandonment dreams.

Then there are other common dreams that we all seem to share, such as simple wish fulfillment dreams — the promotion comes, the lottery is won, the sexual fantasy is fulfilled — and dreams of conquest and victory.

Still, even recurrent dreams that tend to be shared with the populace at large are informative. Some patients will favor distinctive kinds of recurring dreams. Some patients are obsessed, or haunted, by a specific recurring dream theme. This points directly to a dominant type of stress that rules the unconscious of that individual. So while some patients rarely feel anxious, they may feel angry all the time. Recurrent dreams will tell us early whether we are dealing with a primarily anxious, guilty, or angry patient. They tend to pinpoint the predominant emotion through which the patient operates.

"Edward" never had anxiety dreams. Nor did he have dreams of explosive rage. But he was plagued with a recurrent set of dreams that were complex variations on the same theme. Many will recognize the category; what was unique to Edward was the frequency of these dreams. He would suffer the clichéd dream of visualizing from the wings a stage curtain opening, recognizing that he was an actor about to make an entrance. But what were his lines? What was the name of the play? How in the world had he gotten here?

Or he noticed that he was dressed in "white tie." How strange. Where was he? Why, in front of an orchestra of one hundred musicians, in a music hall filled to the rafters with people waiting for the concert to begin. He was the conductor, he who couldn't read a note of music, facing the intimidating pages of a conductor's score! Could he wing it? Weren't the musicians adequately rehearsed by somebody? Could he simply wave his arms and let the orchestra do its thing? Maybe that was all a conductor had to do on the night of the performance.

But mostly these recurrent dreams returned him to his college days. He would be walking through campus on the way to a final examination. He couldn't remember the hall in which the examination was to take place. The campus itself didn't look familiar. He didn't even know where the administration buildings were to inquire as to the location of the exam. And what course was this, anyhow? Had he done any of the readings? Had he attended any of the lectures? How could he have put himself in such a position of imminent exposure and humiliation? What had he been thinking? Where had he been during the previous months? Why hadn't he done his homework? It was this last question that was the key to understanding the significance of these dreams.

Obviously there is anxiety in this form of dream. But the predominant emotions are those of guilt and fear of imminent exposure as a fraud. The situation was always of Edward's making. He had "fucked up." He had "gotten away with it" (whatever "it" may have been) for a long time, but now he was to be revealed for the sham he really was.

Now, what of the real Edward? He was an enormously successful investment banker with at least two other significant activities that would have been counted as careers by almost anyone else: he was chairman of the board of two sizable cultural nonprofit organizations, and he had written a series of thrillers under a pseudonym. By every measurable standard, he was a giant success. The usual comment about Edward was, "How in the world does he find the time to do all of these things?" Yet Edward himself felt that somehow or other he had hoodwinked everyone. He knew that the "real" Edward was a lazy, undisciplined creature who was kept under wraps by a host of activities designed to fool the public.

Edward was the eldest of four children, and the only son. He was the favorite of his father, an extraordinarily hardworking man, who had managed to support his family during the Great Depression by working as a salesman, a job he loathed. Spending six days a week in drudgery, he invested his hopes in his children. Edward was gifted and everything academic came easy to him. He was a voracious reader but totally undisciplined. He never studied for his exams, delayed assignments until the last minute, and managed to graduate valedictorian of his class — which both pleased and confused his father.

Delighted as he was by his son's record, Edward's father was frightened and angry with him. He felt Edward was lazy and was sure that Edward would one day pay a price for his insouciance and lack of discipline. Edward, however, had breezed through high school, playing sports, running the newspaper, acting in school plays, and doing many things that struck his father as frivolous. With no money available to send him to an out-of-town college, Edward delayed until the last day to apply for the qualifying examinations for a scholarship. He won a national scholarship to an Ivy League college.

Of course once Edward went to college, his natural abilities *were* insufficient — one doesn't skip all the labs in a science course and still prevail. On full scholarship, with no ability to pay for his college expenses, he almost managed to flunk out in his first semester and barely avoided losing the scholarship. Frightened, he "conned" the administration into giving him another semester to prove himself, pulled himself together, and went on to graduate school and the successful multiple careers previously described.

Unfortunately, Edward's father died prematurely and never had the opportunity to bask in his son's achievements. But Edward retained his father's image and his father's judgment of him integrated into his own identity. In his unconscious, both the loving aspects and the anxieties influenced Edward's self-image. Edward "bought" his father's definition of him as a lazy person who charmed everyone into thinking otherwise but who would someday have to pay the piper. Edward paid for this internal image with the recurrent dreams of exposure.

All success was dismissed by Edward as another form of "getting away with it." He achieved little lasting satisfaction from achievement, since all was simply sham. It took years of therapy to convince Edward that there was no inner "true self" needing to be hidden from public scorn, that the "real"

Edward was the one perceived by everyone but himself. On the other hand, one would have to say that the determination to hide that "lazy boy" from public condemnation contributed significantly to Edward's great successes.

Interpreting Dreams and Fantasies

Dreams set in early childhood usually have an unbearable reality about them, and since recurrent dreams are usually set early, they too have an intensity that makes them easy to remember on waking. The distinction between waking and sleeping fantasies and events is more blurred in childhood. This makes for difficulty in therapy. When an adult retrieves a memory from childhood, the therapist is often unsure of whether he is dealing with fantasy or reality.

One of the earliest dreams that I can recall occurred when I was about three or four. My father came home late at night after I had fallen asleep with a wonderful present for me, the nature of which I did not know. He put the box in the huge walk-in closet underneath the staircase. That was the dream in its entirety.

This particular closet was five feet tall at its opening and slanted down to the floor, paralleling the stairs under which it was built. It was a catchall closet in which my mother stored extra supplies, seasonal items, outgrown toys. It was a miniature attic.

I recall waking up in the morning and "remembering" that my father had come home the night before with a present for me and had put it in the closet. (Since we had moved out of this house by the time I was eight, I know that this dream occurred before then. I cannot be more specific, but the quality of the dream suggests a three- to five-year-old.) I searched in that closet for what I later remembered to be hours, although more likely it was a matter of minutes, not knowing exactly what I was looking for. Finally I asked my mother, who then informed me that it must have been a dream.

I was incredulous. She just didn't understand. I *knew* that my father had brought a present; it wasn't a dream. I remained unconvinced and continued to search, despite her readiness to call my father and have him tell me that he had not hidden anything in the closet. She tried to comfort me, insisting it was only a dream and reassuring me that my father would bring me home a surprise that night. To no avail. While I had no idea what precisely I was searching out, I returned to that closet for hours to take one more look for my lost treasure.

This dream is a classic dream of childhood. It is direct and simple, a wish fulfillment dream. It reveals the child's difficulty with distinguishing fantasy and reality. But it would reveal even more to a therapist. It defines a special kind of relationship with my father. Further, where was this special gift hidden? *Deep in my mother's closet, where I was forced to explore and search!* What a delight for a Freudian therapist.

Some dreams are so self-evident that they need no interpretation. But others are wonderfully complex and mysterious. How are we to understand the hidden meanings in dreams? Freud and those who persisted in following the classical Freudian line saw all dreams as responses to a sexual wish and the anxiety inherent in the particular wish.

This could not explain nightmares, which clearly could not be seen as wish fulfillment even by the mighty stretches of imagination that early Freudians were prepared to use. Freud struggled all his life in trying to understand how a night terror could be a wish fulfillment, even to the point of introducing a new instinct, "Thanatos," the death instinct, to join "Eros," the sexual instinct. Nothing really worked. Dreams continued to be interpreted as wish fulfillment, and nightmares and traumatic dreams — well, they were "something else."

The simple answer is that once one abandons the assumption that all behavior is a derivative of sexual desire — libido — dreams do not all have to fall within one category. Most therapists these days take a broader view of dreams. We see them as expressing the unresolved tensions that accrued during the day. As such they focus both the therapist and his patient on what is truly troubling.

The first two dreams reported by a former patient of mine reveal the way dreams can define a patient's expectations about therapy. Since starting therapy is usually a significant and disturbing event in an individual's life, the first dreams of therapy are likely to be transference dreams and, as such, are often difficult for the patient to acknowledge. This patient had a major personality disorder — he was tight, obsessive, and extremely anxious in competitive situations — but he was driven to therapy by an acute symptom, his first bout of impotence.

"Robert" was a young man, in his late twenties, and his impotence was particularly threatening to him. After the first week of sessions, he rightly detected my somewhat casual attitude about the impotence and my tacit assumption that this was a transient phenomenon peripheral to his major adjustment problems. This would have a dramatic effect on his behavior. That weekend Robert had sexual intercourse with his girlfriend, and for the first time in months he had no problems maintaining an erection. He felt transformed, and since it was the impotence that had made him seek therapy, he felt cured! His first dream was reported the following

Monday: "I entered the lobby of my apartment and there had been a radical change, indeed, a transformation. The dirty, nondescript lobby space had been converted into a palatial chasm with elegant furniture and artwork. I was astonished and delighted, but confused as to when this all could have happened, and how the super could have effected so dramatic an improvement so quickly."

He reported this dream and surprisingly stated that he had no idea what it was about! After associating for a while, he gradually began to make the connection between his life and the apartment house. The building somehow represented himself and his state of existence. This is a classic dream metaphor. A dirty house, a chaotic and disorganized house, inadequate space, a leaky roof, collapsing infrastructure — all are common symbols used in dreams to express our feelings about our lives and ourselves. Dreams are, after all, elaborate metaphors, and our house is certainly a direct and simple equivalent for our life.

After a period of time, he related this dream to his delight at having been "cured" of his sexual problem. He didn't pretend to understand how this happened, but he felt it was like magic. It *was* like magic; and it is characteristic of the classic "transference cures" that occur during the honeymoon phase of therapy. They are inevitably the product of the magic with which the patient invests the therapist and the process. Not that transference cures are bad. Any cure is good. Miracles occur at Lourdes; and some transference cures are permanent. In either case, however, they are the rare exception rather than the rule. Therapists tend, therefore, to be wary of such instant and dramatic success.

Robert then proceeded to equate the super who was "in charge" of maintenance and decoration of the building with me and indicated his enormous gratitude; he felt that he had made a wise choice in his selection of a therapist and was delighted with the "progress."

Alas, the honeymoon did not last. His problems in relationships, which were central to his neurosis, had not even been discussed. Robert was not a prolific dream reporter, nor did he have the intuitive knack for reading dream symbols that some patients have. This is consistent with an obsessive character with large components of rigidity and literalness. A few weeks later, he reported his second dream: "I had returned from the cleaner with a suit I had taken for the removal of a spot, only to notice that the spot was still there."

This time the patient wanted to dismiss the dream. He said that it was "not really a dream" but was simply a sleeping recall of an actual event. That day he had, indeed, brought his favorite suit back from the cleaner's only to notice the same spot. Whereupon he returned the suit to the cleaner. I encouraged him to associate to this dream, saying I suspected that many annoying things had happened during that day and that there was a reason he would have chosen to select this particular, and seemingly untraumatic, event to dream about.

This is part of the classic understanding of how dreams work. We will tend to take images from the day before — called the day residue — and use these to build metaphors that encapsulate the unfinished emotional business of that day. The daily tensions we choose to dream about are those that are metaphoric, specifically those that are emblematic of our central problems. By analyzing one specific day's dream, we are plugging into a lifelong pattern of tension or despair.

I asked him to continue associating, although his resistance to this dream was much greater than to his first. With difficulty and considerable annoyance, he finally said the only thing that came to mind was the old saying "A leopard never changes his spots."

I asked him what he thought that aphorism meant. Literal individuals have great trouble with aphorisms. When literalism is extreme, therapists refer to the trait as concreteness. Concrete patients have great trouble with metaphor. If you ask them what the expression "People in glass houses shouldn't throw stones" means, they are likely to talk about windows getting broken. So too with this patient. After leaving the world of leopards, he slowly wended his way to the general proposition that it is never easy to change one's nature. Still, he strongly resisted the idea that it had specific significance in his life. Only when I directly questioned him as to whether anything had occurred the night before the dream did he report that he had had a recurrence of his problem with erections. From there he went, laborious step by laborious step, to a despondent conviction that for him change would not come easily: "You are what you are."

When I asked Robert whether there was any emotion in the dream other than despondency, he denied it. When asked if there was any anger during his day, he reported that he had been angry with the cleaner in life, but insisted that there was no anger in the dream. When I asked him if he was angry with me, he flatly denied it. Nonetheless, this eventually led him to his feeling of disappointment in me, and therapy in general, and the sinking feeling that change was going to be a much slower process than he had anticipated it magically would be.

The two dreams jump-started Robert's therapy. They exposed the power of the transference; they served to focus and expose his emotions, through his original delight in me and his later disillusionment. They also revealed a readiness to respond with panic to even a mild suggestion of a disorder in his sexual capacities, while remaining rather sanguine in the face of other forms of reported disasters in his general relationships with women. Although, in all fairness, no young man ever perceives even transient problems with erections as mild.

Interest in dreams on the part of the layman inevitably focuses on the content. But dreams are equally valuable in describing the predominant emotional underpinnings. These two dreams started the process of introducing Robert not only to his unconscious thoughts, but to his emotional life. Robert was predisposed to panic. Edward, with his exposure dreams, seemed to have no anxiety in his everyday life, but was plagued with guilt. He never felt he did enough to warrant his father's approval.

These dreams of Robert's revealed other vital factors besides content and emotional state. The dreams and Robert's efforts to interpret them also presaged the literalness, concreteness, and tendency to denial with which we struggled throughout his therapy.

Like dreams, fantasies are also metaphors for the desires, conflicts, and expectations of the patient. They are useful to interpret in a similar manner to dreams, but they must be approached in a somewhat different way. Fantasies are perceived as being consciously formed and consciously used and therefore much more our "responsibility" than a dream. If a patient was to have a dream of sex with a child, he would be frightened and appalled, but protected by his awareness that dreams are symbols and can mean something quite different from that which their external form suggests. If he has a fantasy of sex with a child, he is more likely to feel terrified and ashamed.

Fantasies occur in a waking stage; therefore they seem more real. Also, we feel we have more control over them; but this is not necessarily true. We tend to choose many of our fantasies — simple wish fulfillment, sexual speculations, hopes, plans, aspirations — but many arise uninvited from our unconscious, just like dreams.

Nonetheless, there are fantasy thoughts that seem to emerge out of thin air and intrude themselves into our consciousness to the same unsettling degree that dreams do, and they should be interpreted in the same way. In addition, there are unwanted and unacceptable fantasies that can plague us in our waking hours: sexual desires for an inappropriate object, thoughts of committing mayhem or of losing control. These are often labeled obsessive thoughts. And all of these are ripe for analytic processing.

Beyond this, remember that almost every account a patient offers the therapist is in one way or another a fantasy, since it is screened through his image of himself and the world he lives in. This is the subjective world of perception in which we all live. A therapist is therefore likely to treat everything a patient says as his perception rather than actuality. Every "objective" account of a thought, perception, or activity will be approached by the therapist with the same concern for distortion and metaphoric implications as a dream event. The therapist will thus be using the techniques of dream interpretation throughout all his dealings with his patient during the course of the hour. Dreams are in every way the prototype of the analytic process, the stuff of analysis.

Further, dream analysis became an early paradigm for approaching the study of the human mind. How does the mind work, and how do thoughts influence behavior?

USING
KNOWLEDGE

II

5 A Psychological Understanding of Behavior

PSYCHIATRIC PROBLEMS were traditionally part of the jurisdiction of medicine, governed by its rules and subject to its methods. Prior to the late nineteenth century, all medical treatment was empirical (trial and error; guided by practical experience, not theory), and most of it was wretched. Physicians and surgeons (barbers), with their excellent knowledge of anatomy and modest awareness of physiology, could limit traumatic damages — broken bones could be set, bleeding could be stanched, gangrenous limbs amputated — but they could do little with infectious or deteriorative organ diseases. Early physicians did that which appeared to work, though they rarely knew why it worked. What etiology (causation) they thought they understood was almost invariably false.

When physicians instituted ambitious therapies, they were inevitably bad therapies — leeches, purging, bleeding, and potions that hastened death in many an acutely ill patient who would have survived if not for the treatments or the deadly infectious environments of the hospitals. Even when I was a medical student in the mid-twentieth century, a brilliant and tyrannical professor of physiology informed a class of ambitious and proud medical students that medical intervention over the years had unquestionably taken more lives than it had saved. More humbling than that was his assurance that this data held true for any given year up until World War II!

The same conditions prevailed in mental illnesses. Certain empirical measures — baths, rest, massage, heat packs, and asylum (protection from environmental tensions) — were effective in that they allowed time for the restorative powers of the human spirit to work. Some of the mental hospitals were disgraceful, punitive and horrible institutions. Nonetheless, the concept of sanitarium, of protection, is an authentic one that is ready to be rediscovered. These treatments subscribed to the first principle of decent medicine, "Do no harm." With patience, time — the precious healer of most wounds — was allowed to operate.

But during Freud's lifetime (1856–1939), all of this would change. The biological sciences, along with all other sciences, were exploding with new understandings, culminating in the brilliant work of Louis Pasteur (1822–1895) and Robert Koch (1843–1910), whose research established the germ theory — proving conclusively for all time that infectious diseases were the product of invasive microscopic organisms. Humankind was finally to achieve the promise of Prometheus and enter a brave new world where man might rival, or even supplant, the gods.

With the physical diseases, a vast body of scientific knowledge about the normal conditions of human organs and tissues had been in place for hundreds of years, awaiting only the discovery of the nature of pathogens and a more exact understanding of physiology. We had had a precise awareness of gross anatomy since Andreas Vesalius (1514–1564). Pathologists understood the site and nature of organ damage, without knowing the cause. With the germ theory, the final piece of the puzzle seemed to be in place.

Unfortunately, with the mind, as distinguished from the kidney or the liver, *no* background science was in place. The mind is situated in — or a function of — the brain, the most complex and least charted of all the human organs. To this day we remain unclear about the most basic anatomical connections of the various parts of the brain that control mental functioning. The physiology of emotions is barely beginning to be understood (what is the chemistry of love?); we have a minimal knowledge of memory and intelligence; and we have *no* understanding at all of the physiology, biochemistry, or mechanisms of an idea or belief. Nonetheless, attempts were made to bring human behavior into the realm of scientific observation.

Freudian Psychology

Any discussion of mental illness, or for that matter any aspect of mental life, must inevitably start with Freud, who left his mark on almost every major branch of intellectual thought in our times, from anthropology to art criticism. It may seem perverse to start with Freud, since his reputation now is probably at its lowest point since he achieved early fame at the beginning of the twentieth century. But he is there and there is no way around him. Love him or loathe him, Freud (if I may borrow words from Shakespeare's *Julius Caesar*) "doth bestride the narrow world [of human psychology] like a Colossus"!

If Freud's reputation were solely dependent on his therapeutic successes, he would not even be a footnote in the world of medicine or ideas. He treated a trivial number of patients, and most of his therapy was left incomplete and unsuccessful. Fortunately Freud was more than a therapist, that is, more than a person devoted to treatment of illnesses; he was also a creative student of human conduct. He was a profound psychologist who brought discipline and imagination to the understanding of the way people feel, the way they interact, the way they perceive, and the way they behave. Here he was master creator, nonpareil, and he remains — despite the current calumny — the father of all modern knowledge of human perceptions and behavior. He was, in other words, a great student of normal behavior, albeit a failure in his understanding of disease.

What has contributed to the diminution of Freud's reputation during the past twenty years? The excessive adulation, almost deification, of Freud during the first half of the twentieth century practically guaranteed a negative rebound at the end of the century. Another contributing factor was the profound disappointment in the exaggerated promise of psychoanalytic therapy, which pledged cures it could not produce and understanding it could not deliver. Finally, there is almost no "politically correct" idea cherished today that cannot be challenged by Freudian thinking. He threatens today's ideologues, with their inflated versions of propriety and truth.

As is so often the way in research, seeking one thing we are likely to stumble across another. Freud's understanding of normal human intercourse came out of his relatively unsuccessful attempts to discover the nature of mental illness. The principles of everyday behavior that emerged from Freud's struggles and observations over fifty years of research stand almost undisputed to this day.

Some may argue that he did not "discover" these principles, that they existed in the past and were expressed in the words of poets and philosophers. Of course they were. From the writings of Genesis, Euripides, Shakespeare, Goethe, Austen, Balzac, Dickens, Dostoevsky, Chekhov, and others we can appreciate and understand the human condition. Similarly, philosophers from Socrates through Hume to Schopenhauer slashed windows into that black box called the human mind. But Freud, the creator of the concept of "mental illness," was also — along with the behaviorists Ivan Petrovich Pavlov and John B. Watson — the father of modern psychology. He brought together in a disciplined fashion, supported by clinical confirmation, many of the poetic and intuitive insights of the past. The major principles of Freudian psychology can be roughly summarized as follows:

- *Motivation.* Behavior is motivated. It moves always with purpose and toward a goal. It is rarely, if ever, just random. This allows for an explanation of each action in terms of some anticipation, some wish, some desire.

- *The psychodynamic principle.* Behavior must also be seen as dynamic. No single piece of conduct can be understood by itself. An example that I have used in the past is the game played with a giant bladder ball where hundreds of students push the ball from hundreds of different angles. At any given moment the ball may remain still. This does not suggest that there are no forces in motion, merely that the forces are in balance. If the ball moves slightly to the northeast it does not mean that someone in the southwest has pushed it there. The balance of forces — hundreds of forces — has led to that result. It may be that someone on the opposing side lost strength or power.

    One cannot ever know why a person chose a specific action without considering multiple aspects of both the person and the event. Three men see a young woman being assaulted by a purse snatcher. One walks quickly away. The second shouts for help. The third directly intervenes. To complicate matters, under slightly different circumstances the various individuals might have changed roles; the action in one event cannot accurately predict action in a seemingly similar one. Such actions are always a complex result of forces and counterforces. This is what psychotherapists mean by "dynamic," and when we talk about psychodynamics, which we always do, we mean the forces and counterforces that operate on an individual to bring about a single piece of behavior. Freud, immersed in the intellectual ferment of his time, may well have borrowed his model from the sophisticated knowledge of force and motion emerging in the burgeoning field of physics.

- *Behavior as developmental.* Behavior can be appreciated only in a developmental context. Nothing that happens can be fully comprehended isolated from its past. Behavior fits into a continuum, or sequence, of events. Determining factors in the past drive us to particular conduct in the present intended to achieve specific goals in the future. There is no way to read today's events without understanding what has preceded them.

- *The discovery of the unconscious.* Freud postulated that we are mostly unaware of these past determinants of our behavior. The motivational forces that drive us to act are as likely — more likely, Freud would have insisted — to derive from unconscious fears and desires as from conscious calculation.

  Even though we are unaware of our unconscious thoughts and feelings and incapable of bringing this material to the forefront of the mind without, Freud would claim, the extraordinary methods of psychoanalysis, the unconscious is the primary driver of behavior. The conscious reasons we offer to explain why we quit our job, broke off our engagement, left home, or took up smoking are likely to be partial explanations at best, or rationalizations (a Freudian word) after the fact. Strict behaviorists do not believe in the unconscious, but very few poets and novelists, and very few ordinary people who examine the follies of their lives, would agree with them.

- *Human irrationality.* Not the least of what offends modern thinkers is Freud's insistence on emphasizing the irrational determinants of human behavior, particularly during this period in which we are basking in the sunlight of our intellectual and scientific achievements. How could it be otherwise, Freud might ask, since so much of our behavior derives from unconscious motivation? Further, the forces and counterforces that dominate unconscious thinking are primarily the passions and the instincts rooted in the biological and animal nature of the human species.

  Against the onslaught of the passions, said Freud, reason and cognition are fragile shields. They mitigate and modify the instinctual drives and forces of hunger, sex, survival, but rarely counter them.

- *Idealism.* Freud was educated under the profound influence of idealism, the philosophical movement that dominated German intellectual life from the time of Immanuel Kant to that of Freud's contemporary Arthur Schopenhauer. Most of us, on first encountering idealism in its starkest form, as articulated by such original idealists as Bishop George Berkeley, struggle with its basic tenet: What does it mean that there is no real world, that the world exists only in our own minds? But when we approach it metaphorically, most of us appreciate the profundity of the recognition that we individuals live in a world of our own perceptions, rather than in some world of objective actuality.

If we emerge from childhood with a deep sense of deprivation, we will travel through life feeling deprived even in the presence of abundant good fortune. We will always see ourselves as somehow disadvantaged. If we feel that we are stupid, no number of IQ tests will convince us otherwise. Similarly, if we perceive ourselves as beautiful, ugly, loved, unloved, it will be the perception, not the reality of our physiognomy and condition, that will drive our behavior. The perceived world is the operative arena in which the patient acts out his life, and is the staging area where psychotherapy must take place.

• *Defenses.* Much of our present behavior involves defensive maneuvers against perceived threats to survival emerging from the unconscious past. In a fascinating work, *Character and Anal Eroticism* (1908), Freud described an "anal character," characterized by rigidity, orderliness, and parsimony. He attributed these personality traits to defenses ("sublimations" and "reaction formations") against anal erotic impulses. If we have a desire to smear feces, we could sublimate it by becoming a painter; "sublimation" means diverting the unconscious impulse to a more socially acceptable area. We could use a reaction formation, denying the impulse by embracing the opposite — becoming fastidious and orderly. We need not accept these specific interpretations (I certainly don't) to accept the legitimacy of defensive aspects of behavior. The point is that defenses lead both to character traits and to neurotic symptoms. Defenses are attempts to preserve our self-respect by allowing us to pursue our shameful unconscious infantile drives in disguised or distorted forms. Such commonplace terms as "repression," "regression," "projection," "reaction formation" — now part of the vernacular — were Freudian definitions of defense mechanisms. Even if one rejects the libido theory, as I have, the idea of defense mechanisms that support our pride and self-esteem by denying unconscious feelings still has immense usefulness.

In treatment therapists focus on defenses as much as dynamics, attempting to substitute healthy defenses for neurotic ones. The man who avoids attachments may desire love and affection as much as the one who pursues them. The unloving person may not eschew love; he may desire it too much. Therefore, in terror of rejection he may reject all who approach him with warmth and affection. The hermit and the hale-fellow-well-met may both be responding to a desperate hunger for love and approval. The problem is not that the recluse lacks the appetite for love and affection. He is merely defending against these passions, which he believes unattainable, by "denying" his desires. Denial is an "ego defense mechanism," as such constructs are now called.

The preceding list is one way to simplify and organize the basic tenets of Freudian theory that seem to have withstood the test of time. Specific terminologies may differ, but it is a rare psychology that does not accommodate itself to these principles. I personally view them as the most profound statements about human motivation to have emerged in modern times. No one since Freud has contributed anything that has lent greater understanding to the ways and whys of ordinary human behavior.

Conspicuously absent from this list are some terms that are generally considered the hallmarks of Freudian psychology: "Oedipus complex," "libido theory," "castration anxiety," "penis envy." These are the catch phrases of psychoanalysis; they do not encompass the basic insights. They are metaphors designed to help organize our understanding of human development. Metaphors are syntactical and poetic attempts to illuminate, by integrating, a body of diverse data. We can have multiple and diverse metaphors, unrelated to each other, that may all prove equally useful. They must only be consonant with all the known facts of human behavior. The story line must include all the pertinent data.

Freud himself was not averse to revising or abandoning aspects of his basic theory throughout his lifetime. Revisionist theories were continually presented by him to his cohort, even though the original theory, when first published, was presented with absolute certitude and authority, a reflection more of the author's personality than the facts.

The Importance of Feelings

One egregious omission from the list of basic Freudian tenets is any mention of the role of emotions as determining forces in behavior. How could this be? People seek therapy because they "feel bad," not because they have become aware of internal conflicts, not because they are messing up their lives or squandering their talents, not even because they have psychological symptoms. If none of the above make them *feel bad,* they will not seek treatment, nor will they do well in it if forced to go. Psychopaths are profoundly psychologically impaired, and they never seek treatment: their symptoms cause distress to *other* people, not themselves.

Given the central importance of feelings in our everyday life, you would think that the psychological and psychoanalytic literature would be dominated by them. It is not so. The reasons for this are not clear. Freud was beguiled by internal conflicts, tensions, and ideation. He even viewed anxiety as a by-product, a derivative of repressed sexual desire. Rage, and therefore aggression, seemed to have no place in his vocabulary. This omission drove Alfred Adler, an early disciple, from the Freudian fold.

Freud certainly recognized the irrational factors in human life, but he ascribed them to the instinctual forces that he perceived as driving behavior. Only relatively recently has affect theory (Freudian language for emotional forces) been introduced into the mix. Why did it take so long? Perhaps to place any value in such a subjective, unmeasurable, "irresponsible" subject as feelings was unsettling in a scientific and logical age. Perhaps feelings are too close to our vulnerable central core to allow for comfortable evaluation. Perhaps it is simply that in a technological society that values the measurable, the visible, the palpable, and the objectifiable, feelings embarrass us by defying our most respected current tools of investigation. Having said all this, the emotions of a patient are the ultimate driving forces of therapy, as they are the driving forces of all his efforts in life.

Emotions are a part of our genetic inheritance as a species, cutting across all cultures, although the expression of emotions will vary from family to family and culture to culture. What is emotionally acceptable on the streets of Palermo would seem aberrant in the cool reserve of Stockholm. The therapist will compensate for the cultural background of the patient, knowing that while the quiet, reserved Scandinavian shares the same emotions as the more demonstrative Latin, he will display them in a different way.

The feelings that the psychotherapist is most likely to deal with are fear, anger, guilt, shame, and pride. But there is a whole repertoire of other emotions, such as feeling envious, tired (often a symptom of depression), upset, touched, hurt, or moved, that offer the therapist a finer-tuned coloration of the patient's current life. One way to look at our own feelings is as signals to us, valuable signals. Even painful signals such as guilt and shame — generally dismissed by self-help books as useless and destructive — are priceless assets directing us to a good and rewarding life. Guilt, for example, tells us when we have betrayed our own standards; shame, when we have violated the community standards.

If there is one rule for conducting therapy, one transcendent principle to guide the therapist, it is the imperative that he must follow the emotion. It matters not where the patient was in the history, where he left off in the previous session; if a patient comes in anxious, humiliated, or enraged over some seemingly trivial, "less important" event, it is that to which the therapist must attend. Unless, that is, he wants to conduct an intellectualized Hollywood type of therapy. If one "interprets" for the patient what one knows about him haphazardly, or when one first gains the knowledge, the patient gets information for which he is unready, and the result will be a totally intellectual and nontherapeutic experience.

The quantitative measurements of our lives do not determine our happiness or pride. Your position, your assets, your loved ones, even the repute with which you are held, are nothing if they are not fungible into feelings of self-worth. It is your feelings that drive you to therapy and it is your feelings that must be changed. The person who is complacent or accepting of the fact that he is a drug addict without a job, abandoned by all friends and family, and living in the gutter, will not make a good patient. But we do not see such patients in therapy. We see those who, while surrounded by the mirrors of their success and worth, perceive only images of failure and worthlessness. The emotions are the road signs that direct us to the areas of conflict that are disabling the patient.

Getting "Scientific"

All of the theories of Freud and others represented attempts to bring the understanding of mental illness into the new world of scientific medicine. They were tired of trial and error — doing what worked without understanding why — and somewhat ashamed of the ignorance implicit in such treatments. Therapists, like all scientists, craved logic and understanding — a direct one-way street between cause and cure, where treatment would always follow etiology (the cause or origin). This was the direction of modern medicine.

But their ignorance of basic mental functioning meant that the minions of science, the psychiatrists (who trained as physicians), would present ill-founded and speculative theories of the causes and cures of mental illness to a lay public enthralled by the new science of medicine. These theories would be offered up in the language and style of science, with the certitude of scientific data — but with absolutely no method of confirmation or corroboration. Often neglected was the kind of valuable observations that yielded an awareness that patients did better when sequestered from the anxieties of their everyday life; that phobias were helped by gently forcing confrontation with the phobic situation; that time healed most depressions. These were useful observations that ought still to be remembered in these days of antidepressant and antipanic pharmaceuticals.

As his theories about normal behavior and its determinants evolved, Freud was also examining abnormal behavior, particularly the grotesque behavior of hysterics. In his earliest writings, specifically in *Studies in Hysteria* (1895, published jointly with Josef Breuer), Freud articulated two seemingly outrageous positions that profoundly offended the medical establishment of his time and transformed psychiatry.

Jean-Martin Charcot, the great French neurologist with whom Freud had briefly studied, had focused his research attentions on the "neurological" condition known as hysteria. It was then assumed to be a *physical* disease of the nervous system that manifested itself in severe forms of physical infirmity: the paralysis of an arm or hand; an inability to hear, see, or talk; epileptic seizures; numbness of whole body sections.

In his studies Freud concluded that the hysteric was "suffering from reminiscences." This outlandish and glorious concept was so radical as to strain credibility. That an actual physical symptom (which was the way the hysterical symptom was then visualized) could be caused by a memory must have seemed absurd. It was hard enough for the laity to buy the idea that a symptom could be caused by an invisible organism, a germ, let alone by a thought, a wish, or an idea. Adding insult to injury, Freud insisted that it was a sexual reminiscence from childhood. Surely children had no sexual life! And wasn't it strange that the patient knew nothing about this until his conversations with the doctor?

The observation that thoughts and the emotions they induce produce symptoms was a transforming idea in psychology. Many therapists now reject the thesis that the unconscious impulse must be sexual. No matter. What was critical was the awareness of the power of the unconscious life and the profound influence of past experiences on current conduct. This early insight that the hysteric suffered from reminiscence had significant implications for the future trajectory of psychotherapy. It set the model for a developmental theory of neurosis. It suggested that self-perceptions can preempt observations of reality. It confirmed that we are authors of our own agony. It implied that the dynamics of the past must somehow or other be confronted to allow a patient to enjoy the entitlements of the present.

Equally innovative and off-putting was Freud's choice of treatment for hysteria. Charcot had discovered that hypnosis could be used to temporarily reverse hysteric symptoms, even while he continued to insist that the symptoms were physical. Freud attempted to hypnotize his patients, but he turned out to be a singularly inept hypnotist. He then settled for simply talking to his patients and managed to get the same result as with hypnosis. He labeled this prototype of modern psychotherapy the "talking cure." Essentially it meant that the patient was simply allowed to talk, a rare event in any doctor's office even to this day. The talk eventually became less directed, more "free associative." An emphasis on fantasies and dreams emerged. What evolved was the nondirective process that is currently a part of all psychoanalysis and most psychotherapies. To the European medical establishment of Freud's time, the idea that talking could cure a physical symptom must have seemed as outrageous as if Carl Jung, the eminent Swiss psychiatrist, had proposed that yodeling could cure syphilis.

By the mid-twentieth century, however, the idea that recovered memories were curative became not only respectable, but de rigueur. The public imagination, as exemplified by movies and novels, delighted in the concept. From *Spellbound,* which introduced us to the most bewitching, desirable, and unlikely of psychoanalysts, Ingrid Bergman, to the more recent *Ordinary People,* with the less glamorous Judd Hirsch, the cure for what ails you seems to be in the rediscovery of memory. The patient recovers an unconscious memory — responsibility for the death of a brother is a particularly popular one — and in the rediscovery the patient learns that he was not responsible for the tragedy. This leaves unanswered the problem of unconscious memories that are for the most part true rather than imagined, but let's not quibble. The patient then hugs his therapist and walks out of the darkness of his illness into the light of health and happiness. Would that it were so! Why this mythology persists to the present is hard to fathom. Freud quickly found that truth would *not* set his patients free. Yet despite that, hundreds and thousands of therapists today still operate on the eureka theory of psychoanalysis.

With each succession of failures, Freud would modify his theory. Through these modifications a much more complex view of mental illness emerged. If one basic insight left the patient unchanged, this must mean that a single trauma was insufficient to produce a full-blown neurosis (now defined as an emotional disorder with no discernible organic cause). He decided that symptoms were "overdetermined," meaning that a single symptom contained multiple conflicts. Only those unfortunate souls battered by a host of traumatic events would succumb to a neurotic breakdown.

The overdetermination principle has its downside. The therapist would return again and again to the same dry well, looking for more information, rather than questioning whether any amount of knowledge would effect a change.

What often ensued was a rambling and prolonged psycho-analysis, meandering endlessly through the past. During the years of wanderings through the labyrinth of the uncon-scious, the patient would learn more and more about himself but with little relief of his symptoms.

This may explain the jaundiced view of my sophisticated college roommate on hearing that I was considering becom-ing a psychoanalyst. He snorted with contempt. "You don't believe in psychoanalysis?" I asked incredulously. "Of course not," said this stoic Puritan New Englander. He then shared with me his vision of psychoanalysis.

The neurotic patient occupies a beautiful house, sound in structure and tastefully furnished, as distinguished from the psychotic patient, whose house is collapsing. The problem, however, is that in the basement of this splendid abode is a mountain of manure, the stench of which makes the house barely habitable. The psychoanalyst equips the patient with a shovel and encourages him to shovel the manure out of the basement — and dump it in the front parlor!

Unkind as he was to confront a budding young analyst with this cynical view of psychoanalysis, he had a point. It was a time when people spouted about their problems, talked analytic jargon endlessly, and assumed that somehow or other their increased sophistication decreased the degree of their incapacity.

Psychotherapy is not a fraud. It does work. Not always, but neither do many medical therapies, as any who suffer from a bad back, asthma, or arthritis well know. We are now — I presume and pray — in a humbler and more tolerant position. It is time to identify the common therapeutic maneuvers that are operative under the general rubric of psychotherapy.

Catharsis

6

WE ALL KNOW from personal experience that in times of anguish "just talking about it" to a friend or loved one often helps. This being the case, why wouldn't just talking about neurotic problems help — or would it? Early psychotherapists, led by Freud, started with the assumption that it would. The problem for them was still a complicated one, since they assumed that the patient was not likely to be aware of precisely what was bothering him.

When one talks to one's friend about a disappointment at work, a health problem, or a sexual indiscretion, the problem being shared is a conscious and explicit one. Freud assumed that the problem underlying a neurosis was unconscious, therefore unavailable for talking out and the relief derived from that. Before talking about "it" could relieve the troubled mind, one would have to discern what "it" really was.

This dictated the first fundamental technique of therapy. Plumb the unconscious, discover what is disturbing the individual, and let him talk it out. Since the cause of all neuroses was then presumed to be wishes or ideas trapped in the unconscious, the assumption was that bringing the bad idea out of the unconscious and into the open would relieve the symptom. This came to be called the cathartic model of therapy. Therapists focused on the unconscious and repressed idea, wish, or memory. They became seduced by the content, the nature of the "it," and never pressed for an examination of the more intriguing question of how *talking* operated to relieve psychic distress, as well as symptoms, that is, how talking worked therapeutically. Early therapists seemed oblivious of the emotional and experiential aspects inherent in talking to another human being.

The editors of the *American Heritage Dictionary of the English Language* have brilliantly managed in one brief paragraph to summarize the various meanings of "catharsis" and in their summary suggest — while not explicating — some of the problems with the use of the word. They list four meanings of the term in a historical order:

> 1. *Medicine.* Purgation, especially for the digestive system. 2. A purifying or figurative cleansing of the emotions, especially pity and fear, described by Aristotle as an effect of tragic drama on its audience. 3. A release of emotional tension, as after an overwhelming experience, that restores or refreshes the spirit. 4. *Psychology.* a. A technique used to relieve tension and anxiety by bringing repressed feelings and fears to consciousness. b. The therapeutic result of this process; abreaction.

Purgation

The psychological definition of purgation is closely related to the medical one. As well it should be. Antisepsis and cleanliness were introduced into medicine through the pioneering insights of Joseph Lister and Ignaz Semmelweis. Perhaps the body could be cleansed and purified by removing the contaminated fluids. Purging was one method to attempt to cleanse the internal environment. If a clean environment was essential for good physical health, why not a clean internal environment for mental health?

The idea that "cleaning out one's insides" is akin to bathing one's exterior is still part of the folklore and home practice of medicine. "High colonics" may be less fashionable now than a century ago, but "regularity" is still considered a physical state of grace, if we are to believe the ads for laxatives that inundate television.

If we stick with the idea of cleanliness and the concept of foreign bodies as causes of pain and disease, we can appreciate how the idea of purging, whether via enemas, bleeding, lancing a boil, or induced vomiting, gained credibility in medical practice. It was not too great a leap to adapt the idea of purging the body to purging the mind. And this was precisely what Freud postulated in his earliest writings.

The foreign body, the toxic material, was a repressed wish. Bring the unconscious thought into consciousness, lance the psychic boil, and — *shazam* — the pain would be talked away. To his credit, Freud quickly modified this early theory. He did so because he was a trained clinician who could not help but observe that the symptom did *not* go away. So he introduced the concept of abreaction, which expanded the simple idea of purgation.

"Abreaction" is defined as the relief of the psychic tension that results from recovering and articulating repressed memories. The process of recovery, the working through, was itself important. Unfortunately, the primary emphasis remained with the early conflict, not the tension or the emotions related to the conflict. Freud quickly perceived that the mere act of making the unconscious conscious would not work, and sought more complex therapeutic models.

Why deal with it here? Incredible as it may seem, a full century later this model A Freud is still clogging the therapeutic highways. It is the foundation for school after school of howling and screaming therapies attracted by the simplicity and economics of the basic assumption that letting it all hang out will cure what ails you. "Don't hold it back." "Let it all out." "Keeping it in is hazardous to your health." These are the shibboleths of so many cult cures of our time. The "it" in all these sentences is invariably rage — certainly not compassion, generosity, or love.

This purgation, or more accurately, emetic, model is sustained by a culture that honors rampant individualism and that has even justified such aberrant and antisocial self-expression as graffiti and urinating in the streets as "doing your own thing." Medicine is a part of that larger culture, and subject to its values and biases. The medical literature has published literally hundreds of articles about suppressed anger and its dangers to health. In *The Rage Within: Anger in Modern Life,* a study of anger I did some years ago, I cited dozens of articles supporting this popular and unjustified position. One paradigmatic research group concluded that "strong support [exists for the] hypothesis that suppressed anger . . . is, in fact, the ideological component to elevated blood pressure, both systolic and diastolic, and consequently to essential hypertension." There are other spurious studies that link suppressed anger with diabetes, cancer, and almost any disease that one can think of.

While a state of anger may play a role in the etiology of some or all of these diseases, it does not follow that *expression* of anger will cure or change these conditions. Expressing anger is not quite like draining a bathtub. In a perverse way, the verbalizing of rage is as likely to leave the person as filled with rage as before the outburst. In fact, recent studies are now indicating that *expressed* anger is hazardous to your health. Men with high hostility ratings have six times as much probability of having a heart attack as average men. In addition, high hostility is associated with the risk of death from all causes.

Expression or repression is not the issue. The mistake that all of the self-expression crowd makes is in assuming that the release of anger is a therapeutic experience. Of course it may momentarily make one feel good. But that does not assault the basic neurotic problem. The problem with angry people, who are certainly more vulnerable to many psychosomatic ills, is not their inability to *release* anger, it is their unlimited capacity to *generate* unwarranted anger. These individuals will summon massive rage in response to meager stimuli. They will perceive even the slightest discourtesy as a life-threatening assault or a damage to dignity and pride.

This capacity to manufacture almost unlimited supplies of anger makes all therapies that attempt cure for one's misery by releasing anger simply ludicrous. Still, there have even been therapeutic schools that have so revered the purgative model that they have baited people who were not demonstrably angry to offer them the relief that comes from the release of anger! The illogicality of this can be demonstrated by a simple comparison. Even if one accepted the concept that fevers are bad and can be reduced by alcohol rubs and aspirin, this hardly suggests that there is something therapeutic in generating a fever in the first place just to permit the administration of the alcohol rub or the aspirin.

What is true of anger applies to most cases of repressed emotions. The problem with people who have pent-up emotions is not just their inability to express them, but their capacity to generate them. They do not need a weekend marathon of provocation and humiliation to express the very emotions which they generate to excess without provocation. I am afraid we are left with a much more complicated problem.

Purification

Purification is often seen as just a synonym for purgation. I have reserved "purgation" for the physical sense of cleansing — freeing one from dirt or pollutants — the meaning with which it is most often associated. I am using "purification" to represent the act of becoming free from sin or guilt. It encompasses the second and third dictionary definitions of catharsis, where the emphasis shifts from removal of toxins (repressed ideas) to a liberating or transforming emotional experience.

In Aristotle's discussion of drama, which held a position in classic Greek society closer to a religious experience than to pure entertainment, he emphasized the purifying or cleansing emotions that are released while experiencing a great drama. What separates the idea of purification from purgation is that with purification the emphasis is placed on the release of emotions, as distinguished from the recovery of memories.

This cathartic effect is unquestionably a part of the therapeutic process, but only because it allows for a release of pent-up and misunderstood emotions. The failure of early therapy to adequately deal with the nature of emotions led to the overemphasis on the unconscious idea. It wasn't the released idea that brought relief, it was the released emotion attached to the idea. And the emotions that are released are more often guilt and shame than they are Aristotle's pity and fear. In our culture, these are the emotions most likely to undermine self-respect and self-pride.

Catharsis in a therapeutic milieu is an effective part of the cure, because along with the talking, which may or may not offer relief, comes something that will usually relieve anguish: forgiveness and implicit absolution. The ability to cleanse one's emotions in the presence of an authority figure who makes no judgments, but interprets misdeeds as the inevitable products of one's development, frees the patient from moral responsibility. Ironically, this purification through absolution of guilt was not readily recognized by psychoanalysis. You would think that early analysis would have dealt with the concept of guilt, but it did not. Freud was slow in discovering a way to integrate guilt into conscience mechanisms, and never successfully did so.

Guilt is a purely human emotion, as Martin Buber recognized: "Man alone is able to set at a distance not only his environment but also himself. As a result, he becomes for himself a detached object about which he can not only 'reflect,' but which he can from time to time confirm as well as condemn."*

An analysis of guilt would have shown its close working relation with fear and anger, both emotions that were early identified with neurotic problems. Feeling guilty informs us that we have failed our own ideals. We try to avoid the feeling of guilt. It is an almost unbearable emotion. We prefer to

---

*See Buber's chapter on guilt in *The Knowledge of Man*, M. Friedman, ed. (London: Allen & Unwin, 1965), p. 133.

feel angry rather than guilty when an action of ours causes damage to ourselves or others. We will ascribe responsibility for the untoward episode to others, so that we can find fault outside ourselves. Thus our first response to a calamitous happening is to assign guilt to someone around us, in a frantic attempt to protect against its being assigned to us.

Even when there is no fault at all, we often defensively assume someone must be to blame. This protects us not only from having the blame ascribed to us, but from having to acknowledge some of the tragic and accidental events that inevitably occur in life. When a child, or friend, or parent dies unexpectedly, the desire to find someone to blame is understandable. The number of people who are eager to find fault with "the system," to find some "rational" explanation for the death of their loved one, is comprehensible. Blaming someone or something is more bearable than the idea that a quixotic fate has picked our child, our husband, our mother, our sister, at random.

Guilt is the ultimate form of self-disappointment. It is the sense of anguish we experience when we feel we have not achieved our own standards of what we ought to be. We have fallen short. We have betrayed some internal sense of a potential self. It is, of course, the most internalized and personal of emotions. If it is only you against you, there can be no villains except yourself. That is why guilt seems to tear apart our internal structure and why guilt is so painful to endure.

This does not mean that guilt is a "useless" emotion, as described by one pop psychologist. Guilt is a socializing emotion. It is a central pillar of conscience. It is the emotion that supports the unselfishness and generosity central to our humanity and necessary for a democratic society. Those who do not feel guilt are less than human; they are the psychopaths who prey upon their fellow human beings with no remorse and no anguish. We want people to feel appropriately guilty (inappropriate guilt is another matter altogether).

Hidden guilt is a torture; guilt craves the exposure of a confession with its promise of expiation and forgiveness. The capacity to express one's guilt to someone in whom we have vested the authority of knowledge and certitude, and to receive a nonjudgmental reply, is a cathartic of the highest order.

The other emotion whose relief is involved in catharsis is shame. Shame is the sister emotion to guilt, and often confused with it. They serve similar purposes: both facilitate the socially acceptable behavior required for group living. In his *Rhetoric* Aristotle defined shame as "the pain or disturbance in regard to misdeeds, whether present, past, or future, which seem likely to involve us in discredit. . . . We feel shame at such bad things as we think are disgraceful to ourselves or to those we care for."

Shame represents the fear of exposure, the fear of dishonor and humiliation. Whereas guilt often seeks exposure, shame retreats into privacy for repair — think of Adam and Eve hiding their nakedness from God. Shame was part of the price they paid for eating of the tree of knowledge. When they were innocent, "the two of them were naked, the man and his wife, yet they felt no shame" (Gen. 2:25).

But what if in exposing our sins, we discover that there is nothing to be ashamed of? This is what happens in therapy, and it happens tacitly and implicitly. Operating under the medical model, the patient is no longer seen as being the responsible agent of evil, but the victim. The sin has been converted into a symptom. Now occupying the sick role, he becomes an object of sympathy rather than scorn.

There is a further comforting and therapeutic effect in talking out one's innermost feelings to another human being. If nothing else, it creates a sense of community, if only a community of two. A sense of community is one of the most comforting things we can have in a society as isolating and fragmented as the world in which we live. The act of talking out in such twelve-step programs as Alcoholics Anonymous, with their expansive and generous acceptance of any and all behavior, has proved to be one of the most valuable means of sustaining abstinence in a drug- or alcohol-dependent individual.

The power of the confessional was early recognized by the Catholic Church, well before the concept of psychotherapy was born. In a religion such as Christianity, which set as its model the perfection of Christ, we will all always be found wanting. A religion that motivates behavior toward an impossible but ideal aspiration must have built within it a model of forgiveness. The Jewish God, Jehovah, did not have to make forgiveness central to His practices. His commandments, while difficult, were achievable, even by mere mortals. Justice and goodness were His concerns.

The confessional allows the less than perfect human being to acknowledge his sins and to share in the blessed and comforting reassurance of confessing those sins to an authority figure who will always find forgiveness. Certainly, penance will be a part of that forgiveness. Although with the fusion of Christian forgiveness and Freudian nonculpability that has occurred in our culture, penance seems to have gotten lost along the way. We seem to move from repentance directly to forgiveness. Statements like "I'm sorry," or "I take full responsibility," seem to be the response to wrongdoing in these modern times, and are deemed adequate in themselves.

One wonders what happened to the concept of penitent punishment.

Penance is a crucial step in the journey from contrition to forgiveness in the parent-child relationship as well as in the confessional. It supports concepts of autonomy, dignity, and personal responsibility.

The psychotherapist occupies a space halfway between the parent and the priest. In many ways he is an easier authority to whom to confess. Here penance seems unnecessary, since by definition no wrongdoing exists. In the amoral world of psychic determinism, no one is responsible for anything, particularly since all wrongdoing has been redefined as sickness.

In the moral world, you are responsible for the evil you do, for the sin against God or man that you have committed. In the medical world, the rules are different. You cannot be held responsible for your tuberculosis, your leprosy, your cancer — or any of your vile behavior that is now defined as neurotic or dysfunctional. This difference explains why the theological model is perfectly compatible with the social concept of autonomy — since all religions demand a sense of culpability — while the psychoanalytic model is not, since it frees one from responsibility. Sick people are victims of their illness, not responsible for it.

It should now be clear that talking does help. The pure and simple effect of talking often offers patients extraordinary temporary relief after their first or second visit with the psychotherapist. But the catharsis that comes with the release of emotions is only effective in certain cases, and only in specific relationships, one of which, but certainly not the only one, is a therapeutic one. To be truly therapeutic it must, among other things, be accompanied by some understanding of the cause of those emotions.

The ability to cry, to express your emotions, to vent anger — or, more important, grief, shame, or guilt — in the presence of an understanding or loving person is a part of the therapeutic process, but only a part. Catharsis alone will never resolve complicated neuroses. The emotions must be tied to a vision of causation, a sense of where this all comes from. The neurosis must be explored in terms of the defensive structure and character armor that the patient has constructed over a lifetime of living with his predicament.

To accomplish real change, patient and therapist together must challenge the underlying false assumptions that the neurotic carries within him about himself and the world he occupies. The patient must confront the defenses built in accordance with these false assumptions, which while false are nonetheless perceived by the patient as truths on which his very survival depends. The patient will perceive each therapeutic assault on his distorted views as threatening, as undermining his security. He will struggle and resist to hold on to his illusions, and his neurosis. He feels safer living in the artificial, constricted, and unreal world he has constructed to serve his anxieties than in any real world of increased opportunities. He will struggle and resist the journey to health. But to unshackle himself from the chains of his neurosis, to grow and mature, he must acknowledge his distortions.

The patient's painful rediscovery and acceptance of the actual world will involve a process called insight.

7 Insight

A PATIENT goes to a physician for relief of symptoms: bloody nose, diarrhea, skin rash, chest pain, shortness of breath, dizziness, seizures, and a raft of other disabling ailments from the trivial to the serious. As I use them here, the terms "trivial" and "serious" refer to the degree of distress or incapacitation the symptom causes the patient, not to the seriousness of the underlying condition, which a patient is unlikely to know.

A sophisticated patient will occasionally seek treatment before physical distress occurs. A woman aware of a small lump in her breast, independent of the fact that it is not deforming nor is it discomforting, will seek treatment. She has been alerted through public education that this is serious business. Similarly, we have been alerted to the importance of pigmented moles; persistent cough or laryngitis; excess thirst and urination. The doctor is charged with interpreting the complaints, determining the cause, and prescribing the treatment.

The first logical step in curing is to locate the damaged system. What isn't working right? Is that difficulty in breathing due to damage to the lungs, the heart, or the brain stem? Just as it is essential to know whether a flat tire was due to a puncture or a leaky valve, the most effective means of curing an illness starts with discovering the cause. Diagnostic evaluations then dictate the appropriate treatment.

In physical medicine, despite the astonishing progress of the last fifty years, we still remain with many unanswered questions. Without such specific knowledge, we are handicapped in selecting treatment, but still not helpless. We can use symptomatic treatment that, while not "curing" the disease, can control life-threatening and painful disabilities. If these restorations of function are permanent, that may be the equivalent of a cure — at least from the patient's point of view. With some physical diseases nothing seems to stay the ultimate course, so we are consigned to relieving pain and suffering while supporting the patient through the rest of his lifetime.

In the case of mental illnesses, we are in the same approximate position of ignorance as with cancer. Actually in a greater state of ignorance. We do not have any anatomic variants that we can locate: no equivalent of masses and tumors; no clearly deformed organs; no identifiable abnormal cells; no changed blood chemistries. We do not even have a universally accepted definition of what constitutes abnormal behavior! Treatment, therefore, abides in an environment of supersubjectivity, totally dependent on what seems to work, independent of *how* it works.

Cause and Cure

Early psychotherapists attempted to solve the crucial problems of emotional distress by asking precisely the same questions asked in physical medicine. How can we relieve the individual of his symptoms and allow him to enter into a more normal way of life? There was a reasonable consensus that one must look into the developmental past of the individual for the causes of his condition. Psychological theoreticians felt confident that their understanding of developmental dynamics could explain where healthy adjustment went astray and direct them to the cure.

These days we are not so sure. Even when a direct line between parental behavior and a psychological symptom can be drawn — take the classic dynamic of a rejecting mother and a weak, inadequate, or brutal father — we know that this is not sufficient to explain any specific symptom, since we know too many people with such a background who seem to be functioning normally. We assume that we will find further elaborations and other contributing factors that will flesh out the dynamic story. And we always do. We enrich our dynamic explanations. (To psychotherapists, remember, "dynamic" refers to the forces and counterforces that shape a person's behavior.)

Even with the emergence of a more complete and elegant story line, a serious problem remained, adding to the therapist's insecurity. Therapists were disturbed by the unresolved matter of "symptom choice," whereby similar backgrounds result in different symptoms. Psychoanalytic theory has never been able to explain why one person with a certain background becomes an addictive personality while another patient with a similar dynamic becomes paranoid.

The attempt to solve the problem of symptom choice was one of the major causes for the diminished respect accorded psychoanalytic theory. In order to differentiate similar backgrounds that led to different results, theoreticians spun metaphoric stories so specific as to become trivial and ludicrous. For example, during the heyday of psychosomatic medicine it was thought that every psychosomatic disease had an underlying and specific conflict. Migraine headache was always a product of repressed rage; an asthmatic attack was interpreted as the infant's frustrated cry for help to an unresponsive mother; and on and on.

Modern-day therapists are less enamored of these specific "causative" formulations, and most sophisticated analysts will admit that we simply do not know why an individual will "choose" one set of symptoms over another. In certain areas of physical medicine, the same is true. Some allergic patients seem to be dermatologically predisposed. If they are going to get allergies, it will be in the form of hives, rashes, and other unpleasant skin eruptions. Others seem to be predisposed to respiratory allergies. A third group to gastrointestinal responses. It is clear that airborne allergens are more likely to cause respiratory allergies, while contact allergens are more likely to cause dermatitis, but that is not the question. The question is why some people seem more susceptible to one than the other.

The same problem can be visualized in a different way. Every psychotherapist has had the experience of curing a patient with a specific symptom such as agoraphobia, a fear of public spaces. The same therapist will also have dealt with an agoraphobic who has steadfastly resisted his treatment. Even Freud was only too aware that his understanding of therapeutics lagged severely behind his assumed understanding of etiology.

My own experience with patients has been a humbling and invigorating one. It has forced me to challenge my preconceptions, question my dogmas, and rethink the entire enterprise of psychotherapy. It has kept my practice of psychotherapy a constantly stimulating and provocative activity.

I must admit to a bias against those whose theory is always abstract and never practical. There are a number of distinguished psychological theoreticians who have never treated a patient. They exude a confidence that eludes those of us who have sullied our theories by dirtying our hands digging into real-life neuroses. In the early days of the Hastings Center, a research institute devoted to the study of ethical problems in medicine and the life sciences, I recall having great debates with one of the young staff members, a sociologist, who had unflinching convictions about the proper treatment of the dying but had never seen someone die. He had never been to a hospital — literally never — having suffered no diseases and having been spared diseases of his parents. The other administrators and I arranged to take this naively self-confident individual and subject him to some firsthand experience.

Our young sociologist visited a terminal-care facility for the near dead and dying on a Monday and did not show up at the office for the rest of the week. He was so visibly and emotionally shaken by the experience — a rather rough and perhaps insensitive introduction to hospital life — he could not gather himself to return to work. When he did return, he was reluctant to discuss his experience, although we had heard about his distress — he had actually fainted — from the Sisters who had conducted his tour. This incident remains a part of the mythology of the Hastings Center — our equivalent of the mystery of what actually happened in the Malabar caves, a pivotal event in E. M. Forster's *Passage to India*. Without explanation he simply abandoned the area of death and dying as a locus for his ethical studies and applied his energies and inquiries to the area of health care allocation.

Freud never allowed the theoretician in him to obstruct the clinician. Many of his theories may strike us as naive or half-cocked today, but they were always shaped by and tailored to the presence of a suffering patient. They were always rooted in the reality of sickness. One thing remained constant, however. To Freud, as to all dynamic therapists to follow, the sickness observed in the here and now was inevitably the product of problems from the past.

Searching the Past

Even though Freud was prepared to abandon old and treasured ideas for newer ones, the thread of the old ideas was often incorporated into the fabric of the new. Constant to all of his theories was the conviction that the child was father to the man. The past held the key to both formation and resolution of neurotic conflict. Neurosis was never explained in terms of current external conflict. Your misery, if it was neurotic, could not be a product of the present and did not emerge from the world of reality. It was the result of an internalized past conflict. Except for a few fringe groups, this remains close to a universal assumption among therapists.

In his later theories, specifically the libido theory, the symptom was related to an unconscious desire on the part of the patient rather than an actual seduction, as had been his first contention. The symptom symbolically contained within it both the unconscious wish and the defense against it. For this he coined the term "compromise formation." So the dreaded urge to masturbate, then considered shameful (not the sign of sexual liberation it is now held to be), could be controlled by developing a hysterical paralysis of the hand.

To attempt to resolve a symptom, the patient and therapist are obliged to identify the "basic cause." This requires plunging into the unconscious and making the offending wish conscious. The unconscious wish, festering like some foreign body within the tissues of the human brain, must be extricated and brought to conscious awareness and into the control of the ego, or the self. This was Freud's original concept of "insight," with its implicit message that making the unconscious conscious would be the central therapeutic maneuver. The unconscious thoughts would emerge through the use of free association, dream interpretations, and a nondirective approach. The difference between catharsis and insight was significant. In the earlier theory, merely talking about the repressed wish was expected to be curative. With insight, what was required was the identifying of the problem in order to emotionally come to grips with it.

When one uses the word "insight" outside psychoanalysis or psychotherapy, it has two related meanings. One is the discerning of the true nature of something, so that if one says that an author of a book about the Supreme Court has shed insight into the workings of the Court, it means that his research has brought us to a fuller understanding of the true nature of the activities of the Court.

Insight is also used in common parlance to mean an elucidating moment, a flash, a "sudden insight." One thinks of that profound moment in Henry James's *Portrait of a Lady* when Isabel Archer, the naive American heroine, sees her husband, Gilbert Osmond, seated in the presence of a standing Madame Merle, a woman friend. Given the mores of the time, and the manners of appropriate behavior, this informality provides Isabel with an instant insight. Isabel recognizes that her husband is in the presence of his lover, not his friend, and Isabel, in that recognition, perceives that her husband is not the man she had thought him to be: "Under all his culture, his cleverness, his amenity, under his good-nature, his facility, his knowledge of life, his egotism lay hidden like a serpent in a bank of flowers." This was a moment of insight as we would use the word today. A flashing truth that washes away self-deceptions and false illusions. An epiphany. Isabel Archer would never again view her husband as she had perceived him before.

In the traditional three-act drama, the first act is devoted to the introduction of characters as one might first see them. The second act introduces the essential conflict, and traditionally the second act curtain brings the conflict to a crisis point with some shattering insight; the profound moment of truth is the classic second act curtain. The third act must demonstrate the changes wrought by that insight. The resolution of the conflicts established in the first act and elaborated in the second must transform the characters and their lives. In the classic theater, this always happened. The staggering insight of Oedipus involves the literal nature of his identity, and the play's resolution explicates the awesome transformations consequent to that identity.

It is not just by chance that so many current plays flourish through their first two acts, only to falter in the third. It is easier to identify a conflict than to resolve it, even in the theater, where the author has command of all of the variables of his characters. The author wants a play that is "true to life," or at least one that will touch the reality of his audience. But transforming knowledge is hard to come by these days.

Freud — as well as every therapist who was to follow him — had third act problems in good measure. Persnickety and stubborn patients often refused to respond to his brilliant theories by getting well. This is a disappointment that I have experienced myself all too often.

One of the most insightful statements about insight itself was made to me in the course of working closely with a powerful mentor who influenced my early thinking. I spent one entire summer as an unpaid research assistant helping to draft a book (which never emerged) for this sardonic, cynical, depressed, but brilliant and innovative psychoanalyst. During the course of this particular summer, he said, almost as an aside: "I wonder if insight isn't really the product of change rather than the cause of it."

This offhand remark was a stunning insight for me. He was suggesting that the recovered unconscious memories which were presumed to initiate the process of change were actually the products of unconscious changes that had already occurred! Many other factors during the course of therapy, which he did not elaborate, must make the unconscious memory less threatening, allowing it to emerge. The insights signaled that the patient was now secure enough to face and deal with past memories and feelings that he had been incapable of acknowledging before.

This was a startling departure from the conventional wisdom of the day, which perceived the insight itself as *the* therapeutic maneuver. This new construction conforms more to the reality of therapeutic change. No patient has his symptom disappear with the emergence of the insight. Insight is only a step in the journey toward change. This reevaluation forced me to examine the multitude of unexplicated and unexamined interactions in the relationship between patient and therapist. Obviously, something in the ongoing relationship with the therapist allows the patient to feel safe enough to observe the once terrifying aspects of his past experience.

Even accepting this dramatic reversal of the relationship of insight to change, the emergence of an insight, however it arises, is a significant event. The insight can be useful as reenforcing knowledge, helping the frightened patient to step out of the confining and restricting perceptions of his past and forcing him to experience the real world. The insight is still essential in locating the area and the nature of those past distortions. It will show us, for example, whether his present sexual timidity is related to a seductive mother or to a competitive and threatening father.

Perception and Reality: Insights from the Present

Insights emerging from past memories serve as markers that define the distorted lens through which the patient's perceptions are filtered. They may be understood as dynamic insights that relate the way we were treated in the past to the way we are behaving today. These dynamic insights focus our attention on the specific areas of the past that must be explored to effect change. They are invaluable tools for narrowing the scope of therapy.

But an insight does not have to be about something covert, or something in the past. Nor does it have to be a revelation of an event — a seduction, a brutalization, a rejection or humiliation. There is an insight that I will call an adaptational insight. It emerges from examining our interactions in the present. This insight can force a new perspective on the self, a new view of the way one behaves with others. The moment that a therapist confronts a patient who views himself as the soul of generosity with the fact that he has so far demonstrated nothing but the most self-serving of behavior in and out of the therapy is a true moment of insight.

I recall the first time that I suggested to a middle-aged man that he was angry with his wife. He simply denied that this was true. "I never get angry," was his response. When I pointed out that one need not "get" angry to feel angry, it was to him an epiphany. The amount of rage he had been harboring then poured out in the therapy and spilled out into the marriage as well, frightening both him and his wife. It was necessary for both of these somewhat controlled people to recognize that anger did not imply the absence of love. Whom else are we more likely to get angry with than those we love? They have the greatest power to threaten us.

An awareness of the unconscious distortions that plague a patient can be as central to relieving his symptom as the discovery of an early trauma. The usefulness of this kind of insight lies in forcing the patient to conform his perceptions of himself and the world about him closer to reality. Experience is still the great teacher. Behaviorists would claim it is the only teacher. The patient must test his insight through changed behavior in the real world.

One way of defining a neurotic is as a person who seems incapable of learning by experience. These patients have absorbed lessons from the past so profoundly distorted that they dominate the present. The patient fails to learn from experience for two reasons. One, he will avoid all experiences that he anticipates as leading to pain and failure. He will, for example, not seek out loving relationships if he "knows" that they will end in rejection. Therefore, his conviction of his unlovability will never confront those experiences that alone could contradict the painful "truth." Second, when involved in the real world, he will distort experiences to conform to his expectations. For him, psychological expectations are always self-fulfilling prophecies. He will reject the offer of love before it can even be tendered. The patient who is trapped in his past can never learn from the present, since he is never experiencing the actual present. To the paranoid, every glass is always half (or more) empty, and every generous offer is a poisoned apple.

An insight can be truly transforming when derived from observation of everyday behavior — when the therapist confronts a patient about his distorted self-image and the true nature of his conduct. If a patient who views himself as the soul of generosity, someone who is always given less than he gives, is transparently begrudging and ungiving, stingy, or niggardly, the therapist must point this out to him. Even in the context of a nonjudgmental therapy, this can lead to outrage and denial. But it will prove to be therapeutic. It will initiate a journey into the real world. First the patient must accept the reality of your statement. He must give up his illusions about his life and himself. This is often most safely done in the context of the transference, where the proof is at hand and can't be denied. Then it can be extended into the real world.

I had one patient who simply could not understand why she had so much difficulty with fellow employees. When I suggested that her sardonic manner and patronizing attitudes might play a part, she denied that these descriptions applied to her. I responded by listing all her critical remarks about the way my office was furnished, my choice of haberdashery, the "tackiness" of the patient who preceded her, ad infinitum. She was horrified, and insisted that surely I was aware of the humor implicit in these comments. I assured her that I was, but added that I interpreted the humor as a defensive protection against the hostility of the comments. We were on our way to a significant insight.

Victorians used to say that the last thing a fish was likely to discover was water. And the last thing a patient is likely to discover is the distortion of reality that informs his self-perception. A talent for self-deception is the one attribute that we all share. I've had beautiful patients who thought they were ugly. Interestingly, I have also had unattractive patients who thought they were beautiful. Whether the latter should be analyzed or not is an intriguing question.

An adaptational insight can often be derived exclusively from analysis of the patient's everyday realities. By becoming aware of his constant self-defeating behaviors, the patient will be forced to finally confront the major distortion in his perceptions, and to recognize that he alone is author of his despair. That is an insight derived from the present.

In the course of therapy there are powerful means of "forcing" the patient to confront a new reality. The transference — the relationship with the doctor — will be one encounter that he will not be allowed to bend to his neurotic expectations. This is one relationship that he cannot control or manipulate. The experienced therapist will insist that the patient take this seemingly unique experience with him back into the real world — *the only place where real change can occur* — to learn that it is not singular or idiosyncratic.

At one time the distinction was made between the neurotic and the psychotic on the basis of their reality testing. The psychotic was defined as living in his own world, unrelated to the actual world around him, while the neurotic was seen as living within the real world. In fact, both distort reality. It is only the nature of the distortion that distinguishes the two.

Some psychotics will form delusions. For example, one might be convinced that he is the agent of God, or is God himself. These delusions are the rules of reality under which the psychotic will then operate. They are the kind of rules that permit an insane man to commit an act of murder and perceive it as an act of grace. He has destroyed the Antichrist or raised someone into the Kingdom of Heaven.

The psychotic is seen as making a break with reality. One of the great creative perceptions of Freud was that, in his way, so does the neurotic. So do we all. George E. Vaillant, in his intelligent book *Adaptation to Life,* rephrased this by proposing that for all of us, sick or well, the naked truth of life is intolerable, and that we all devise adaptive mechanisms and reality distortions to make life palatable. The way we choose to distort reality for our benefit will define how successful we will become.

Each of us, therapist and patient, child and adult, essentially conforms to the philosophical idealism that shaped Freud's basic theories: perception is everything. We all live in a world of our own perceptions, a world partly of our own design. Of course, this does not mean that we are hallucinatory and delusional; the distinction between the psychotic and the neurotic still stands.

Here a comparison of the paranoid schizophrenic (psychotic) and the paranoid personality (neurotic) can be helpful. An individual paranoid schizophrenic may suffer from delusions of persecution often combined with delusions of grandeur. He may believe that enemy aliens have occupied the bodies of his fellow employees, that the CIA is sending signals directly to his brain via electronic impulses that no one else can hear. He believes that he alone is capable of detecting these impulses, and his actions are totally appropriate to the situation *as he perceives it.*

The paranoid *psychotic* makes this rupture with reality in a delusional form that is easy for us to recognize as "crazy"; paranoid *neurotics* do not form delusions or hallucinations, even though they have their own equivalents of reality breaks. These individuals on the border of paranoia are distrustful and provocative, convinced that they are always taken advantage of and given less than their fair share. Ironically, they are often right, as there is something about the defensive attitude of a paranoid personality that invites just such behavior.

Such people go through life feeling deprived. So much so that they may be threatened by, and therefore avoid, any success that brings into question the accuracy of their life view. Deprivation is often welcomed as confirmation of their most profound suspicions. Their wives, children, friends, have accused them of being "paranoid," meaning overly suspicious, overly cynical, untrusting. Therefore, each event in which someone has taken advantage of them becomes a triumph for their bias. They are grievance collectors. They are the beachcombers of misery who see each grievance as a treasure to add to their collection. They are always given the worst table in the restaurant, the worst seats in the theater. It is their bad luck to be in the longest line at the ticket counter, and their room *never* has the best view.

They are even able to interpret neutral acts that occur to the group at large as being specific and punitively directed toward themselves. They see these events as happening only to them and because of them. It rains because they had planned a picnic that day. They are convinced that deprivation is their due, and they conduct their lives in such a way that deprivation will be their lot.

To protect themselves from further hurt, they anticipate the negative event. Pain is mitigated when it is expected, even more so when it is self-inflicted. Instead of being disappointed, they accept their bitter lot. They may even romanticize it, viewing their endurance as a tribute to their courage and tragic nobility, romantically joining them with the legendary Tantalus and Sisyphus. But what a price they pay to maintain this illusion! They must avoid genuine love, affection, or generosity when it is offered to them. They manage to protect against disappointment, but only by paying an enormous price in lost pleasure. This is a pathetic, often heartbreaking, adaptation. They make sure they will never be hurt again. They will never be used again. They will never be humiliated again. But in order to do this they must go through life with an armor that will defend them against every gracious or gentle approach.

Every analyst, at one time or another, encounters a paranoid patient who will test the limits of his self-control and professional discipline by succeeding in provoking him to anger. I recall the first time this happened and my humiliation at venting anger on a patient who after all was "sick" and needed, indeed was entitled to, my understanding. What I remember besides my own chagrin was the sheer joy and pleasure the paranoid patient demonstrated when I finally did get angry. After months of provocation, he had won. Winning confirmed his view of himself as a deprived and unloved person. After all, if a professional who is paid to take abuse, and whose training focuses on controlling his own emotions, succumbs to anger, it certainly must prove that the patient's feelings of poor usage are not simply his imagination. Such paranoid individuals are surely destined for deprivation.

Patients need not be paranoid to suffer from feelings of deprivation. I remember one particularly bright and charming young physician, one of six siblings, who emerged out of childhood convinced that he was the least loved and most deprived of the six. After hearing his history and the nature of his rather aloof parents, I was convinced that every one of his siblings, if questioned, would see herself or himself as the unloved member. His parents were immigrants, preoccupied with the struggle for survival, and intrinsically detached people by nature.

This young physician was ready to perceive deprivation in every aspect of my relationship with him. In actuality my struggle was quite the opposite. I had to defend against desires in me to be "maternalistic" toward him. I felt sorry for him and protective, seeing him as a decent person who was draining away his potential for happiness in his readiness to feel isolated and rejected. Nonetheless, he was sure I was judgmental, punitive, and definitely less interested in him than in the "beautiful girl" who preceded him.

The woman who preceded him was indeed beautiful, a successful young actress. She happened, however, to be more truly paranoid, with a greater sense of deprivation, than he. He would have been shocked to know that she had fastened on him as a rival for my affections, seeing him (in his white jacket with stethoscope hanging out) as someone with whom I could more readily identify and therefore unquestionably more favored by me than she was.

I use the paranoid personality as a paradigm to illustrate the distortions of reality that occur with neuroses as well as psychoses. Even with "normal" people, images from the past are built into our sensibility and will inevitably distort our perception of the present. I recall a shared revelation from a colleague. This woman was an accomplished and successful scientist who almost single-handedly created a new area of research. Brilliant by almost any person's judgment, she was an acknowledged leader in her field.

She described returning to her hometown after a prolonged absence. During the time of that visit, she herself was in her early fifties. She was met at the train station by an elderly taxicab driver. He looked at her closely and said:

"You're one of the Smith girls, aren't you?" She was delighted to be recognized, since she had not been home in at least twenty years. She told him so. He continued, "Which one are you — the pretty one or the smart one?" Without a moment's hesitation she answered, "The pretty one." It was the role she had been assigned in prepubescent days. Her older sister had been designated as the brilliant one, while she was assigned the role of cute and charming daughter. To this day, this woman thinks of herself as less than gifted, attributing her success to hard work and luck. She shared with me the fact that she has recurrent dreams of being exposed as a fraud.

Most of us have experienced dreams in which we find ourselves exposed in a sexual or naked form. We are in school and suddenly notice we are nude or without pants or shoes or an article of clothing or inappropriately dressed. These are generic dreams of exposure. But there are specific dreams that define a quite different form of exposure, the feeling of being unmasked. These dreams tend to occur in successful people who feel that "somehow or other" they have "gotten away with it." Their fathers always told them they were stupid; their mothers told them they would never amount to anything; it was suggested, if by inference only, that nothing much was expected of them as compared to their more industrious sibling. They therefore see their achievements as a fraud that they have successfully perpetrated.

The woman scientist that I have just described is absolutely convinced that much of her success has been due to her attempt to prove that she was just as smart as her sister. Her sister, being quite assured of her own intelligence, and with nothing to prove, has managed to live a conventional, presumably happy, but uneventful and intellectually unaccomplished life.

Dreams of exposure are common enough that I have heard them from almost every patient of high achievement. Perhaps the most profound insight for such a patient — and it does not come easily or quickly — is the awareness that he is not what he thinks he is but what others perceive him to be. He has not deceived anybody except possibly himself. His successes are genuine and deserved. To force a patient to recognize that he is better than he thinks is surprisingly as difficult as to force him to be aware that he is less. With neurotics, we are dealing primarily with those who sell themselves short, so while the insight is difficult for them to accept, it is liberating when accepted.

The very first insight that some patients must face is a recognition of the symptomatic nature of their behavior. Before explaining this, I must ask for indulgence in using technical language. Psychoanalysis has a penchant for the use of jargon and unattractive, sometimes unintelligible, words. Often they are convenient obfuscating devices used to cover lapses in knowledge. Over the years I have largely abandoned the use of such terms as "cathexis," "object relations," "affect theory," partly because I have abandoned the theory (the libido theory) that necessitated their use. Even when I have continued to accept the ideas, I have found simpler terms. I will now have to burden the reader with the terms "ego-syntonic" and "ego-alien" (or "ego-dystonic"), for which I have no better language.

Before a therapist can even deal with the patient's specific symptoms, he must deal with the patient's attitude about his symptoms. Take a patient who arrives at my office for the first time, breathless from having walked the four flights of stairs rather than taking the small self-service elevator. He explains that he is frightened of elevators. Were I foolish enough to indicate to him that elevators are the safest form of public transportation in New York, certainly safer than the taxi or subway that he used to get to the elevator, I would get one of two general and opposing responses. The first might be, "Why, you idiot, don't you think I know everything you said? If I weren't aware that being afraid of going into an elevator is crazy, why in the world would I be coming to a psychiatrist?" That response is one that would be a joy to a therapist's ear. It means that already the symptom is alien to the patient. He knows it is "sick." It is not a part of his identity. It's attached to him like some unattractive and unnecessary foreign body, and he wants it removed. This represents an ego-alien symptom, i.e., one that he cannot accept or rationalize as a part of himself.

Were I, on the other hand, to get the response, "Why, you idiot, that's as much as you know," and then have him present a list of data — an accurate one — summarizing all the dangers inherent in riding an elevator — the number of deaths in elevators; the number of people traumatized by an elevator out of service and trapped between floors; the number of people accosted in elevators — I would be disheartened. If the patient insists that only the foolhardy ride in elevators while prudent people eschew them, I know that I am dealing with an ego-syntonic symptom, one that has been rationalized and incorporated into his sense of self, his ego.

If progress is to be made with the second patient with the elevator phobia, the therapist has his job cut out for him, and it is not a short, sweet one. He must somehow or other "prove" to the patient that this is an aberrant fear, metaphoric in nature, not a real survival mechanism. The ego-syntonic symptom must be converted into an ego-alien one. The patient must be forced to acknowledge the difference between his perception and reality. Not an easy task.

The great Belgian surrealist René Magritte painted a realistic image of a pipe and painted a caption under it reading, "Ce n'est pas une pipe" — "This is not a pipe." Most viewers of this painting are bewildered or annoyed by this statement. Caught in the web of their own perception, they ask themselves, "What the hell does that mean? If it isn't a pipe, what is it? It's certainly not a bowler or a green apple." The viewer may dismiss this as some kind of Dada absurdity. It is not. Magritte is making a statement about the difference between perception and reality. Of course it is not a pipe. It is a combination of paint and brush strokes that will generally be perceived as a pipe, but it is only a representation, a symbol. Don't try to smoke it. This is the essence, the central thesis, of this chapter.

While all viewers will perceive Magritte's representation as a pipe, we will not all view Rorschach inkblots as the same representations. Some will see a butterfly where others see a monster. So too in life. We will all make conventional and generic assumptions about the world, assumptions we will share in common with most other people; and we will also make some idiosyncratic or personal constructions that may differ from those of others. In the areas of our own neuroses, we are making idiosyncratic *and harmful* misperceptions. We are living in a world of our own perceptions.

Insight as originally conceived meant transforming self-knowledge — knowledge derived from the past and buried in the unconscious — whose very exposure and revelation would alter maladaptive attitudes, perceptions, or behaviors. Today there is real doubt as to whether knowledge in and of itself has the power to perform such actions. Surely the epiphanies of stage and screen are rarely, if ever, replicated in the therapist's office. The "recovered memory" of your brother's drowning and your exculpation does not in that instant transform your personality nor alter your lifelong patterns of behavior.

Knowledge alone does not inform conduct. Insight is rarely a transforming event. Still, insight is a useful, perhaps necessary, ingredient for change. Whatever it may be called — self-knowledge, self-awareness, insight — it is still central to most schools of psychotherapy. An abandonment of past grievances, injuries, hurts, and deprivations, and of the behavioral consequences of those attitudes, is a mark (or a consequence) of the improved patient.

What has changed over the years is the new awareness that insight need not be arrived at only through exploring our developmental past — our psychodynamics — but also through our awareness of the defensive maneuvers we have adapted to protect ourselves from the perceived dangers of those long-gone realities, and the price we are paying to defend against a danger that exists only in our perceptions. To fully change self-awareness, we need both "id analysis" — delving into the dynamics of the past — and "ego analysis" — examining the characteristic defensive maneuvers in our present-day life. We need both kinds of insight to perceive how each contributes to our self-inflicted miseries.

8   Psychodynamics: Looking to the Past

A PATIENT comes to a doctor with distress that he presumes to be medical. The doctor is charged with "curing" the condition. To accomplish this he attempts to determine the underlying cause, if he can. While to the patient a cough is a cough, to a doctor it is only a symptom, not a disease. The doctor wants to know the specific cause of the cough, since there are different treatments for different coughs. If the cough is due to tuberculosis, we now have antibiotics to treat it. If the cough is due to congestive heart failure, the doctor knows that the primary problem is not in the respiratory system at all, and he treats the disabled heart. If the cough is due to an allergic response, we have no specific treatments except to ameliorate the symptoms.

The mental patient seeks help for the same reasons that the patient with physical disease does: he desires relief from his distress. He too is suffering from symptoms or dysfunctions. He is depressed; he is having delusions or hallucinations; he is having serious psychosomatic illnesses; he is incapable of forming personal attachments. With mental illness we do not know the cause. Even in depression, where we are on the threshold of finding chemical "cures," we are dealing in empirical symptom relief. We do not know *why* one specific drug works with some patients and not with others; we do not know *why* it works with some patients for years and then stops working; we do not know *why* two quite similar drugs will prove to have different results in different patients seemingly suffering from the same depression. We are nowhere near meeting the criteria of scientific evidence of cause and disease. We don't have to be apologetic about this. Many of the ultimate and final pathways of chemical treatments of physical diseases are equally unknown.

The physician treating a physical disease takes the presenting complaint, attempts to identify the cause by locating the organ or system that is dysfunctional, and attempts to cure the underlying pathological condition. Locating the source of the symptom directs him to proper treatment.

With psychological illness we identify the symptoms as dysfunctions of the mind. If we were even reasonably close to understanding the workings of the *brain,* we might get close to understanding the physiology or chemistry of mental processes. We are nowhere near that point, so it seems more appropriate to talk of mental (or psychological, or emotional) illness rather than brain disease. Here, as in physical illness, the therapist takes the complaint of the patient — say, inability to maintain an erection — and determines if it is psychologically grounded (as distinguished from a primary problem in the genitourinary system), thus locating the dysfunction in the mental system. Next, he seeks a cause.

Since psychotherapists from the most conservative to the most radical all tend to believe in the psychodynamic concept — that is, that a piece of behavior must always be seen as the result of many forces and counterforces — they will search for multiple causes. Beyond this, almost all therapists take a developmental point of view. Behavior in the present is always rooted in the past; what one does in a particular moment is determined by all the previous experiences that have been "programmed in"; the observed piece of behavior is seen merely as the end point of a sequence of behavior preceding it. Given these assumptions, therapists will define the "disease" in terms of present-day dysfunctions, and look for the causes in the developmental past. Therapists have problems in both areas.

What is dysfunctional, and who says so? In physical medicine the doctors say so, and more often than not, in one voice. They may argue about the level of blood pressure at which one ought to intervene and the nature of the intervention, but high blood pressure will be generally defined as a disease requiring medical attention, even if the patient protests that it is not bothering him at all. With mental illness it is not that clear. Definitions of mental illness are more likely to be subject to influence by political and sociological conditions, particularly when not dealing with the major psychoses. Not that physical medicine is immune to such pressures. Deafness has been defended by advocates of the hearing-impaired as an alternative and not inferior lifestyle, and they have gone to court to prevent the correction of hearing impairment in a child. Still, the problem of defining a mental dysfunction is less controversial than that of identifying its causes.

Different Ways of Looking

When it comes to cause, while all dynamic therapists will look to the past, they will look for different things. They will describe the causative factors in different language, emphasizing different historical events, different conflicts. They will tell a different "story." How should one reconcile the different stories of the different schools of therapy with the fact that most of them achieve similar results? While they tell different stories, they are not necessarily contradictory. In many ways, the various therapeutic stories may be seen as equivalent to the different biographies of distinguished figures.

The great biographer must take the available data and construct a narrative consonant with the known facts. Yet the George Washington that emerges from James Flexner's brilliant biography is a different man from the one we meet in Douglas Southall Freeman's monumental work. Both men are serious scholars, determined to define the man accurately. Even more variation will occur in the interpretations of figures of the past where little remains of record. Is Richard III the monster depicted in Shakespeare? Who knows? But most of us will always view Richard — as well as Julius Caesar, Cleopatra, et al. — as Shakespeare defined them.

With the mental patient there is also little documentation. We are dealing with a subjectively perceived and nonverifiable past, allowing the therapist to more readily impose his personal template in designing the final form and appearance of the emerging material. Not just any personal template, mind you. But one which accurately captures an aspect of the person that will define his total personhood. Since any human being is so complex as to be ultimately beyond description, all that we can hope for is an emblematic sketch. Even the multiple self-portraits of Rembrandt vary dramatically, but they all somehow capture the essence of the man.

The differences in the scenarios dictated by different schools of thought should not be distressing, therefore, if we acknowledge that no human being can be encompassed within any single theoretical framework. While each theoretician may cut a different window in the same black box of the past, they should all see an accurate, if incomplete, image of the person. But each theoretician must cut a window broad enough and clear enough to reveal a true and significant aspect of the patient. Each will then be equally useful for therapeutic purposes. The difficulties arise when each school insists that its story is *the* story, the gospel truth. Well, even the gospels vary. The Jesus of Matthew is not identical to the Jesus of Mark, or Luke, or John.

Therapists from different schools sometimes seem to be dealing with entirely dissimilar subjects. This should not be so. If each theory conforms to the accumulated knowledge of human development and human biology — as biographers must correspond to known data on the lives of their subjects — each will simply be telling an aspect of the same story in a different language, employing different metaphors. Any structure that allows one to hold together the details of a history will be helpful in therapy.

The common elements to which all authentic psychodynamic therapists subscribe is the recognition that the present is not all that it seems; that unconscious determinants in operation must be uncovered; and that these elements are likely to be discovered by exploring the patient's past — his psychodynamic history.

To undo the symptoms of the neurotic patient, we must understand the causes. To understand the causes, we must return to the past by delving into the unconscious of the patient, where the conflicts of the past still rage. But the only reason for looking into the past is to modify a piece of neurotic present-day behavior. When the therapist can change behavior without this circuitous journey, he should do so. Therapists are not historians, nor biographers, for whom past knowledge is an end in itself. Too many therapists forget that, and wallow in the past as though the journey itself is sufficient. The principal purpose of psychotherapy is to treat the patient and relieve his suffering.

The Libido Theory and Its Successors

Different schools of therapy have different images of the past. This would seem to suggest a chaotic and random attitude about causality, but as I have explained, it need not. Even starting from different theoretical perspectives and arriving at somewhat different destinations, each successful theoretician will paint an acceptable, recognizable, and useful portrait of the patient. To clarify this seeming paradox, I am going to contrast two theories that were at one time seen as antithetical: first the classical Freudian libido theory, which dominated psychoanalysis after World War II; then the neo-Freudian views of the Columbia Psychoanalytic Center, where I trained.

The libido theory, originally postulated at the close of the nineteenth century, played a prominent role in psychoanalytic therapy for more than seventy-five years. It was Freud's first attempt to find a unifying and universal theory to explain not just neuroses, but human motivation, cultural phenomena, character formation, social institutions — nothing less than the totality of human endeavor and human experience.

Freud now rooted all behavior in the biological and genetic composition of the human being. He visualized people as being driven by two instincts: the instinct for survival and the instinct toward pleasure, which was encompassed in the drive for sexual pleasure. Late nineteenth-century philosophy (think of Nietzsche, Schopenhauer, Bergson) was obsessed with the idea of a "life force." Freud's driving force was labeled eros. It was the motivator for all behavior beyond mere survival. The energy of this instinct was the libido.

Freud was attempting to find something that drove the human being in a fashion similar to the way steam drove a locomotive. He finally concluded that libidinal energy was the exclusive force behind all elective human behavior. Thus activities such as stamp collecting, horseback riding, smoking, gardening — well, *all activities* — were sexually driven and therefore disguised sexual activities.

Understandably, then, Freud felt that all neuroses were sexual in origin, products of flaws in the biological development ("vicissitudes") of the sexual drive. Since all neuroses were sexual, all symptoms must be viewed as disguised sexual activities — deviations and perversions of the normal development. All neuroses ultimately became centered on and channeled through the Oedipus complex, a conflict originating in our sexual attachment to our parent of the opposite sex. This forced a competitive struggle with the parent of our own sex. All of this, Freud felt, was part of the genetic endowment of our species.

As expressed here it sounds simplistic, but the elaborations fill volumes, indeed libraries, of textbooks. It was the heart of the orthodoxy that emerged after World War II and that dominated not just psychiatric thinking, but the worlds of literature, art criticism, anthropology, sociology, psychology, and history.

Almost from the beginning of the psychoanalytic movement — with the defections of Jung and Adler — the libido theory came under assault, and a fragmentation of the psychoanalytic community followed. Each splinter group resisted the exclusively sexual characterization of neuroses. Followers of Harry Stack Sullivan, Karen Horney, Clara Thompson, and Sandor Rado, to name some of the American leaders who specifically challenged Freud's obsessive attention to internal conflict, began to emphasize interpersonal relationships and the adaptation of the individual to his environment, thus broadening the Freudian theory by forcing closer examination of the everyday present. Relationships with others, not just the relationship with ourselves, became legitimate areas of examination.

All of this occurred before the sexual revolution proved how perversely wrong the theory of sexual liberation would be. If sexual frustration was the root of neuroses, a liberated sexuality should have eliminated the pesky things. We are all now denizens of that golden age of sexual liberation. Everything is now acceptable, and anything goes. Among the empirically measurable results of this revolution so far observed have been: the introduction of new and horrible diseases like AIDS; an increase in cancer of the cervix; an epidemic of teenage pregnancies (fortunately now abating); and the trashing of all standards of social order and decorum. What we have *not* observed as an outcome of the sexual revolution is any diminution of neurotic behavior.

Sandor Rado (1890–1972), the great Hungarian American psychoanalyst and educator, was one of the major defectors. Rado did not believe in fixed human instincts. By the end of World War II, the energy aspects of the libido theory were already hopelessly outdated and embarrassingly simplistic. He abandoned them. Rado thought too much attention was being paid to sexual development and insufficient attention to other aspects of development. He felt that too much emphasis was being placed on internal conflict and too little on adaptation to the real world. Something of value is learned about a flower by dissecting it and examining it microscopically, but observing a rose in a garden provides equally valuable information of a different sort. The same is true with people. Rado wanted to examine the patient in his environment with others, in addition to examining the internal environment.

In *Inhibitions, Symptoms, and Anxiety* (1926), Freud had said that the crucial factor in human development, particularly from the biological standpoint, was "the long period of time during which the young of the human species is in a condition of helplessness and dependency." Rado focused on childhood dependency as his central concern. The human being is helpless beyond any comparable creature. The prolonged dependency period wherein the human infant is totally reliant on others for his survival is the crucible in which self-image and self-confidence are established or destroyed. This theory also elevates the emotional life — particularly problems with handling fear and rage — to a position of central relevance in therapy, as fundamental as the psychodynamics derived from the past. The child views abandonment by the parents on whom he is totally dependent as tantamount to a death penalty. The fear of separation is in this theory the equivalent of Freud's castration anxiety. Anger with the parents threatens the loss of their protective love and also imperils a survival that the dependent child knows is beyond his capacity to handle. Love and ingratiation, more than power, are the tools of survival during infantile dependency. The family — the only community of which the infant is aware — is everything.

This was the cornerstone of Rado's theory, and it allowed him to sojourn outside the narrow paths of sexual development into broader areas of family life. He placed questions of identity and relationship at the center of the adaptational process. Having said that, I have done as egregious an injury in simplifying Rado as I did to Freud.

Differences notwithstanding, any competent theoretician can fashion a story that will be useful in understanding most symptoms. From my student days onward, I was under the influence of both of these presumably alternative and antagonistic theories, and it became apparent to me that the differences were less than the heat that they generated would have indicated. Unacknowledged common features joined these two antagonists at the hip.

In going to Columbia, the psychoanalytic center founded by Rado, I had chosen a new and deviationist school which only by the power of its faculty had avoided the excommunication visited on other deviant institutions. It held tenuously to its approval by the American Psychoanalytic Institute. By attending Columbia, I could become an "approved" analyst while still holding a skeptical approach — in accordance with my rebel personality at that time — to the revealed truth of the established church.

As part of standard psychoanalytic training, every student must himself be analyzed, and this must be done by a senior analyst who has been ordained a "training analyst" qualified to treat candidates. Since the Columbia Psychoanalytic Center was new, it had not graduated sufficient students nor attracted sufficient defectors to have a solid core faculty of training analysts. Therefore, some collaborating training analysts from the more orthodox and established schools were deemed acceptable. That suited me to a T. Since I was going to have my training in a nonconformist school, I wanted to have the experience, through my own personal analysis, of the classical Freudianism.

From Theory to Practice: My Training Analysis

I made an appointment with a physician who was a training analyst at the New York Psychoanalytic School, the bastion of orthodoxy, but who was still acceptable to the rebels at my school. He was tall, slim, courteous, and reserved — and to my delight spoke with a pronounced Viennese accent. That lent an air of authenticity and romance. I would be experiencing an *echt* analysis, the real thing, in the tradition of Freud. I had been told that my analyst had been analyzed by the great German psychoanalyst Karl Abraham, who himself had been analyzed by Sigmund Freud, thus making me a great-grandchild of the founder of psychoanalysis!

I was not prepared for the fact that my analyst, assuming that I was getting somewhat distorted and inadequate training, would take it upon himself to see me as a wayward child, and see his mission as converting me to the true faith. This could have been a total disaster, but I was protected by the character, personality, and moral integrity of the analyst I had chosen. I was lucky.

I met my analyst first for the briefest of meetings, in which we established the hours of treatment and the hourly fee. Since I was in full-time residency and had daytime classes at Columbia, I requested early evening hours, so that I could leave my residency and still get home early enough to spend time with my wife and baby daughters. He made such arrangements, a kindness that at the time I had no way of understanding, let alone acknowledging. He gave me hours that are precious to a psychoanalyst: six o'clock at the end of the working days, hours that had a great commercial value. My hourly fee was fifteen dollars, less than the prevailing fees in the 1950s, particularly for the services of a well-known psychoanalyst.

"Training analysis" is a confusing term. The word "training" suggests that the analyst in the course of the therapy gives tips, advice, or direction to the young candidate, indicating what he is doing and the purposes of his interventions. Nothing could be further from the truth. It is an analysis conducted in exactly the same way as a therapeutic analysis. Instructions and directions are done separately during supervisory hours with another senior analyst, appropriately called a supervising analyst. In the training analysis, the candidate is the patient. In supervision, he is the therapist.

While a training analysis is treated as the equivalent of a therapeutic analysis, there are two significant differences. One, the analyst must be designated as a training analyst by the psychoanalytic school; sometimes an analyst is even assigned to the candidate. Two, the patient, since he is a candidate working toward a degree, is something of a captive to treatment. Unlike an ordinary patient who may be dissatisfied or find the passive approach of traditional psychoanalysis more than he can take, the psychoanalytic candidate cannot leave his therapist. It is part of his training and must be completed before he can be certified.

Knowing this, the training analyst can conduct therapy in the most traditional and demanding way, adhering to a trying classic technique that might be intolerable for a freer patient. Thus the therapy becomes a model, an ideal, to help the student shape his own behavior when he is conducting analyses. The irony is that in his practice, the young therapist will confront all the sloppiness of the real world and rarely be able to conform his conduct to the model set by his analyst. He will face all the constraints of a restless patient who will not sit (lie) still for a passive treatment; the economics of patients who can rarely afford four or five sessions a week; and the problems of dealing with a patient free to depart for greener pastures at any time.

The primary purpose of the training analysis, however, is not to set a model, but to give the student a firsthand view of the workings of the unconscious and the dynamics of the therapy through exposure to his own unconscious and his own internal distress and turmoil, and to make the candidate as unneurotic as possible.

By my definitions I had no neurotic problems — an assumption that was less than completely accurate. Nonetheless, I went to my analyst prepared to be introduced to unconscious dynamics that were influencing my behavior, and here I was not disappointed.

Analysis is conducted by exploiting three primary sources of information: free association, dream interpretation, and analysis of the transference. Often, particularly at Columbia, a period of history taking would proceed the patient's lying on the couch for the free-associative sessions.

As I entered my analyst's office for our first working session, I noticed from the corner of my eye a couch with a napkin on the pillow. I asked him whether during these first few sessions he would prefer my sitting in the chair near his desk or lying on the couch. He gave no answer. He was prepared to teach this young apostate from a heretic school the way things were really done in the temple of classicism at which he normally conducted his business. With a shrug of my shoulders I went over to the couch and lay down.

I asked him if he preferred that I give him a history — the biographical data of my life — or simply begin free associating. No answer. I gave him a history as briefly as I could. This was the start of my therapy.

The next crucial step was my first dream. I was not a great dreamer, or more accurately, I could not remember my dreams, being a sound sleeper at that time. Occasionally I would have dramatic dreams. Certainly nightmares were remembered, although they were few in number. I hoped for some dramatic dream with which to launch my therapy. After all, Freud, in one of his major cases, "The Wolf Man," analyzed one dream through the entire years of his analytic process with the patient.

My first dream was pathetically unimaginative and, to my naive mind, totally irrelevant. The dream was simply this: on glancing down I happened to notice a small cut in my necktie. That was it. So undramatic; so unromantic; so unsophisticated! I was so disappointed that I was prepared to dismiss this dream and wait for a second, more elegant and literary product with which to start my journey into my unconscious. Having related this meager offering to my analyst, I started to talk about events of the day, but my analyst had other ideas. He made his first intervention in my therapy. He asked, "Why do you ignore the dream?" My analyst had me devote an entire week to that dream. Every time I would turn away from the subject of the dream, he would say to me, "Why do you avoid the dream?"

My first instinct was to relate this to a common variety of dream that I had experienced, exposure and unpreparedness dreams — being in the wrong place at the wrong time for the exam, not being dressed appropriately for some occasion. But my analyst dismissed this idea, indicating the specific nature of the dream was not that I was shoeless, naked, or tieless, but rather that the tie had been cut. This sparked my first recognition of the central metaphor of the dream, leading me to the dream's relationship to the upcoming holidays.

My wife, our baby daughers, and I were alone in a strange city with no friends or family. Indeed, the ties had been cut. I had been raised in a close-knit, protective, somewhat provincial family, bound even closer by the restrictions on travel and independent pursuits imposed by the Great Depression. During childhood much of my social and emotional life was involved with extended groups of uncles and aunts, cousins and kinfolk. Once married and involved with my own children, away from Ohio, I rarely thought of my extended family — or even my own parents.

I certainly was not aware of being lonely. My wife would have to prompt me to the telephone once a week for my casual hellos to my parents, and it was she who would write the letters. Whenever I was reminded of my parents, I thought of them with love and affection, but in all truth, it was only with their later deaths, and the contrasting degree to which they have occupied my thoughts since then, that I became aware of my isolation from them. I was overworked and too occupied with my struggle to fulfill my obligations as a student, husband, and father to be concerned with being a son.

In articulating these feelings of being cut off, I experienced my first insight, an awareness of an unconscious, emotional state other than that which was part of my conscious awareness. More than I was prepared to admit, I missed family connections. Dreams were important. I had learned something. Now I was prepared to leave the dream and get on with all the real distress of my work life. My analyst was not satisfied. And by refusing to acknowledge anything that didn't pertain to the dream, he encouraged further associations.

The specific connection of the dream to my father, as distinguished from my family in general, should have been immediately self-evident. The fact that it wasn't became a further subject of discussion about the nature of denial and defenses against recognition of unconscious feelings. My father loved ties — as do I. Racks and racks of ties hung in his closet. It was this hardworking man's only self-indulgence. The tie that was cut was my tie to my father.

Friends tell me that I must have been extraordinarily close to my father, since I mention him frequently. These are current friends. I suspect that the friends I knew between the ages of twenty-one (my marriage) and thirty-three (my age at my father's death) would not have heard frequent allusions to him. I did not perceive him during that period as a significant "player" in my current affairs; he no longer held the authority over or responsibility for my life that he'd had during my childhood and teens. I assumed, without thinking much about it, that I loved him. I never analyzed that love. Had I done so at that time — in my scientific, objective, analytic way — I might have come to the painful and false conclusion that I did not love him. What I am trying to describe is the fact that in my day-to-day life I was not aware of any *feelings* of love.

How would I have defined my relationship with him? Respect, affection, duty, and "love" in an undefined way. But I did not live with any feelings of love or longing for him. Those emotions were reserved for my wife and our daughters. Obviously, my unconscious knew better.

During that period, I had come to New York and was struggling to survive in an unfamiliar and hostile environment. I must have felt an enormous sense of loss, separation, and helplessness: still in residency training; desperate for money; leaving our apartment after the children were asleep to work at a clinic, often until midnight, to make extra money; two children under fourteen months of age to tend to; nowhere a helping hand; no one to spell us even for an evening; and no means to buy the comfort and surcease that were so often given casually and freely by family.

All of this emerged in response to this simple dream. A wellspring of affection for my father came tumbling out, feelings that could never have been articulated to someone as reserved as my father by a son equally reserved and barely out of his teenage years. Again, I felt a sense of accomplishment in the analysis and wanted to get on with my life, to talk about some of the problems I was having with my residency. But again my analyst would have none of it. He pressed me for further associations.

From somewhere in my unconscious emerged an association of a ritual at a Jewish funeral, that of cutting the black ribbon worn by a mourner. Through this association arose a whole flood of denied and repressed emotions I had felt at leaving home and finding myself in a city whose attractions were beyond my reach, but whose disadvantages were constantly imposing on my life. Repressed feelings of deprivation began to surface.

I was indeed mourning the loss of my father. The cut tie was *my* mourner's ribbon. While acknowledging the authenticity of my emotions, I was totally bewildered. The emotions seemed alien and preposterous; I found my feelings irrational. After all, I had been independent of my father since I was seventeen. I had supported myself through college with a full scholarship and later the GI Bill, and once married I was supported through the medical school years by my wife's teaching and by the part-time jobs we both took. We worked together as soda jerks during weekends and ran a school playground in the summers.

More precisely, what I was mourning was not the loss of my father, but the death of my childhood and the loss of my home. For now, in this alien place, *I* was the father. And I was starting to feel the pressures. My self-confidence was beginning to be challenged.

This part of the interpretation was confirmed from an amusing corroborative source. During that fall I found myself haunted by an unnamed melody that obsessively played in my mind but whose identity eluded me. It was a popular song, obviously, but what song? I simply could not identify it. I hummed it to a few friends, who also failed to recognize it, either because my humming was so bad or because it was somewhat obscure for a pop song.

Sometime shortly after the beginning of the interpretation of this dream, I remembered the words. It was the Leonard Bernstein song from *Wonderful Town,* whose lyrics, by Betty Comden and Adolph Green, began, "Why, oh why, oh why oh? Why did I *ever* leave Ohio? Why did I wander to find what lies yonder, when life was so cozy at home?"

Now that I surely had milked the dream for all of its multiple meanings, I was eager to leave the dream and get on with my problems: my money was running out, we were exhausted by the responsibilities of parenthood, and we couldn't afford baby-sitters, diaper services, or the simplest of self-indulgences. I wanted someone to whom I could complain about my troubles. I wanted comfort and reassurance. But this was not allowed. My analyst wanted me to stick to the dream. Good God, what more could there be in that simpleminded dream? My analyst was waiting for something more: Where was the sexual content?

Since my psychoanalyst was a good old-fashioned, European, orthodox Freudian, it was necessary for him to tie this dream into the structure of the libido theory. This was particularly essential for him because, as I was later to learn, central to his research thesis was a theory that the first dream presented by the patient foreshadowed the entire analysis. It would not do to have this be other than a sexual dream.

The absence of specific sexual content would certainly not have bothered my supervisors and teachers from the Columbia Psychoanalytic Center. My dream would simply have been interpreted as an expression of separation anxiety, which would have been more than consonant with Columbia theory, since Rado saw the central core of neurosis as being the profound influences of dependency.

After much urging, my analyst in frustration asked me about the shape of a necktie. Was this not, he suggested, an obvious phallic symbol; why was I resisting the obvious? Why indeed? I had no objections. If it pleased my analyst and let me get on with the analysis, let it be a phallic symbol. This allowed him to translate my frustrations and exhaustion into a sense of castration and impotence, and laid the ground-work for analyzing an Oedipal struggle between my father and me for the affections of my mother.

I am not prepared to say this was wrong. Certainly I felt helpless and alone. Is this not the equivalent of castration anxiety? I was constantly anxious about money and how we could survive the financial difficulties of my training period. Surely it was fair to say that I was confronting my "impotence." It did not strike me with the force of truth as had the earlier interpretations of being cut off. Nor did it bring me the kind of delight and relief one feels when one is brought into contact with unconscious feelings, the exhilarating response to catharsis.

I know that the dream brought me into contact with my unconscious, my fears, and my male competitiveness. This was enough for me. If my analyst insisted that the competition for survival in the jungles of New York was essentially sexual competition, this was not bothersome, since I knew that for him the only way one could visualize competition *of any sort* was in the sexual terms of the Oedipal triangle. I began to understand his language.

Often during the analysis there were explicit and specific sexual elements to life's struggles that I would deny, and his frame of reference proved supremely helpful there. Often there were clearly no sexual elements. But if my analyst felt dissatisfied with a sundae slathered with hot fudge and whipped cream, seeing it as incomplete without the cherry on the top, I would make him happy by "seeing" the cherry. He had ladled up the ice cream, poured generously of the sauce, topped it off with whipped cream. He had given me a profound insight into my current despair. That was good enough for me. Conceding the cherry would let me get on with other concerns.

Let me emphasize that the "conflicting" views of my teachers and my therapist led to very similar interpretations of the dream that I presented. Let me also emphasize that either interpretation of the dream would be ultimately in the service of illuminating the dynamic roots of my disabilities. And lest I be seen as minimizing what was done by my therapist, I should acknowledge that after these sessions I felt an uncommon sense of relief. Defining what it was precisely that offered me such relief proved more complicated than acknowledging that there was the relief. I suspect that it was the beginning of a sense that my therapist understood me. I felt grateful. I had begun the important process of identifying with him. The dream interpretation also supplied a positive and rational explanation for my strange feelings of melancholia. All of which was comforting and reassuring.

Now, what about reality? The kind of help that we were desperate for would have been more adequately supplied by my mother. She could have pitched in, relieved us of chores, cooked, cleaned, shopped, cared for the fourteen-month-old while we were attending the newborn, far more efficaciously than my father. This contradiction was ignored by both me and my therapist. My analyst must have been aware of this. Still, the patient must lead; I made the association to my father. My relationship with my mother could wait. There would be plenty of time and occasion. The dream would be stored away in the therapist's memory file, so that when my mother emerged as a figure in my dreams or fantasies, he could recall the dream and raise the question as to why my isolation was first visualized in relation to my father rather than to her.

The selection of my father emphasized that the dream's primary thrust was in terms of my shaky confidence in being "the man" of the family. It was primarily a dream of identity and identity crisis. In an orderly analysis, we prefer to deal with identity factors before problems with relationships. In the long run, most problems in attachment and relationship — problems with others — are secondary to problems with oneself.

This dream started me on an exploration of my past through my relationships with my parents. It started the process of seeing my current loneliness as a product of past relationships. In both frames of reference, by using the dream I had entered the world of dynamic analysis, beginning the process of building psychodynamic bridges between current feelings and past events. But how would it change anything? Knowing about my anxiety and loneliness surely would help me to feel better. But how would it remove my symptom?

Well, for one thing, I had no symptom. Wilhelm Reich, a true genius of early psychoanalysis, declared that symptoms were not necessary to define a neurosis, that the problem for many neurotics lay in the nature of their character. He coined the term "character neurosis." This suggested that the symptom-free individual could still be neurotic when the nature of his character, which normally determines the sources and scopes of pleasure, becomes a limitation to pleasure and performance. The emphasis on character neurosis as distinguished from symptom neurosis inevitably drives therapists more and more into an analysis of adaptive maneuvers and ego defenses.

Like most candidates, I was considered to have a character neurosis. No one was allowed the luxury of being "normal." Loneliness might be defined as neurotic behavior, but not an organized symptom like a phobia or an obsession. There's the rub. For the most part, the analysis of the dynamic forces in the unconscious was designed to resolve symptom neuroses, and among the worried well who seek treatment nowadays there are very few patients with traditional psychological symptoms — compulsive hand-washing, hysterical blindness, agoraphobia. For the most part, we are dealing with character neuroses.

The Move Toward Ego Analysis

It was the absence of symptomatic patients and the expansion of the definition of mental illness to include all sorts of symptomless impairments that drove the direction of modern therapies in the 1960s and 1970s toward what has come to be called ego analysis. This is an attempt to understand mal-adaptive behavior through the character structure of the person, his identity, his emotions, his distinctive ways of behaving. It is not that the unconscious dynamic is unimportant, but we must know how the patient chooses to handle the dynamic to assess his problems. What would be a necessary adjunct to my dream would be to analyze the way I defended against my feeling of impotence. Did I collapse in self-pity; blame my wife for our distress in a paranoid rage; develop migraine headaches; become a workaholic eschewing all pleasure? How did I *defend* against anxiety?

Therapists gradually began to spend as much or more time examining the character armor (Reich's term) of the patient, his characteristic behavior when he felt threatened, as they did looking for the internal conflicts that generated the feelings of anxiety. This is the stuff of ego analysis.

Ego analysis evolved from an original Freudian insight, the concept of ego defenses. Freud had originally described the primary defense against an unsupportable and threatening unconscious impulse or desire — almost invariably, according to Freudian theory, an incestual sexual feeling — as repression. This meant that you pushed the desire into your unconscious, where it would lie buried and unacknowledged. Later he elaborated numerous other defenses: denial, projection, sublimation, reaction formation, and the like. Freud suggested that the symptom expressed both the unacceptable wish and the defense against it. The therapist can start with either of these in the process of undoing. In the early days of analysis, infinitely more time was spent on the dark, repressed dynamics of the id, the world of unconscious instinctual forces. These days we are most likely to emphasize the self-defeating defensive maneuvers of the patient. In other words, there is less concern about your impulses and more attention on how you deal with those impulses.

Traditional Freudian therapy has also been moving in the direction of the here and now, although their infatuation with the stuff of internal conflict makes it a struggle for many classical therapists. The interpersonal and adaptational schools made it easier to do this earlier.

Of course both dynamics and defenses are significant sources of self-enlightenment, and neither should be ignored. But note that the sexual interpretation of the dream did not bring me into contact with my love for my father. Love was not a topic one dealt with in a classical analysis — except the pain of its absence or loss, or the love for one's mother, always cast in terms of sublimated sexual desire. But love is more than lust. And love for one's child, one's mother, one's friend, one's country, is trivialized by casting it in terms of disguised and distorted sexuality.

Emotions generally were given short shrift in classical libido analysis. Emotions are too directly related to life experience and ongoing relationships. Think of my original dream. I missed my friends and family, or at least I missed their help and services. There is no way to handle this in the old frame of reference. So the classical libido analyst quickly moves away from the emotional stuff and into the internal life. Ideas, sexual desires, conflict, these are the "authentic" stuff of analysis. Or so the classical analyst thought. Only recently, with the advent of affect theory (jargon for the recognition of the power of emotions to influence behavior), has traditional analysis found a way to deal with the specific causes that bring all patients to therapy: pain, anguish, distress, despair, fear, rage, guilt, shame, humiliation, loss of pride, and anxiety about the future.

The power of the more modern and eclectic forms of therapy, as distinguished from libido theory, was not in the difference of their stories — both scenarios allow one to cover similar ground — but in their readiness to accept the primacy of the emotional life and their focus on interpersonal relationships. The distinctions among the various schools are now becoming blurred, and that is good. All modern therapists these days will focus on the defenses as well as the dynamics.

9

Defenses:
Looking at the Present

W HEN WE LEAVE the internal world, when
we attend to the patient in the real world
of the present, what looms largest is the
awareness of the patient's defenses and the perversity with
which they operate. In trying to defend herself against pain and
disappointment, the neurotic seems hell-bent on getting less out
of life than is her entitlement. She must examine her defenses;
recognize that they are expensive relics of the past, denying her
pleasure in the present; recognize that they "defend" against a
reality that no longer exists. And she must be helped to find the
courage to change them. She must be led to understand the
degree to which she is the instrument of her own undoing.

Freud's fertile imagination and his ambitious reach often
became his own undoing. He had defined neuroses as the
product of the sexual instinct's being arrested at an early age,
such as the anal-erotic period. In his classic early work
Character and Anal Erotism (1908), he described an anal-
erotic character type. These people displayed three primary
traits: they were especially orderly; they tended to be parsimonious; they were obstinate. The term "anal" persists in
common parlance as a description of such behavior. Freud
decided that these traits were the patient's means of defending against his desire for perverse and neurotic anal-erotic

sexual activities. This is comparable to stating that the bacteria that cause pneumonia could, in some cases, cause ambition or laziness instead; that is, that an "agent" of disease could at times simply change your personality.

If the healthy and the sick individual share the same impulses, what is the defining difference? The difference is the way the impulses have been handled; the difference is determined by the nature of the defenses used to deal with the impulse. The defenses, it would seem, will determine the outcome. The treatment of choice, then, should be an attempt to change the defense mechanisms — the means of contending with the infantile impulse — rather than the more difficult, often impossible, goal of expunging the impulse.

Take the example of the infantile sexual impulses of exhibitionism and voyeurism. One person defends against (or satisfies) his exhibitionistic tendencies by becoming a performer, thus exhibiting himself nightly to enormous advantage and general admiration. Another, less fortunate exhibitionist becomes a street flasher and gains only opprobrium where his counterpart receives approbation. One individual with anal fixation becomes an accountant or statistician, gaining fame and fortune; another develops spastic colitis. These simpleminded examples are only intended to indicate the rationale that drove psychotherapy more and more toward analyzing the defensive structures of the ego rather than being preoccupied with instinctual drives. This dictated concentrating more on current behavior than on past mishaps.

Ego Analysis

Ego defenses are now a part of common parlance. We accuse each other of "repression," "sublimation," "reaction formation," "denial," and so on. We implore our lovers to "stop being so defensive." We tell our angry friends that they are just "projecting." We see repressed rage in sardonic humor. We have, willy-nilly, all become ego analysts in our everyday assessments of our friends, colleagues, and loved ones.

Ego analysis now thrives in the therapeutic community in great part because of the changing definitions of mental illness and the consequent altered nature of the population that comes for treatment. As discussed in the last chapter, traditional therapy was rooted in the treatment of the symptom neuroses. The classic patients presented with debilitating and often bizarre symptoms: delusions, hallucinations, paranoia, phobias, hysterical blindness or paralysis, obsessive handwashing. These are no longer the bread-and-butter issues of office psychotherapy. These symptoms flourish with naïveté and self-deception, and the modern patient is too savvy for a hysterical seizure.

The patients we see do have symptoms, but these days they are rarely classic mental symptoms. A patient will come in for migraine headaches, impotence, premature ejaculation, marital problems, work inhibitions, personality and adjustment problems, or generalized complaints of unlovability, inadequacy, or low self-esteem. We are deluged with a healthier population with a broader range of dissatisfactions. Their disabilities are stated in their lack of a capacity for pleasure; or a dissatisfaction with their relationships or lack thereof; or their inability to perform well at work. These inadequacies and the anxiety they generate are now treated as mental illness.

Ego analysis focuses primarily on examining the patient's operative self, the ego, the personality; his characteristic methods of adjustment or adaptation to the world at large; his relationships with others; and his emotions. The only emotion one needed to deal with in the early days of id analysis was the lust that drove the sexual impulse in all of its disguised forms.

Once one abandons the classical focus on the libido, other motivating forces become readily apparent. Sexual pleasure is not all. Pleasure is not all. Survival issues can take their proper place both as a primary force directing human conduct and as a source of anxiety. Aggression can be recognized as an essential component in the battle for survival. Competition is given legitimacy beyond the confines of Oedipal competition.

The craving for dependence, the need for love, the fear of rejection and abandonment — all become primary fields in which to dig in search of the roots of insecurity. Further, anxiety is given its rightful place as a central, not derivative, phenomenon of human existence. The therapist is forced to deal with other emotions as well: anger, pride, shame, and guilt. A richer and more complex psychohistory emerges. And a more difficult and complicated therapy.

Only the diehards persist in defining all pleasure in sexual terms. A good cigar may simply be a good cigar after all. Today's therapist is likely to perceive the struggle for survival as at least as central a concern as the pursuit of pleasure. When pleasure and survival are in opposition, pleasure — even sexual pleasure — will usually be abandoned. The oak rod erection of a teenage boy will wilt like a noodle when the girl's parents burst into the sexual sanctum. Survival does count.

By abandoning the libido theory, with its assumption that everything is a transformation of sexual desire and sexual energy, one is also freed from the need to base all neurotic conflict on the vicissitudes of the sexual instinct, or any other instinct, for that matter. There are plenty of other sources of tension for the growing child. The environment is once again introduced as a primary player. The underlying conflict can now be visualized as external as well as internal; can involve relationships with others as well as a battle between parts of the self. The increasing struggle of the growing child for more and more independence while still clinging to parental love and approval is a natural medium for culturing all sorts of conflicts.

Misguided Repair

Sandor Rado, whose jargon became as clumsy and arcane as the language he was trying to replace, introduced one very useful concept — the idea that a neurotic symptom is a "misguided repair." In this view the neurotic prototype is as follows: major conflicts arrive in childhood, particularly in the struggle for independence; we attempt to reconcile our pleasure and our security needs; a conflict arises and we attempt to repair it; when the repair is such that the patient is left in worse condition than he was with the original problem, we call this misguided repair a neurosis. If the repair works, *we do not label it neurotic*. Misguided repair becomes the primary determinant and hallmark of neurosis. The flasher is sick; the actor is not.

To understand the reparative aspects of a symptom, it is easiest to explore a dramatic one like a delusion. A man is in despair and panic, and then comes to the delusional conclusion that his wife is trying to poison him. What possible problem could such a delusion solve, and what possible utility could such a symptom offer the patient? To understand this, one must start with the concept of generalized dread and anxiety. There is something totally terrifying about fear that has no apparent cause, a free-floating and persistent anxiety. It is ceaseless; it cannot be limited; it cannot be controlled. Its very irrationality makes one feel there is no predictability in the world, that all is chaos; disaster lurks at every corner independent of where we turn; and if we are foolish enough to disclose our fears, we are perceived by our friends as hopelessly crazed. With no blueprint, no logic, no rationale for his general terror, the patient will find it almost impossible to deal with everyday life.

Suppose, then, that this patient with generalized panic delusionally decides that his wife is trying to poison him. The immediate response is one of instant relief. It rationalizes the symptom. "I am not crazy after all," the patient feels. Who wouldn't be frightened if the person he most depended upon was trying to poison him? Beyond rationalizing the anxiety, the delusion also limits the time and area of his anxiety. Instead of a pan-anxiety, he only need be anxious when eating at home. By defining the danger and locating the enemy, alternative and ameliorating safety mechanisms become available. Don't eat at home, eat elsewhere. Switch plates. Make sure your wife tests the food before you eat, and so on. Such a delusion temporarily helps the patient design a prudent, relatively safer, albeit eccentric, way of life. The catch is that rarely will the single delusion hold.

Delusions are misguided repairs at their worst. The price the patient pays for temporary relief of anxiety is a break with reality. The person he would normally turn to for solace and comfort is converted into the enemy. In order to justify the ubiquitous nature of the anxiety, the delusion must always involve someone central to his life. It must involve a wife, husband, mother, or other omnipresent figure. Eventually he will try the patience of even the most loving relation and find himself in a state of increased isolation and vulnerability. Sometimes, to protect close relations or when there are none, the delusions involve God, the FBI, foreign agents, or extraterrestrials. In any case, the patient loses control of reality, and to little avail. The precautionary maneuvers will eventually be extended until they seep into every aspect of daily life. All work and play will be sacrificed to security. Finally the anxiety will not be controllable or contained even with total vigilance throughout the entire twenty-four hours of the day.

A symptom is nothing but a bad bargain. It controls anxiety — but at an excessive cost. On the other hand, when the defense actually works, we do not call it a symptom! When function is preserved or enhanced, we define that as a healthy adjustment. We do not examine the dynamic causes that led a person to become a successful businessman, carpenter, banker, writer, lawyer, or psychoanalyst *unless* the success was purchased at the expense of equally important functions in other areas of life. We do not analyze the roots of efficiency, pleasure, joy, and success. We have better things to do with our time. We analyze that which we wish to undo. The fastidious man who obsessively follows the bottom line to success is not generally labeled neurotic, even though his obsessiveness may serve a symptomatic purpose. If the same obsessiveness had driven him to washing his hands fifty or more times a day, intruding on every work and pleasure function, we would define this defensive maneuver as neurotic.

Whatever the definition and whatever the theoretical frame of reference, the dynamic therapist is constantly faced with two choices in the course of a therapeutic hour: whether to focus on the cause of the symptom, which requires directing the patient to examine his past, or to focus on the results of the symptom, analyzing the defenses mobilized to control the problem. With the latter we examine his current behavior in order to force recognition of the inordinate price he is paying for his defenses against anxiety. Most therapy involves shifting from one to the other, interpreting the cause of the anxiety and insecurities during one session and the responses in another.

Each therapist varies, and each patient experiences a different mix of interpretations. Knowing when to concentrate on the present and when the past is part of the art of therapy. Many patients seem happier when dealing with the past. Most are delighted with dynamics — isn't this, after all, the stuff of psychotherapy? Conversely, they are threatened by examination of their defensive structures, for here you are confronting their very personality and behavior, requiring active and painful changes in habituated modes of operation: give up food; stop taking dope; get out of bed; get a job. I had one passive male patient who finally left therapy with me, disgusted with the fact that I seemed "preoccupied" with his failing marriage and his shattered career, and avoided getting into the "important" things buried in his past.

The problem with pure id analysis (focusing on past dynamics) is that it often encourages a passivity on the part of both the patient and the analyst. The patient, generally, has more than enough passivity to begin with. Unfortunately the same is often true for the therapist. The problem with pure ego analysis (dealing with everyday defenses) is that it can deteriorate into coaching or, worse, hectoring the patient, which will simply not work. An understanding of the unconscious distortions that led to the passive avoidance of life, or to a quick-fix mentality, is an essential step in restoring the self-confidence that will be necessary to actively engage life's challenges and make painful changes.

Obviously ego analysis also deals with internalized problems. One does not go to a psychotherapist to solve real problems unrelated to character or past. If the stock market is falling and his portfolio is a mess, the patient can't expect help from his therapist. However, if the patient takes it a step further and sees the financial problem as a problem in himself (if he really is a contributor to the debacle), we are in a therapeutic milieu. When the patient says, It is really my fault; I should have known better; Why am I always so reckless, or so pathetically conservative; Why am I always following other people's advice, or refusing to follow that advice; Why am I always so arrogant, or so timid — one has opened the door to therapeutic interventions. Psychiatry deals not with injury, but with self-inflicted injury. And self-inflicted wounds are grounded in past experience.

Once symptoms are perceived as reparative maneuvers, the therapist is forced to enter the general emotional life of the patient. What is the patient frightened of? What is the symptom meant to protect against: Competition? Rejection? Emotional dependence? Sexual involvement? Or even aberrant or perverse sexual impulses, as the libido theory suggests?

Remember, a characterological flaw is like a faulty thread running through the entire pattern of the cloth of character. The therapist must patiently tease out the aberrant strings of character. This is much different from finding the single encapsulated trauma buried in the unconscious and abreacting it (bringing it to the surface). Dealing with the broad aspects of basic character would be an interminable task if therapists were forced to work their way through all of the characteristic response patterns of the patient and change them. They do not have to do this. Change need not be, indeed cannot be, the conversion of an individual into something other than what he is. Therapists do not have to "turn a patient around" one hundred and eighty degrees. For the most part all they need to do is to change the tack slightly. As any sailor knows, a small change in tack over a period of time will alter the destination sufficiently to take us from the land of despair to the shores of pleasure. A five-degree tack leaving New York and traveling eastward can make the difference between landing in Africa or in England. Only relatively minor adjustments are usually necessary to get the patient functioning better.

Traditional therapists, particularly those trained in psycho-analysis, used terms like "hysterical" and "obsessive" or their equivalents, "oral" and "anal," to describe character. These represented a classic polarity, and all of us are presumed to be a combination of the two, having both oral and anal characteristics, but often with a preponderance of one over the other. The hysterical personality at its extreme was seen as someone emotionally insecure, strongly suggestible, imaginative, with unstable emotions, urgent needs to be loved and admired, and a strong dependency on the approval of others for self-esteem. In contrast, the obsessive was considered to be work oriented, perfectionistic, emotionally constricted, and with a strong conscience mechanism. What determines the direction the child will take?

What I suspect happens is that the developing child is prepared to try *all means* of satisfying the parent and gaining his or her approval. Remember that in the prolonged dependency period, the child is helpless and finds solace only in the knowledge that powerful adults are there to protect him. These strong adults, however, must love him in order to protect him. This is the early lesson of dependency that we all sustain through life. If the child finds that being cute, charming, ingratiating, or cuddly invokes a response of approval or forgiveness for wrongdoing from the parent, he is likely to use those mechanisms more and more as means of handling confrontation and conflict.

If, on the other hand, the parent responds to such ingratiation and charm with distaste because she cannot tolerate it, the child will find alternative means of winning approval. The way to this mother's heart may be through "being a good boy" and doing all that implies: tidying his room, playing quietly by himself, attending to the "work" of his specific age period. This child will obviously see performance and achievement rather than charm and ingratiation as a primary means of gaining approval and will tend more and more to use these to please the parent.

The hysteric therefore learns that the direction to security is through *expression* of his emotions, while the obsessive learns that security is gained by the *control* of emotions; the difference is profound in determining which emotions predominate. In addition, the obsessive feels safe because of what he *does* and therefore is threatened when his performance fails. The hysteric feels safe because of what he *is* and is threatened when he feels unloved or unwanted.

The hysteric seems implicitly to go through life saying, "Take care of me." The implication is that "you" will take care of "me" because I am lovable and worthy of being taken care of. The you is always brought into consciousness, and the hysteric tends to be a person who relates emotionally and who needs contact with others. The obsessive seems to be saying, "I know I will be taken care of when or if I am good," meaning obedient and dutiful. The figure by whom he is to be taken care of is repressed or abstracted. He will feel safe by being a good boy.

It is interesting to consider how much more tolerant most parents are of ingratiation and cuteness on the part of a girl than on the part of a boy. At least it was so before the feminist movement and the consciousness of gender disparity occurred. I suspect it still is so. Fathers particularly have difficulty with boys who are coy, seductive, and cutesy. The father is likely to be threatened by overt affection, warmth, demonstrativeness, on the part of his son, since this is patently "unmanly." Thus he will help to continue the artificial gender stereotype that has existed for so long in our culture. It is not surprising, therefore, that more women are driven into hysterical behavior patterns and more men into obsessive. This is also a possible explanation for the differing aspects of national character. Obviously genetics plays a part in determining temperament, as any parent can affirm, but we do know that cultures differ in the way they express or handle emotions. The stiff upper lip of the Anglo-Saxon is alien and often anathema in the "hotter" Mediterranean cultures.

Lessons learned in childhood are carried into life, long after the parents are not in a position of power and authority, or even are deceased. Surrogates — employers and the like — will be invested with the powers of the parents and treated with the expectations learned from the parents. For all of us, there will always be figures of authority who must be pleased. Through abstraction and metaphor the ultimate authority figure may be visualized in religious terms as God.

The persistent defiance (or seduction) of authority figures, independent of who they are, is often a manifestation of the manner that worked in our childhood; that is, we assume that these authority surrogates will react as our parents did. The patient will not only impose these assumptions on neutral cases, he will distort actual experiences that contradict his perceived reality. He simply will not see such behavior, nor believe it. In his mind these people will be responding to him as his parents did, even if all the evidence contradicts this. Believing that what worked with the parents must also work with others is a disastrous unconscious formulation; employers are unlikely to be devastated or feel guilty if we pout and refuse to eat our dinners (or finish our reports).

The Past as Prelude

Understanding the survival mechanisms developed in childhood and their inappropriateness in adult life is a significant step in the process of abandoning these maladaptive and self-destructive patterns of behavior. A major part of therapy lies in obliging the patient to look directly into the face of life absent the distorting lenses of the past. If he is to understand that the present is not always mirror to the past, he must be encouraged to enter into what he will perceive as threatening areas in the real world. To unlearn the lessons of the past, one must learn from experience. To learn from experience, one must enter the world and perceive it as it is, not as one assumes it to be.

In addition, the risks entailed by misjudgments in adult life are never equivalent to the consequences perceived by the child on losing the love of the parent. The child only too well perceives the degree of his dependency on his parents, seeing them for what they actually are, the instruments of his survival. Abandonment by the parent is seen as a form of death to the child. That is never true in adult life, even when the authority is the boss with the power to fire. There is always another job.

Confronting reality, the primary instrument in ego analysis, does not imply that actions in the present are not conditioned by past events. Ego analysis fully subscribes to a developmental point of view. What it does is expand the areas of the past that must be examined. Ego analysis doesn't simply round up the usual suspect — the sexual drive — it allows for other culprits in the patient's past. They do not have to be sexual. They do not have to be instinctual. They do not have to be linked to a reprehensible impulse originating from within the patient. The event in the past does not have to be self-selected. It can be a traumatic event visited on the child.

I am reminded of two patients who were in treatment at roughly the same time. Both of them were highly successful performing artists. Each had suffered the premature loss of his mother. Both of the men experienced immense feelings of guilt over the loss. One mother died while the patient was thirteen and the other when the patient was twenty and away at college. As different as their backgrounds were, both shared a feeling that there had been insufficient time to express to their mother their gratitude, their appreciation, and finally their love. And both carried into adult life a guilt-ridden need to compensate to other women for their "failure" in relation to the original woman in their life, their mother.

While they entered treatment with quite different presenting complaints, the focus of their early therapy was on their relationship with women. I do not want to offer a detailed history of either but merely to use both as examples of how the therapeutic process works. Neither man sought treatment because of guilt over the loss of his mother. Both entered treatment years after the event. One came because he was feeling depressed and could not recognize the source of the depression, and the second came because of a vague dissatisfaction with life in general despite a "happy" marriage and a brilliant career. He suffered from severe insomnia and a general sense of lack of satisfaction with his choice of career.

Intriguingly, both of them married intelligent, companionable, and attractive women who proved to be cold and sexually rejecting wives. One was actually living in a celibate marriage. He indicated that his wife had never been a very sexual woman, although as treatment progressed he began to suspect that she had an active sexual life outside the marriage, which eventually proved to be the case. He too had casual sexual affairs, but scrupulously avoided any true romance or commitment. For him, whose mother had died when he was thirteen, one such loss in a lifetime was all he was prepared to endure. The thinness of the current attachment to his wife suited him fine.

Early in the course of therapy, both referred back to their maternal loss. Each followed a strikingly similar pattern. With little resistance, a profound sense of guilt emerged. It was hardly "repressed." Memories of maternal sacrifice, affection, service, trust, and confidence emerged, which had been accepted and taken for granted in typical boyish fashion, without any verbal acknowledgment of gratitude or appreciation. They both felt immense regret for their casual indifference, so typical of a male adolescent toward maternal giving.

Only later, with significant resistance, were they capable of facing their anger with their mothers for "abandoning them" at a time when they were still in need. Abandoning them before they could display their successes and indicate that the mothers had done a good job and that they were good sons. Abandoning them before they were fully men and could complete the normal cycle of life by becoming protective and maternal, or paternal, to their mothers and could experience that reciprocity of spirit that expands the sense of self and fills one with self-confidence and pride and self-esteem. Premature death had denied them the role of giver and caretaker, leaving them feeling forever indebted as takers and users.

In both cases, and only after extensive exploration of guilt, love, and anger in their relationships with their wives, did the anxiety they felt after their mother's death emerge. This anxiety became fused with the guilt they experienced, and led to dreams and fantasies of being "responsible" for their mother's death. Both related their different stories of how it was in part their fault that their mother had died. The one who was in college was convinced that his parsimonious father had stinted on medical care and denied his mother the services of a big-city specialist who might have saved her. He should have intervened, he felt, although what role a college-age son could have played here was questionable.

Recurrent dreams plagued both patients over the years. With the kind of quasidelusional thinking that occurs during dream states, they were convinced that their failure to reciprocate in kind the loving displays of their mothers must have obliquely and mysteriously been a contributing factor in their deaths. These specific feelings of guilt generated a profound pain well beyond that experienced with the guilt they had so readily acknowledged earlier in the treatment.

The emotion of fear experienced at the time of the maternal death had been repressed by both. Being afraid to face life without a mother is unseemly in a "man" of twenty, or a young man of thirteen, for that matter. The terror of abandonment — the fear that to love someone fully is to put oneself at agonizing risk — was a central dynamic that significantly shaped the lives of both men.

The penultimate step was to convince these men to take a good look at their marriages — one incomplete with no sexuality in it, and the other detached with little emotional commitment. Facing those realities was no easy task. Both had idealized their wives and were reluctant to examine them as they really were. In addition, both men had to be convinced that it was not an accident that they had selected their wives not for love, but to protect against loving. After all, both were attractive, successful men who had more than their share of opportunities. Both had to come to grips with the fact that they had purposely selected detached women. The very incompleteness of the relationship was designed to protect them from the crushing loss they had once experienced with the death of a mother. A loss of either wife would inevitably be difficult, because loss was difficult for these men, but not the tragic blow to self and pride that the loss of the mother represented. This is the trench warfare of psychotherapy.

These dynamic insights forced the patients to reexamine all their relationships — with friends, colleagues, children — and what emerged was that with all their charm and seductive appeal, each had built a transparent wall, a protective shield, around himself to defend against a threatening intimacy. Both were deeply reserved and private men. But both craved love. Where would they get that? As performing artists, both were adored by a massive public, millions of surrogate mothers and lovers.

One might infer that the choice of career allowed them to gain love and approval without commitment or attachment to any one person. This is certainly a possibility, but I am reluctant to suggest that their choice of career, and certainly not their success, can be explained on the basis of this one specific dynamic. Talent is — or once was — an essential to success as a performer. Had they not, each in his own way, been extraordinarily talented individuals, they would have had to find alternative modes of working through this dynamic dimension.

This brings up an unfortunate distortion that inevitably befuddles reason when approaching unconscious dynamics. There is a tendency to think of "psychodynamic" and "psychopathological" as identical terms. There is a proclivity to believe that if we find a dynamic explanation for behavior, that makes that piece of behavior sick or neurotic. This is not true. Discovering complex symbolic reasons rooted in infancy and childhood that are determinants in a patient's becoming an actress or musician or conductor does not make such achievement neurotic.

Basic psychoanalytic theory assumed that *all* behavior was psychodynamically determined, and most derivative psychologies do the same. Nonetheless, there is that infuriating and erroneous tendency among both laypeople and psychotherapists to see an unconscious determinant as somehow or other discrediting the conscious action. I suppose this is a residue of the fact that traditionally the exposure of the unconscious has been incidental to, and in the service of, psychotherapy. There we start with a neurotic symptom and work back to discover its origins. If we started with a healthy adaptation, we could also work backward and find dynamic determinants.

Since all behavior is psychodynamically determined and rooted in the past, what determines which behavior therapists should attempt to change? Obviously they will pick "neurotic" behavior to probe rather than healthy behavior. But how will they know one from the other? As I have previously indicated, if an individual has exhibitionistic tendencies or a need for public acclaim or is a narcissistic personality — all of which cover similar ground in different frames of reference and different orientations — he can become an exhibitionist and expose himself in public, or he can become an actor and also expose himself, in a different way, in public. We define the person who drops his trousers in public, coveting the admiring glance of the woman to whom he has exposed his precious endowment, as a sick individual. We define acting as an honorable art form. Therapists have a value system, based on functional utility and culturally determined attitudes about proper conduct and decorum, that shapes their definitions of normal and abnormal.

Unlike physical medicine, where most symptoms are objectively defined, in the emotional area our definition of "sick" is highly subjective and notoriously culture-bound. Psychotherapy is littered with abandoned definitions of neurosis. Actions that were once seen as sick are now seen as healthy. The same act of masturbation that was originally defined as onanism, a sin against God, was defined by early psychoanalysts as an essential youthful form of sexual expression to be abandoned in the mature adult. Later it would be seen as permissible in adults provided it did not preclude intercourse. Still later it would be defined by certain radical feminists as a *superior* form of sexuality since it liberated women from the disempowering aspects of sexual relationship with men. Similarly, homosexuality was seen by early therapists as an immature, arrested, and fixated sexual development, while now it is regarded by a majority of therapists as an alternative way of life.

We are constantly redefining what is sick and what is healthy. This means that the therapist decides what warrants intervention — what must be "treated" — and what is to be left alone. Since this involves *his* definition as well as the patient's, the values of the therapist will have a profound influence on the conduct of the therapy. This is a truth that has too long been denied and must be recognized by the therapeutic community as well as the community of patients. I will go into this matter in detail in Chapter 12.

The Danger of Oversimplification

When one focuses on a specific dynamic, as I chose to do with the two performers I have been describing, it will inevitably be given excessive weight in defining the patient's life. This has been the crime of oversimplification that has brought such recent discredit to modern psychoanalysts. One dynamic, regardless of how dramatic, does not "explain" a human being. Beyond that, were all the dynamics of an individual discoverable — which they could never be — they would still not define the person.

Take the two performers. My description of their cases begins to make them sound like Tweedledum and Tweedledee. Yet their dissimilarities were far more extensive than any similarities. No one knowing them would have identified them as remotely similar. And the course of these two therapies that shared this common central dynamic could not have been more diverse. What differentiates us one from the other is not dynamics — after all, most of us from the same culture share many dynamic patterns — it is the way we integrate the dynamics into our character and personality. It is the way we *use* those dynamic factors. It is the way this one dynamic, combined with other dynamics, shapes our personality and our characteristic means of dealing with people and problems. Discovering dynamics is never an end in itself. They are but overtures to the opera of life. They introduce the therapist and the patient to the active and executive ego. They define the self (a late-emerging concept in psychology) and all its operations in a very real and ongoing life.

The concept of the unconscious introduced by Freud offered a new source of information and new perceptual model for understanding behavior. But here an unfortunate distortion has been introduced by many therapists and writers. There is a tendency — particularly elaborated in the burgeoning field of psychoanalytic biography — to think of the "inner" man as the real man and the "outer" man as an illusion or pretender. Like magnetic resonance imaging, the unconscious offers us a new means of illuminating the person. But few of us are prepared to substitute an MRI of Grandfather's head for the portrait that hangs over the mantel. The unconscious represents only another view, not a truer one. A person may not always be what he appears to be, but what he appears to be is always a significant part of what he is.

To probe for the unconscious determinants of behavior and then to define a person in these terms exclusively, ignoring his overt behavior, distorts the true individual more grossly than does ignoring the unconscious altogether. Saint Francis, in his unconscious, may have been compensating for and denying destructive Oedipal impulses identical to those which Attila projected and acted on. It is not by their unconscious dynamics that we know these two men, but by their behavior. I do not want to hear that Hitler had a tough childhood. I know what the man did, and no amount of explanation matters; no psychological justifications are warranted or desired. How an individual chooses to defend against his impulses will define the man in action, the man perceived, the man as he was — the real person. In short, a knowledge of the unconscious life of a man may be an invaluable adjunct to understanding his behavior, but it is not a substitute for his behavior in understanding him. For these reasons, one dare not separate dynamics from defenses.

The therapist must use everything at her disposal to create change: knowledge of dynamics, the nature of defenses, behavior in real-life relationships, observation of the evolving transference, every implicit aspect of the intense, volatile, and powerful relationship that emerges between herself and the patient.

The scut work of therapy is getting the patient to examine the wall of obstacles that he has built around him that separates him from his basic needs and desires — to break down, brick by brick, the defensive and self-defeating structures of his life. The often interminable time spent in therapy is explained by the fact that change demands not just knowledge of the unconscious; not just knowledge that we are the authors of our own misery; not just knowledge of the unconscious ways in which we manipulate the environment to conform to our preconceived notions of what we are; not just *knowledge.*

To change behavior, knowledge alone is never sufficient. To undo the powerful perceptions infused into the very substance of our identity during the critical formative years of childhood requires our going beyond the limits of knowledge.

BEYOND
KNOWLEDGE

III

The Therapeutic Alliance

10

THERE IS an implicit assumption in the minds of the uninitiated that there exists a considerable — if not an absolute — relationship between knowing good and doing good. That certainly was an assumption I carried around with me when I first started my psychotherapeutic training, and beyond. Had not Socrates assured me during my undergraduate days that moral knowledge would lead by a straight (if not short) route to just moral conduct? Well, let's just take moral conduct as an engaging example.

In 1969 I entered the Byzantine world of moral philosophers when I cofounded the Hastings Center, an institute for bioethical studies. During my first workshop with what were then the leading lights in normative philosophy (ethics), a number of unpleasant incidents arose that were called to my attention as one of the organizing directors of the meeting. One of the distinguished philosophers, a married, middle-aged man, was sexually involved with an undergraduate assistant working for him. Another distinguished philosopher managed to use this (and subsequent workshops) as an occasion for sexual pursuits of a nature aggressive enough to be labeled sexual harassment by current standards.

Beyond these sexual misdemeanors, our moralists demonstrated a degree of hostility, lack of spiritual and emotional generosity, level of personal calumny and gossipmongering, and a proclivity for both backbiting and public humiliation that were, charitably speaking, at least equal to the prevailing academic norms in medicine, law, and social sciences. Yet I know that morally unsophisticated individuals, who would not know a utilitarian from an electrician or a deontologist from an endodontist, are capable of acting with grace and goodwill.

Over the years I have come to the inescapable conclusion that philosophers, despite a considerably higher degree of knowledge of ethics, comport themselves by no higher set of moral standards than do nonphilosophers. With moral behavior, then, I had been reluctantly driven to recognize that a direct quantitative relationship between knowing good and doing good does not exist.

I should have listened to Saint Paul instead of Socrates. He understood human behavior, as is evident in the passage from Romans I have already noted: "I do not understand my own actions. For I do not do what I want, but I do the very thing I hate. . . . I can will what is right, but I cannot do it."

Perhaps moral behavior operates on different principles from neurotic behavior. In the moral sphere we often ask that one sacrifice self-interest in the service of others. Neurotic behavior has already been defined as self-destructive behavior, although I would argue that part of the definition of a healthy person is that he be capable of generous and selfless actions. Still, for the purposes of this inquiry, let's assume that the behavior we want to change is self-damaging. The question is, would the knowledge of where our best interests lie be sufficient to change our conduct? The evidence is disheartening.

The Limits of Knowledge

By now there is no one who does not understand that smoking is bad for one's health, that drugs kill, that the sun's rays can be destructive to the skin, that AIDS is a deadly disease transmitted by sexual intercourse or other contamination with body fluids. Yet this knowledge does not stop people from exposing themselves to these dangers, even though no one wants to die. We pour hundreds of millions of dollars down the drain in "educational" programs — the noncontentious, politically safe, and politically correct response to such frustrating, wide-ranging self-destruction — when coercion and manipulation would be more effective. Despite all experience, we want to believe in the perfectability of man through logical discourse. We hate admitting the degree to which our behavior is driven by our irrational impulses.

Aren't some educational programs effective? Yes, but rarely because of their cleverness in transmitting information. After all, for the most part the data are simpleminded and readily at hand. What is passed off as an effective educational process is often a covert coercive maneuver that works by engendering not cognition and logic, but emotion — for the most part fear, shame, or guilt, and occasionally pride. We shame or frighten a person into giving up many of these self-destructive pieces of behavior. The emotions motivate an individual much more than does mere knowledge.

Knowledge is not, however, irrelevant. It is for the most part a necessary, if not sufficient, condition for changing behavior. If a person wishes to migrate from Stockholm to Helsinki it is important that he know where Helsinki is. But it is equally important to know where Stockholm is. In initiating any action in life, it is necessary to know not only where you want to go, but where you are starting from. Besides knowing where you are, it is equally helpful to know who you are.

Knowing where you want to be still does not get you there. There are multiple questions about *how* to get there. To continue our metaphor: Do you take the arduous thousand-mile trek up the western shore of the Gulf of Bothnia, only to return the thousand miles or more down the eastern shore? Or do you take the two-hundred-mile shortcut across the Baltic Sea? Are seaworthy boats available? If not, are you clever enough to construct them? Is that boat-construction project just a pipe dream, an effort to avoid an arduous journey by finding a quick fix? If so, then the slow but sure slogging land trip may actually be quicker. Further, if a boat can be fitted out, is that particular sea navigable? And are you a competent sailor? All these questions raise facts of knowledge that are essential to determine before the journey can begin.

Beyond that, a series of other questions must be addressed. Why do you want to go? What do you expect there? What are the differences between where you are and where you think you want to be? Ought you be making this journey in the first place? Is it safe? Is it prudent? Is it even accomplishable? And if it is, why now and why there? Is it "right" in addition to being feasible and reasonable? And what does "right" mean, and who decides? There is a great deal of useful knowledge to be acquired.

A major part of therapy, as has been demonstrated, involves defining the problem. The patient does not always know right from wrong, or, in the language of therapy, that which is sick from that which is healthy. This knowledge is essential in focusing the attention and efforts of the patient in the right place, on what is causing his torment. Differentiating the sick from the healthy in a patient's behavior is required for most patients, since they come for therapy not because they have identified some neurotic behavior, but because they are in a state of emotional distress.

The knowledge that is accumulated during the course of the therapy goes beyond defining the neurotic behavior: it also includes understanding what led to such neurosis. Why the patient has, over an entire lifetime, chosen a maladaptive course, when a healthy mode of action would by definition serve his pleasure, his welfare, and his security much better. The patient is led to understand why he chose his symptoms.

The paranoid individual comes to therapy asking why "no one likes me"; why "I'm always taken advantage of"; why "I'm always cheated." The knowledge that is transmitted to him during therapy is not the answer to these questions, but rather the awareness that he is *not* always cheated, even though he always *perceives* himself as cheated. Or he may learn that no one likes him because he likes no one else; or that he projects his own anger and hostility toward others; or that he encounters rejection and mistrust because someone who always feels cheated manages to create an environment of distrust and hostility. Such knowledge is certainly productive; it distinguishes the true nature of the problem from the perceived nature of the problem.

The next necessary accretion of knowledge involves an understanding of the why's. Why does the patient behave in ways that thwart his pleasure or productivity? When the paranoid patient begins to be aware that his symptoms are an ill-fated attempt to protect himself against pain, rejection, humiliation, and hurt, we are on our way to change. When he fully appreciates that the neurotic activity is actually creating more pain, more isolation, and more failure, we are in a position to talk of insight rather than just knowledge.

Another kind of understanding, often beyond self-awareness, involves the degree to which we are the author of our own despair. Acknowledging the executive power we possess in creating our own misery is greatly reassuring. It suggests that we are not passive victims. We are not impotent. We have power that, while now used for bad, could be used for good.

Another use of knowledge is in explicating for the patient the emotional life he is experiencing. People do not often properly identify what they are feeling. One of the most illuminating insights is the recognition of their own true feeling. Most people can generally recognize the primary feeling of fear. But even with as basic an emotion as anger, a widespread amount of denial abounds. Many people do not know when they are angry, let alone why they are angry. *"I am not angry,"* said between clenched teeth or even shouted out in rage, is emblematic of an angry person. Confusion about guilt, shame, or humiliation is even more complex. Explicating the emotion that a patient is actually feeling is of significant benefit in clarifying his motivations, since emotions are the driving forces of behavior. The emotions, for good or bad, also fashion our state of mind.

A further amplification in the world of emotions involves identifying the unconscious feeling that is frequently screened by the expressed emotion. One of the most informative and useful commonplaces is the polarity between fear and anger. I will often tell patients, particularly in the later stages of therapy, to ask themselves when they are feeling angry: "What's frightening me?" And when they are feeling fear: "What am I angry about?" A variation on this theme involves a similar relationship between anger and guilt. More often than not, an angry patient is defending himself against his own feelings of guilt — better to blame someone else than assume personal responsibility. This is a particularly crucial insight, for the appreciation that he is dealing with a sense of guilt will direct the patient to the possibility of expiation and relief through appropriate acts of penance, whereas anger would drive him in almost the opposite direction.

Were all of this knowledge available to a patient through the use of some elaborate diagnostic software package installed in one's home computer, I seriously question whether it could change fixed patterns of neurotic behavior. It might provide an efficient preliminary to a therapeutic process, but I doubt even that. Such abstract knowledge is more likely to produce intellectualization, an enemy, not ally, of insight.

Emotions are the underlying root of neurotic behavior. And emotions occur in the contexts of survival or relationships. Fear of the hurricane sweeping down upon us, fear of the Nazis pounding at the door, is real fear and not the stuff of neurosis. The fear of abandonment, the shame of humiliation, the anger at rejection, the perceived disrespect that erodes pride, the sense of impotence in relation to others, the despair of failure, the sense of guilt in wrongdoing — all of these are experienced in the context of relationships with others. All of them exist in a social world.

The treatment for this neurotic distress, these maladaptations, these misguided repairs that undermine our self-esteem and define neurosis, must also occur in a social setting — must be part of a communal effort of one person with another. An individual deprived of human relationship during his formative years will not even develop the traits that define humanity. Personhood is defined in relationship to others. The ego is developed through contact with others. Given all of this, neuroses will be formed, and must be resolved, in a social structure.

The Power of Community

We human beings do not choose to live in social relations; we are obliged to. Writing in *Animals as Social Beings* (1964), the great biologist Adolf Portmann said: "Man comes to 'sociability' not by 'arrangement,' by rational decision, but by the natural primary disposition which he shares with all higher animals. Attraction to other members of the species precedes all hostility and repulsion. Solitariness is always secondary, a flight from the natural bond."

For survival the human being requires nurture, warmth, and protection from predators. To ensure such needs — given the helpless state of the human infant at birth — he requires the existence of fellow creatures. In addition, to survive as a human being, not just as another form of animal life, to develop a conscience, a capacity for love, and a moral sense — in other words, to be fully human — requires interactions with other human beings.*

Freud certainly knew this. Much of his early writing was devoted to the biological awareness of the social nature of the human being. His early book *Totem and Taboo* (1913) was devoted specifically to this subject. Yet psychoanalysis, flourishing during the rise of individualism in the twentieth century,

---

*The pioneering work of such researchers as Harry Harlow, John Bowlby, and Marshall Klaus, among others, has clearly established the detrimental effects of early childhood deprivations and separation.

progressively turned its back on environment, relationships, and feelings to focus almost exclusively on internal conflicts.

Where therapy is concerned, two is company but three (or more) is not necessarily a crowd. Group therapy is an effective device particularly for social problems in relationships among people. The individual therapist is handicapped by not seeing his patient in action (the group therapist directly perceives the way his patient relates to others), and he must extrapolate from what the patient says to what actually occurs outside in the real world, in the process often missing some of the subtler points. This is most telling at the beginning of therapy. In time the therapist will eventually "catch on"; he has a check on the reporting biases of his patient. The therapist can utilize his own relationships with the patient, and through the mirror of the transference, the therapist is capable of recognizing the characteristic distortions with which the patient will view other relationships.

Why be dependent on the transference? Why not conduct all therapies in groups, as some would advise? The profound limitations of group therapy are only too apparent to those who have been involved with it. There is no privacy in a group or from the group. One of the most horrifying aspects of group therapy is the degree to which confidences are broken. In addition, therapeutic intimacy is lost. Things that can barely be revealed to one person will never be offered to an assemblage. The group of two is still one of the most profound and complex vehicles for human intercourse, and it can suffice. William James, the great pioneer of American psychology, speculated that although the moral life demanded relationships with others, the complete moral life could exist with but two people:

Were all other things, Gods and men and starry heavens, blotted out from the Universe, and were there left but one rock with two loving souls upon it, that rock would have as thoroughly moral a constitution as any possible world which the eternities and immensities could harbor. . . . While they lived, there would be real good things and real bad things in the Universe; there would be obligations, claims and expectations; obediences, refusals and disappointments; compunctions and longed for harmony to come again, and inward peace of conscience when it was restored; there would, in short, be a moral life, whose active energy would have no limit but the intensity of interest in each other with which the hero and the heroine might be endowed.*

It is doubtful whether there can be such a thing as self-analysis, although many respectable people (including Freud) have credited the idea. Certainly Saint Augustine seemed to manage. And C. S. Lewis handled his grief at the death of his wife by writing his extraordinary journals. Yet it is easier for all of us, and necessary for most of us, to act out our neuroses in relationship with another human being, a trained therapist. In such an environment we are prepared to see more clearly and more honestly, to recognize the destructiveness of our neuroses and the price we pay to maintain them, and by so doing prepare to resolve them. By experiencing these insights in the presence of another, we can — to use the splendid distinctions of William James — convert "knowing about" something into

---

*"The Moral Philosophy and the Moral Life," in *The Writings of William James,* J. McDermott, ed. (New York: Random House, 1967), pp. 618–619.

"knowledge of" it. We can transform the intellectual into the experiential. We can convert knowledge into insight.

For this to happen there must be a special community. It cannot be any two people. It must be a therapeutic community.

A Special Community

All of the knowledge, all of the self-understanding and insight, all of the accumulation of data, acquire special meaning, and true utility, only when shared with another human being. This capacity to share and the relief it affords are an essential component of community. The first service the therapist supplies is as the voice of that community — the voice of the other. But it is a special voice. It is a nonjudgmental voice.

The special nature of the therapeutic community is embraced by a broader context, the medical model. The medical model stands for a number of things. The physician views illness as something that is imposed on a patient rather than something he created; he is not "responsible" for his symptom. The medical model casts the patient in the role of victim rather than victimizer even when he actually shares culpability (the alcoholic, for example) in the creation of his own condition. Assuming the sick role brings him into a setting in which he can expect care from a collaborating ally in fighting the common enemy, the disease.

Although the therapist speaks in a nonjudgmental voice, hers is not a value-free voice. She is constantly forced to make judgments defining what in the patient's conduct will be considered healthy (the psychological equivalent of good) and what will be perceived as neurotic (the psychological equivalent of bad). She will never ascribe culpability to the patient for any of his behavior, healthy or neurotic, any more than a doctor would pass moral judgment on the patient for physical symptoms.

Whenever a physician defines something as a symptom, she is making a value call, forming a judgment. Blood pressure of 140 over 70 is preferable to a blood pressure of 240 over 120. High blood pressure is unhealthy (bad), a symptom of a disease. We do not, however, hold the patient accountable for the symptom, even when we find that he shares responsibility for it. Even when we know that he could have altered his behavior to ameliorate his high blood pressure — low-salt diet, reducing tension, losing weight, stopping smoking — we do not condemn the patient for the salt in his diet nor the tension in his life. We do not cut him off from health benefits — yet.

All that is true with physical symptoms is doubly true with mental symptoms. We know that people do not choose to have a common cold, let alone cancer. But what of that behavior that we are now defining as neurosis? Is it a work block or indolence, obesity or lack of willpower? The mere assigning of the mentally "ill" patient to the sick role is singularly relieving of both guilt and culpability. The power of the medical model is an extraordinary comfort to the mentally ill.

There is profound relief in simply being able to talk about things that were formerly perceived by oneself as shameful, disgusting, unacceptable — and might well be so perceived by the community at large — to a fellow human being who will receive whatever one says in a nonjudgmental manner. To a person who will listen with an air of compassionate neutrality — beyond neutrality, a person who is supportive and reassuring, an ally. The therapist and patient form an alliance against the common enemy, the sickness.

The alliance is not one of two people who are equals. The therapist is not just any representative of the community. Hers is not a random voice of the "other"; hers is a special voice. The therapist is an authority figure, the voice of expertise, status, and power. In coming to a therapist, whether the therapist is a physician, psychologist, or social worker, the patient will perceive the therapist in terms of the power and authority of the expert.

The doctor, or any health provider, is an authority. It has always intrigued me that we speak of following doctor's "orders," as distinguished from the "counsel" of our lawyers and the "advice" of our friends. Orders are to be obeyed. And we tend to be more obedient to orders from the health provider because he bears with him the imprimatur of life and death.

In the early stages of therapy, such authority often passes unacknowledged even as it is being exploited. By the end of therapy, the knowledge that the patient is treating the therapist as an authority figure must be made explicit. The overestimation of the power of the therapist must be analyzed away before analysis is terminated. Prior to that a clever and confident therapist can find a playful use for the magical endowment that the patient ascribes to his therapist.

One specific example that delighted me involved a former teacher of mine, the gifted and innovative psychoanalyst Dr. Lionel Ovesey. He was a small — one might say diminutive — man, slight, small-boned, with fine features all contained within a miniaturized frame. He kept a stock of small, inexpensive carved stone lions in his office. To phobic patients who would say that they wished that he could accompany them on a particularly frightening trip, he would offer a carving, the implication being that they had the "little lion" (Lionel) with them at all times. It was offered tongue-in-cheek, and yet it was a powerful emblematic statement, saying, "I am with you, and while I am with you harm will not come to you." I envied him his freedom in doing this, but in those early days of my career I never emulated it, being wary of any suggestion of magic.

In recent years I found myself doing something not terribly dissimilar. One of my patients was a mildly phobic actress who of necessity had to fly back and forth between New York and Los Angeles and had managed to at least control her intense fear of flying. Nonetheless, she once called me from Los Angeles in a panic. She had to take a flight to a location for an important picture and was sure she could not do it. I talked to her on the phone, trying to reassure her, telling her that she had overcome most of her other anxieties and this fear of flying was common enough that she could join the multitude of others who shared in it and endured. This time, she insisted, she was sure that the plane would crash. I told her there was no way she could be "sure" it would crash, and quite the contrary, I was "sure" it would not. She laughed, recognizing the inanity of my remark, and said: "Do I have your word on it?" I knew the laughter intimated her awareness of the foolishness of both her statement and mine, suggesting that the amelioration of her anxiety had already begun. In the spirit of the game, I replied: "Unequivocally!" She said, "Do you guarantee it?" And I did.

She terminated treatment some time later, but periodically visited me for a "touch-up." In between times she would occasionally call in anticipation of a flight to some obscure place, asking me how the prospects looked. Like a newspaper astrologer, I always found the timing of such flights propitious. We would take these occasions to chat and get caught up on her family and career. Inevitably the conversation would end with her saying: "So, I have your guarantee." And I would wryly assure her she did. By this time it had become an affectionate joke between us, but wrapped in the banter was a vestigial remnant of the magical transference.

This badinage is not the analog of seemingly equivalent playfulness between two friends. This is the kind of relaxed moment that often occurs after successful therapy in which the authority of the therapist has been demonstrated by his capacity to help the patient through a difficult time. Even when the therapist takes pains to indicate to the patient that it was she herself who made the change, the patient is always overly generous in sharing credit for the success with the therapist.

This little ritual may seem not much different from touching wood, crossing oneself, or keeping one's fingers crossed. They too may suggest the implicit power of some authority (chance, God, the gods, nature) that influences our destiny. There is never any question that for therapy to have any chance of success, the patient must vest the therapist with the powers of authority.

As mentioned earlier, this becomes most manifest in the various, often contradictory, uses of the therapist in the transference phenomena. During the course of therapy, the therapist will become, in the patient's perception, the doting mother, the intimidating father, the lover, the husband, the submissive sibling or the dominating one. This is encouraged by the peculiar stance that characterizes the analytically trained therapist in particular, the nondirective attitude. Part of the value of such a pose is precisely to allow the various transference feelings to be played out, but it is only part of the value of this posture.

I have suggested before that there is no way the therapist can be nondirective short of abdicating responsibility for the treatment. A therapist has to have a plan. More often than not, she will understand the structure of the patient's problems very early. Most therapists within the first month or two — often within the first week or two — will have a complete sense of the key dynamics of the patient. If knowledge alone were enough to modify conduct, she would simply inform the patient of his conflicts, elucidate their sources, and effect the magical cure. But premature knowledge is often harmful, coming before the patient is prepared to face it. The insights must come when the patient is ready to receive them, and they must be revealed in the passion of the present-day struggle.

"Nondirective" really indicates that the patient, not the therapist, must be allowed to choose the subject for discussion during any particular session. He is entitled to this authority and freedom. He is unlikely to get such indulgent attention anywhere else. The therapist is reassured by the certitude that the patient always chooses the most useful subject, whether it appears so or not, since his choice will be dictated by his unconscious and his emotional state.

It is the emotional state that we therapists must attend to. Even if it is not the subject which preoccupies the therapist at that moment, the "more important" subject is the one that engages the emotions of the patient. Knowledge cannot be utilized when it is not fired by the emotions of the patient. It is that fire that fuels motivation. If the patient is in a rage over a betrayal at work, at that moment he cannot effectively deal with all of the questions that may have been gradually and carefully prepared in the preceding weeks of analyzing his tenderness or lack of tenderness toward his wife.

The patient must be allowed to pick his own subject matter despite the well-laid plan of the therapist. First off, because it is the only way that will be effective. Second, in the long run it will not matter. The labyrinth of the unconscious can be traversed through a number of paths, each journey illuminating a different aspect of a similar problem. The therapist simply has the extra burden of keeping in mind the number of stories that have unraveled, at what position they are currently, in order to eventually bring them all together in one grand design.

The patient will perceive the nondirective approach as giving him greater power over the therapeutic hour. He feels the dignity of being in charge. This is in itself in such dramatic opposition to the authorities of childhood, where the parent was always in charge, or the workplace, where the boss sets the agenda, that it forges a new and special kind of alliance between patient and therapist. The therapist represents a unique model of authority. An authority who is prepared to be led. An authority who is nonjudgmental. An authority who is never overwhelmed with anxiety or anger, or for that matter, solicitude or compassion, the latter being just as much a threat to the therapeutic alliance as the former.

For most therapists, controlling their anger is easy. They are trained under the medical model to do so. No matter how "disgusting" a wound may seem to a layman, a surgeon approaches it with interest. He will not shun a patient because of the presence of a smelly abscess. So too is the case with the therapist in the face of mental symptoms that might be received with revulsion or rage in the lay community, even the community of loved ones. In the therapeutic milieu, symptoms are observed dispassionately and with interest. This alone is sufficient to label this relationship a singular one.

A more difficult task for the therapist is to guard against maternalism, protectiveness, compassion, and empathy. She is, after all, a human being and desires the best for her patient. It is hard to see someone for whom you feel compassion suffering without exhibiting that compassion. A therapist who feels no compassion cannot be a good therapist. The therapist who indulges that compassion is not doing her duty. Therefore, the therapist who does not have to struggle is not one I would trust. The maintenance of the therapeutic alliance demands control of benevolent emotions as well as pejorative attitudes. We must avoid killing the therapy with kindness.

Of course, this cautionary refers to the ongoing stance of the therapist in relation to her patient. Within the course of the many hours shared, there will still be appropriate times for sympathy, encouragement, and compassion. I cannot imagine a therapy where the therapist does not feel free to engage her patient at this level. This is, after all, still a shared encounter among fellow human beings.

The Therapeutic Alliance

This special and singular relationship, this idiosyncratic community of two, constitutes what has been called the therapeutic alliance. No other community can supply what it offers. Even with loved ones there are antagonisms and conflicts, expectations and disappointments, competition and betrayals. Not in the therapeutic community of two. The therapeutic alliance is limited in nature and limited in time, setting special conditions. The patient is expected to reveal everything, to share every impulse and idea with his therapist. The therapist is expected, required, to withhold her feelings and desires. The stuff of the therapeutic hour has nothing to do with the analyst's health, life, aspirations, needs. I recall the moment I heard of the death of my mother during the course of a workday. It disrupted only one patient's session: I had to dismiss one patient while I made the necessary travel arrangements. Successive patients came into my office, completed their hours, and left, presumably unaware of my distress. I say "presumably" because just as children are finely attuned to their parents, many patients are extremely sensitive to the moods of the therapist.

The power of this alliance allows the patient an honesty that is impossible in any other relationship. The patient is freer and more revealing than with her closest friend. She is protected by the narrowness of the therapeutic goal, and by the fact that her interests, not the therapist's, will always drive the therapy. She is protected by the awareness that she will not be hurting the therapist's feelings, regardless of what invective or abuse she may heap upon her. She will not be accused of calumny or ingratitude. These conditions allow the patient to face problems she could not face by herself or with a loved one who might be accomplice to the problem.

If insight is indeed the product of change, rather than the cause, it is only within the safety of the therapeutic alliance that such insight and self-awareness are likely to emerge. Armed with an ally vested with the power and authority to destigmatize all aspects of self-loathing, the patient finds the demons of the unconscious less daunting. In the Catholic covenant one is urged to hate the sin but love the sinner. In the world of psychotherapy, where no sin is recognized, one neither hates nor loves either the actor or the act. Here is a confessional that leads to absolution without penance. There is no price the patient has to pay, no propitiation to the judgmental gods, for this god is nonjudgmental. All that is asked of the patient is that he enter the world of actuality and confront the illusions that bind him to his neurosis.

The therapeutic alliance arms the patient with the requisite credence and courage to face his unconscious. The therapeutic alliance supplies the patient with the essential instruments necessary to convert understanding into action.

11 The Corrective Emotional Experience

"C ORRECTIVE emotional experience" is a term I borrow from Franz Alexander. Alexander was part of that great influx of Hungarian Jewish refugee psychoanalysts who came to this country fleeing the Nazis and so enriched the intellectual life of the psychiatric community. While Alexander originally referred to a conscious maneuver on the part of the patient to conform his behavior to specific norms, I have expanded the concept to include the entire effect of the ongoing relationship between therapist and patient.

What is encompassed by the term "corrective emotional experience"? Each word is carefully chosen to specifically describe the phenomenon that Alexander observed in the ongoing alliance between patient and therapist.

- First, it is a form of *experience*; it is an encounter, an engagement with another human being, the therapist. An experience, as the dictionary states, is "an active participation in events or activities leading to the accumulation of knowledge or skill; an event or series of events participated in or lived through." This is already distinct from insight, whereby knowledge is perceived as emerging from introspection and self-examination. Insight suggests a cognitive

217

activity (learning *of*), while experience suggests action (learning *through*). Alexander invites us into the world of implicit learning that occurs in a relationship, as distinguished from explicit learning that could just as well be garnered from a book.

- It is an experience of an *emotional* nature. An individual learns all manner of things from his relationships, but not all of them are of emotional import. Without explication, or even awareness, we may adopt a style of dress, a manner of speech, an attitude or an idea, from our involvement with others, particularly those whom we respect and admire. This may happen in the therapeutic relationship too, but the exchanges that will prove therapeutic are those that engage the most profound emotions of the patient.
- Finally, I suggest, the very process of undergoing therapy will *correct previous misconceptions* that were determinative in former relationships. The nature of the therapeutic relationship, where all activity is driven to serve the health and welfare of the patient, challenges the patient's entrenched anticipations of what to expect from those around him — usually abuse, exploitation, disrespect, and diminished self-esteem — by offering a powerful alternative that resists falling into the pattern of the destructive stereotype. Good therapy is a corrective emotional experience.

Since this process spans the entire time frame of the therapy, rather than being a specific event, it is difficult to offer an example short of an entire case history. Still, two cases in my experience were so dramatic in their nature that they may prove illustrative, even in an abbreviated and fractured form.

Sarah's Story

"Sarah" originally came to me only for consultation and a referral. She had had two previous experiences in psychotherapy, the first in Chicago, where she attended an upscale suburban high school, the second while in college in the East. Both had ended disastrously when the therapist made sexual advances to her. She was determined never to be involved with a male therapist again. She came for an evaluation that she expected to lead to a referral to a female therapist. I, however, had not been apprised of this.

Sarah had been referred to me as a case for treatment directly from another therapist — a woman who was treating her closest friend. This referring therapist gave me an outline of her take on Sarah's problems, her feeling that Sarah urgently needed therapy, and asked me in advance if I would have time to treat her, since she wanted to avoid her being bounced around from one consultation to another. I happened to have time to take on a new patient and therefore saw this as the beginning of a therapeutic process rather than a diagnostic interview. When Sarah called, I simply made an appointment.

After an hour or two of history taking and evaluation, which was indeed complex, I attempted to set hours. She was startled and indicated that there must have been some miscommunication. She had only come to me for referral; she felt she required a woman therapist. I apologized for the misunderstanding and indicated that this was not a problem; I told her I would make preliminary calls to some women therapists whom I respected to see who had available time to treat her and then would give her their names.

After I said this she seemed flustered and hesitant, almost disappointed. This was what she had asked for, but not necessarily what she wanted. Sarah then said that since we had already spent two good hours together, perhaps we could give treatment a try. I said she still had the option of a referral; there must have been reasons why she preferred a woman, and she was entitled to her choice. I suggested that she take some time to think about it. I told her that she was free to leave with no commitment on her part; I would hold the time open for her, and she could notify me within the week whether she wanted a referral or preferred to continue treatment with me. I then called the referring physician, who apologized for the confusion, saying that while Sarah had indicated a preference for a woman, she had not perceived it as a fixed resolve and felt that Sarah would be better off in treatment with me.

Sarah called me that same day to say she was determined to continue treatment with me. She was an emotional and expansive young woman who quickly formed a magical transference with me, if not an exclusively positive one. The treatment would be haunted by that early ambiguity and dominated by considerations of my gender and what that meant in terms of trust and safety in therapy.

In the first session after this confusion, Sarah told me of an early seduction by a teacher that had occurred when she was in high school, and described her sense of panic and betrayal. Only after this did she reveal that sexual advances had been made to her by her previous therapists as well. One often has to question the validity of "coincidences" of this nature, but I have no doubt that these were actual events, based on her descriptions and the emotionality that accompanied the revelations.

Sarah was indeed a contradiction. Witty, expansive, ebullient, and flirtatious, she was at the same time frightened to the edge of panic, had severe performance anxiety to the point of being incapable of getting up in public even to state her name. She described this as a symptom dating back to grammar school, when the panic of getting up in class was so terrifying that she would have to leave the classroom. She indicated that she was sure she would expose her inadequacy and stupidity. Only much later in treatment was "exposure" associated with sexuality.

She had been recently offered a place on the board of a community service group in which she served and had refused despite her pride at being invited and her desire for status. She could not bear the anticipation of the moment when she would be asked to introduce herself to her fellow board members. She was also too frightened to look for a job. What she would have preferred at any rate was to continue her education, but she could not conceive of going on for graduate education, although she had a great passion for this. She was a brilliant and sensitive person who would have benefited from it. Her background was so unsettling, so destructive of self-confidence, that it was guaranteed to frustrate initiative and to keep her operating at a fraction of her abilities.

The key figures, as one might expect, were her mother and father. Her mother, a self-styled sculptor, was a borderline psychotic and alcoholic who vacillated between extremes of paranoid rejection of her children and effusive embraces. She had the qualities of a diabolical and unpredictable Auntie Mame. She flaunted her sexuality in front of her children, often walked around nude in their presence, and freely discussed with them the inadequacies of her sexual life with their father, contrasting it to her experiences with her various lovers. Sex was discussed in the family at all times, by both mother and father, and since the sexual proclivities of both parents led them to many affairs (not without rancor and acrimony), it was a sexually saturated household.

Her father was an enormously successful advertising man, albeit mildly psychopathic. He was ingratiating to everyone and was universally perceived as a "lovable soul." But this cuddly sweetheart was capable of exploding into almost uncontrollable rages in the bosom of his family. He was extraordinarily seductive to his daughter. She adored the affectionate qualities of her father, in marked contrast to the flamboyant but detached emotionality of her alcoholic mother, but was terrified that her father's affection masked a sexual interest in her. No evidence emerged that her father actually involved his daughter in sexual activities. I was as convinced as one can be that this did not happen. But I am also convinced that given another therapist and another time, Sarah would have been converted into a "sexually abused child," since her suggestibility was enormous, with an anxiety to match.

Her manner in therapy was bewilderingly contradictory. If it truly mirrored her relationships in life, she would have been a confounding paradox to any man with whom she was involved. Obviously here the transference carried extra weight. An older man with power and authority who could both support and betray her was a paradigm in her life. She was open and revealing about the most intimate aspects of her history and her unconscious, excepting always her feelings about me. Her suspicions of my intentions and motives were always manifest. She was ready to interpret all attention as sexually motivated. Once on the couch she felt safe. The moments getting to the couch at the beginning of the session, and leaving the office at the end, were stilted and painful.

I observe every patient as he or she comes in. I am interested in the way my patients look and dress, their facial expression, their body language. I would have no reason to avert my eyes, which would itself suggest something indecent or voyeuristic. Still, I do not conduct a visual inspection or review. The greeting at the beginning of an hour is consonant with normal social form and simple politesse. When Sarah, however, observed me looking at her as she walked into the room, she would angrily ask, "What are you looking at?" or "What's wrong?" or simply say, "I don't like you to look at me," explaining that it made her uncomfortable. When I would ask, "What would you have me do?" her delightful sense of humor would come to the fore and she would say sardonically, "How about standing in the corner and closing your eyes."

Routine entries and exits eventually became less troublesome, but there were times when it seemed to me some comments were appropriate. One of my most formal supervisors would not have agreed. He once chastised me for questioning a patient who came in severely bruised with a black eye. I admit that I immediately asked her what had happened (a fall down a flight of stairs), though I could have waited until she lay on the couch and started associating. It seemed unnatural, even rude, not to acknowledge her injury. Still, this same supervisor had been incredulous, and highly critical, when I reported helping a patient with a broken arm into his coat. The rules are not clear nor universal.

I have always operated on the principle that while the therapeutic relationship is not a social one, certain social amenities still prevail. The omission of certain conventional behaviors would be more bizarre and open to misinterpretation than simply following social convention. Were a patient to offer me an expensive Christmas gift, I would not accept and would analyze the possible meanings beyond the generosity. However, when one patient included me on her list of people for whom she dropped off some homemade cookies, I accepted without searching the unconscious motivation in the action. This led to a severe reproof from yet another supervisor.

Dramatic changes in a patient's appearance are things I traditionally raise questions about, for at least a couple of reasons. When a brunette patient of two years showed up as a blonde, I commented. To "not notice" would be a pretense and an affectation. The *absence* of comment would be provocative. It would seem perverse, and could justifiably be perceived by the patient as an affront. Were a patient to come in bandaged or on crutches and not discuss it immediately — a rare and unlikely event — I would ask about it. Marked changes in the appearance of a patient are important to me and are always introduced by me when they are not mentioned by the patient.

I was particularly careful with Sarah, recognizing her special sensitivities. So that even when she came in one day with a dramatically altered hairdo, I waited patiently before eventually commenting, albeit with calculated neutrality and significant trepidation. With Sarah, any comment, even about a changed hairdo, could lead to rage, sobbing, and hysteria, followed by the statement that I was not supposed to be noticing those things or looking at her "that way." She had no inkling that it was her overreaction to such an ordinary comment that sexualized the interchange.

Similarly, she could not acknowledge her own seductiveness. And seductive she was! That she was unaware of this was a part of her problem that would become apparent to her only relatively late in her treatment. It occurred to me that she had most likely sent such conflicting messages to her previous therapists. This *did not* in any way make her an accomplice to their reprehensible behavior, nor excuse their violation of their professional role. She was entitled to behave this way — she was expected to behave this way. It was part of her symptom complex and her personality.

The active sexual approaches of her previous therapists were in flagrant violation of the tacit contract between therapist and patient. There is never any justification — never any — for a therapist's having sex or making sexual overtures to his patient. This is a specific violation of the code of ethics of the American Psychiatric Association and most other professional associations. And it is *always* antitherapeutic, despite the persistence of rationalizations to the contrary. It is significant that such incidents generally involve older male therapists with younger women patients. If these advances were made in the interest of some therapeutic goals, we all would have heard of at least one case of a forty-year-old male therapist having sex with a seventy-year-old patient.

Sarah expected sexual seduction and betrayal, and she assumed it would come in the guise of protection. Her father was supposed to lend some stability in a household dominated by the mood swings of the alcoholic mother. But he too was capable of occasional incidents of terrifying rage, accompanied by vitriol and verbal abuse of his daughter. While admittedly he was not as volatile as her mother, his emotional outbursts were more threatening. A child raised by a psychotic parent is like a child raised beside the railroad tracks. The noise of the passing locomotives is assimilated into everyday life. Sarah handled her mother's bizarre behavior with a maturity and sophistication that were surprising and admirable.

With her father it was different. He was generally soft, seductive, ingratiating — sufficient to lull her into a false sense of security — when out of nowhere an explosive rage would emerge. Her transgressions and misdemeanors, her inadequacies and failures, would be piled one upon another, ending always with the message of her inadequacy and how disappointing she was as his daughter. Naturally she expected the same of me.

I was sensitive to her fragility and attempted to phrase all interpretations in the least threatening language. Perhaps I was too sensitive. There was that occasion previously mentioned when Sarah arrived with a total makeover, her blond ponytail having given way to a sophisticated short cut. I initially treated it with complete disregard. This then led to a rebuke, allowing her to comment: "I can't believe you didn't notice I cut my hair." I then patiently said that my previously noticing even such a simple thing as the fact that she was dressed up for a job interview instead of in her usual jeans had been seen as a threat and as having potential sexual overtones. Through such gentle exchanges Sarah began to see the confusing signals that she herself sent to men she encountered in real life.

I must caution that I am selecting just one thread out of the fabric of a complex transference relationship to focus on, thus running the risk of oversimplifying Sarah and her therapy. This element hardly embodies the richness, the intricacy, and the full emotional range of our relationship. Nonetheless, one thread can be followed clearly, whereas depicting the total involvement would require the length of a Victorian novel and the talents of a George Eliot or Charles Dickens.

Sarah's preparedness to feel betrayed by me came up weekly. Small things — a changed inflection in my voice, a slight shift in tone, or even moving in my chair — were seen as a lack of interest and a readiness to discharge her. She always expected rejection. I was determined she would never get such from me, and when occasionally I had to cancel appointments, I would always make sure they were not hers, that her therapeutic hours were sacrosanct, at least during the beginning phases. Nonetheless, Sarah found her betrayal.

I usually interrupt my practice for four to six weeks in the summer, and my patients are informed well in advance. I leave a phone number where I can be reached and encourage my patients to call me. I also leave the number of a therapist on call when I have particularly volatile or fragile patients such as those suffering with depression. In late May, I reminded Sarah, along with the rest of my patients, of the exact dates of my summer leave, extending from late July through Labor Day. Despite the fact that she had experienced such a break the previous summer, this time a pivotal and explosive event occurred between us.

Sarah was horrified by the news and said I had not told her before of my taking off this summer, and had not given her sufficient notice now. I said that I thought I had, and that in addition, it was made clear the previous summer that I always take an extended break in the summer. She countered by saying that last summer I had only taken the month of August. This year involved an extra two weeks, and it was outrageous that she should not have been better prepared for this. She felt it was a betrayal of the analytic situation and a breach of therapeutic ethics. It should be said that Sarah was in no particular crisis during that period, but actually seemed to be progressing in all aspects of her life, except the ability to find a boyfriend. I was seeing her on a twice-a-week basis, and except for major holidays like Christmas and Thanksgiving I take no holidays. Sarah would on occasion take a winter break of a week or two.

She felt that my behavior was "inexcusable," and this was supported by the views of her friends and family. Her mother, who wavered between seeing me as a god who had saved her daughter and an ogre who would destroy her, was in one of the latter moods and supported her outrage.

Returning for her next session, Sarah announced that the therapy could not continue and that she wanted a referral — this time to a woman therapist. I would be happy to arrange this, I told her, assuring her that a patient is always entitled to a second opinion. I reassured her not only that was she entitled to see another therapist, but that something good often resulted from a change. I suggested that we continue meeting to discuss her feeling of betrayal during the period she was having her consultation. In addition, I told her that I was prepared to reserve her hours until after her new therapy was under way. She stated that she would never trust me again but that she did not want to stop treatment until she was in the hands of another therapist.

During the transition period, Sarah continued questioning how I could have "done this" to her. Considering her response, I was more than prepared to admit that I might well have made a tactical error in not informing her earlier, but I refused to accept the extreme nature of her response as proper or proportional, seeing it rather as a defense against some emerging and threatening feelings. While I allowed that she might view me as careless or derelict, I could not understand how this could be interpreted as ignoble or villainous or in any way a betrayal and breach of trust. Sarah was enraged by my refusal to admit that what I had done to her was reprehensible and a moral wrong; and, paradoxically, she seemed equally angered by my willingness to support her change of therapy.

I supplied her with the names of some women therapists whose work I respected. In addition, I cautioned her that, given her present frame of mind, she might prefer a referral from someone else, perhaps her friend's analyst. She checked my names out — with whom I am not sure — and went to see one of them, who was also on a list of referrals from another source. She started seeing this other therapist, and I left for my summer break. It was to be more than a consultation, more a trial therapy. Nonetheless, Sarah asked if I would reserve her hours. I said that I would.

She saw this therapist almost the entire time that I was away and expressed her feelings that I had committed a massive and inexcusable offense. Sarah was later to tell me that the most therapeutic response of the new therapist was her obvious confusion and inability to understand the source of Sarah's outrage. Why the sense of betrayal? Even if Dr. Gaylin could be judged negligent, how could that be escalated into villainy? How was any of this "iniquitous"?

Sarah at first answered that it must be the emergence of her old separation anxiety. When the therapist asked Sarah to focus on these anxious feelings, the result was an outpouring of worries and concerns, but the anxiety not related to separation. Sarah had been terrified by intimations that I had become sexually interested in her. Her new therapist asked her how she knew this to be true — in what way had this been demonstrated? She responded that although she had no evidence, she was sure it was true.

After some delays, she reported to the therapist a dream she had while still in treatment with me of my actively seducing her. The therapist pointed out that this was her dream, not mine, and that it suggested *her* emerging sexual feelings about me, not the opposite. Surprisingly, Sarah accepted this interpretation with little difficulty. It is questionable whether she would have from me. She then expressed fear that she might succeed in seducing me. In a way that might not have happened in a traditional therapy rather than in this prolonged trial therapy consultation, the therapist laughed and told Sarah that she had the wrong man — that "hell would freeze over before Dr. Gaylin would do such a thing!"

The spontaneity and directness of the response proved both liberating and reassuring to Sarah. She continued to discuss her relationship with me, and what emerged was that she had started to have sexual fantasies that would have been so painful and difficult for her to discuss with me that she had not reported them. Sarah called me during the summer, telling me that she would continue to see the woman therapist during my absence because it was proving so useful, but that she wished to continue treatment with me on my return. And so she did.

The consultation was a transforming experience. It freed her to examine her own confused sexuality. Throughout the therapy with me, Sarah continued to question, to find doubts, to be hesitant, to have anxiety, to have nightmares of my either abandoning her or seducing her. In fact, of course, I did neither of these things, and over a period of four years her life was transformed. Her anxiety diminished; she began to relate to her father better; she courageously (not without trepidation) enrolled in an incredibly demanding graduate school program, came through with shining colors, and received her professional certification. She accepted a leadership position in many of her areas of interest, actually acting as a spokesperson for one important cause that she believed in.

Sarah's whole life had been one of unreliability and betrayal of trust. It was not surprising that she anticipated the same from a therapist. More important, she *needed* it from her therapist to convince herself that she was not crazy, and also to convince herself that she was in no way an accomplice to some of the seductions in her past life. There had been many, and they had been betrayals. A date rape, a teacher, two therapists, and others. She could not bear to believe that any man could behave differently, because that would then introduce doubts about the reality of her past perceptions. Her mother's confused sense of reality was frightening to her, bringing into question her own reality testing. Sarah had to be sure that she was right about men, all men, including her therapist. But she was not right. And this single community of two, this single experience with a therapist who did not subscribe to the prototype of her father — a prototype she both sought and encountered her entire life — proved to be a transforming, corrective emotional experience.

Despite all these successes, and they were many and manifest, when she felt it was time to think seriously about a permanent romantic attachment with a man, she decided she wanted to work this out with a woman therapist. She went on to have a second successful therapy with a woman therapist. I have had modest knowledge of Sarah after that and am always delighted to hear about her progressive maturation in life. Once a corrective emotional experience destroys the consistency of the past, the patient then is capable of going into the real world and, using the therapist as a bridge, reapproaching situations with a new and more trusting anticipation. This was indeed Sarah's story.

John's Story

A briefer example of the way the corrective emotional experience works may be seen in my relationship with "John." John was my first supervised psychoanalytic patient (four times per week), while I was still in training. He himself was a resident in medicine while I was a resident in psychiatry. Normally this would not have happened. One was expected to be well into, or to have completed, residency training before admission to an analytic school. But I was a young man in a hurry. I had talked the director of the Columbia Psychoanalytic Center, Dr. Rado, into bending the rules and admitting me to psychoanalytic training concurrently with my starting my residency training in psychiatry. Rado was intrigued, I think, by my youth, my early marriage, and by my audacity and my financial plight. He was himself a rebel and may have responded to a kindred spirit. He admitted me. John, who had once thought of psychoanalytic training himself, assumed that anyone who was well into psychoanalytic school had completed his psychiatric residency.

John had profound problems with a terrifying and punitive father and, consequently, intense problems with male competition. He was plagued by nightmares. Every failure in his everyday life would — in his dreams — be seen as castration and vulnerability, with scenes of his being sexually raped by a stronger man. These were nonerotic dreams in the sense that John was not aroused by them. Indeed, he was terrified, and the terror was further enhanced in everyday life by his assumption that this must mean he had latent homosexual impulses. In the heyday of libido theory, every dream was a wish fulfillment, so homosexual imagery in dreams was thought to be evidence of the latent homosexual impulses that we all — even the most confirmed heterosexuals — were supposed to have in our unconscious. This concept proved disastrous and was the father of the idea that anyone raped — man or woman — must have "asked for it." A dream of a homosexual rape was assumed to be a desire for it. But when a man says, "Boy, did I get fucked today," he is rarely describing an erotic pleasure. The same may be said for a dream.

There are people with true latent homosexual impulses, but John was not one of them. His competition with other men was mirrored in his distortions that inevitably exaggerated their powers vis-à-vis his. He was constantly measuring and always finding himself coming up short. His capacity for distortion in terms of other men was mirrored in his perceptions of me. John was tall and lanky like myself (in those days), perhaps an inch taller. Yet he perceived me as three or four inches taller. And he imagined me as five to ten years older than I actually was.

Two unpredictable and unplanned events occurred during the course of his therapy that would change its direction and speed the therapeutic process. The first took place early in therapy. I was seeing John in an office at the Columbia Psychoanalytic Center. That was the way we did it with clinic patients. He paid the clinic directly, not me, and we used offices set aside in the clinic for therapy. This was fortunate for me, since I had no private office and no private practice. So John had no illusion about my having completed my psychoanalytic training. But since that could occur five to ten years after residency, it did not alter his view of me as a senior physician.

One day, six months into therapy, John needed to reschedule a session. He called me at the clinic, which then gave a forwarding number to reach me. He expected that this was my private office. Instead it was the ward of the Bronx

VA Hospital that I was rotating through during my residency, and the phone was answered by the ward nurse. When I came on the line, John told me of his need to cancel an hour. At the beginning of the next therapeutic session, he quizzically said to me, "I don't understand. Where were you?" I explained I was at the Bronx VA Hospital. He said with horror, "You're not still a resident, are you?"

The temptation to lie was enormous. I dreaded having to reveal the truth. I knew this would shatter John. I had no idea what it would do to the therapy in which we both had invested a significant amount of time and in which a certain amount of progress had been made. There were selfish reasons why I didn't want the therapy to go belly-up. In order to graduate I had to have at least two completed psychoanalytic cases. John was my first. If I had to stop with him, I would be set back another six months. But a blatant lie would have been difficult if not impossible for me. Beyond that, it would have undermined the implicit assumption that a patient makes — and the explicit reassurance that I am always prepared to offer my patients — that I will never lie to them and that I will always strive to serve their purposes.

I might have rationalized an evasion if not an outright lie. The analyst is expected to protect his own privacy. He is instructed not to reveal too much to the patient. This serves a therapeutic purpose. The therapist becomes a tabula rasa on which the patient is then free to write his own story, or so it was then thought. This was as much a part of the tradition of the Columbia Psychoanalytic Center as of the other schools.

I would have given anything to have been able to call my supervisor at that time, but one doesn't simply dismiss a patient and say, "Excuse me while I go ask my supervisor what to do." I argued in my own head that it was in John's interest at this stage to be unaware of my limited training. I stalled, asking him what he thought it would mean were I still a resident, what difference it would make, allowing him to associate for the entire session. Yet when he persisted at the end of the hour, I felt that refusing to tell him would be a form of lying that would itself undermine the therapy.

The therapist refuses to answer most personal questions raised by a patient, not just because it allows the patient room to speculate and fantasize, but also because the knowledge that the therapist is not required to answer will facilitate the patient's asking other painful questions. Armed with the knowledge that the therapist is not required to answer, the patient can raise questions about the therapist's personal and sexual life, whether he has been divorced, whether he has had gay experiences, whether he has extramarital affairs, still masturbates, et cetera. When free associating, such thoughts occur. If a patient is still masturbating regularly, even though he is a married adult, the thought may enter his mind: "I wonder if my analyst does." This is profoundly embarrassing to express. In addition, the patient really doesn't want to know, any more than he is really interested in the sexual details of his parents' life. If the therapist were required to answer, the patient might repress such thoughts and screen the flow of associations. The failure to answer protects the patient from knowledge he often does not want, thereby allowing him to fantasize and continue to say whatever comes to mind. The patient must always be made to feel free to raise doubts about his therapist, to express his anger and disappointment with his therapist, and to raise the most personal questions.

Still, it has long seemed clear to me that certain questions *must* be answered. It was part of my code that at the beginning of therapy if a patient asked me if I was a physician, was

I certified in psychiatry, was I an analyst, he was entitled to this knowledge as much as any patient going to any medical specialist. To hide from the truth, particularly in the area of training, was more likely to serve the interests of the therapist than the patient. This was what John was asking me. Had he raised the question at our introductory session I would have had no doubts as to where propriety lay. I steeled myself and answered John: "Yes, I am still in my residency."

I saw my supervisor shortly after this hour. I went there with alarm and foreboding, sure that he would chastise me for having messed up what had to that point seemed like a successful beginning of the therapy. Quite the contrary, he felt I had handled it in the proper way. I was immensely relieved. I know for a fact that other supervisors would have seen this as an egregious breach of proper technique, a violation of the anonymity that assuredly is a facilitating factor in successful therapy.

This unexpected event turned out to be a turning point in the early phases of therapy. It forced John to confront his own distortions, his evaluation of himself relative to other men, his need to see himself always as the child in relation to the stronger father. Here he was engaged with a therapist his own age and in his own position, and still he had endowed him with paternal authority and paternal attributes. Predictably, this event did not appreciably alter John's specific transference. He continued to idealize the therapist on one hand, while continuing to perceive in me the negative image of his rejecting, cold, competitive, and austere father.

What did change was his view of himself. There began to emerge feelings that he could assume a direct masculine role in his life, his profession, and his sexual activity. This patient continued to mature, growing rapidly in self-confidence and self-esteem, eventually winning a highly coveted role as chief resident in his specialty.

Nonetheless, during the entire course of the therapy, John persisted in seeing me as a cold and rejecting personality like his father. Certainly the therapeutic role is one of detachment and in that sense is hardly warm and fuzzy. The absence of any true demonstrativeness was an obstacle for John. He needed a new model of manhood that combined strength *and* softness. He did not understand how to deal with his own affectionate and tender emotions, which seemed to him unmanly, manliness being a fixation with him. He had no other models except his father and me, and I too was cold and austere. Then, much later in the analysis, a second serendipitous event occurred.

By this time I had a full load of three patients in supervised psychoanalysis, three patients in supervised brief psychotherapy, and a smattering of private patients. John was my last patient of the day. He had left my consultation room — I was now in a private office of my own — and I thought he had left the suite of offices. Waiting for me in the small waiting room were my wife and two daughters. My girls were two and three at that time. I was working long hours, and when I couldn't get home for dinner and their bedtimes, my wife would bring the children in so I could see them. It was a typical unguarded affectionate moment, hugging and embracing my wife, with both girls in my arms, laughing and giggling. This went on for perhaps a minute before out of the corner of my eye I saw that John was still in the office fussing with his coat. He had observed the scene. He quickly left the office, flushed with embarrassment.

This event had a powerful influence on the course of therapy, and in the long run it was all for the good — John was forced to see me in a new light, which then offered a new model for his behavior. In the short run, however, there was true anguish. Originally my austere demeanor was seen as a part of my persona; this was the kind of man he had chosen for his therapist. Now my coldness was not just the way I was, but reflected my lack of affection for him specifically, since I was obviously capable of giving affection. I would never become the loving father he craved to replace his remote true father; he would never have the loving father he so desired. But of course he would not, nor should he have been seeking that. Deprived of such a caring father in childhood, he must not search in vain for that which was unacceptable and unneeded in this phase of his life. John must get his pleasures in the alternative role by *becoming* a loving father.

The corrective emotional experience necessitated his seeing that men could be concerned about him without being paternal; that not all male relationships were competitive; that there was an egalitarian friendship available between men in which neither was the dependent one; that deprivation of childhood fathering was never reparable in kind; that the love of a father-child relationship would reemerge only when he was prepared to take the *paternal* role.

John worked through these insights. He was now ready to understand the nature and limits of the therapeutic session and recognized that what was missing in his life could not be supplied in the transference relationship but must be sought "out there" in the real world. John's therapy armed him with the new awareness that a man can be loving, affectionate, warm, and devoted while still being a man. He found himself secure in both the sexual and the affectionate role.

So fortuitous were the results of this chance event that I raised with my supervisor the future possibility of staging such "accidents" with other patients. My supervisor with John was an experimental and confident man, willing to test orthodox limits, and he agreed with me that this unplanned event had dynamited a logjam of some six months in which John seemed to make no progress in his affectionate relationships in life. But he drew the line here. He was, as usual, correct. Even were one capable of planning the appropriate event (not at all predictable), the very calculated nature of such action would represent something quite different from serendipity. It would be an artifact, a form of fraud. An artificiality of this sort would be manipulative, violating the Kantian imperative of never treating a person as an object, of always respecting the special dignity and autonomy inherent in being human.

Later I did come close to breaking the rule, and may have actually crossed the line. At one time I had in treatment a remarkably attractive woman. Narcissistic beyond belief, she was convinced that she was the most beautiful woman in the world and expected to be treated with the awe and admiration to which she was entitled. She used her beauty not to attract men, but to control them. She was pathetically isolated and alone. Her expectations were enormous. During the same period, I had another patient who was so breathtakingly beautiful that she caused a disturbance in my male patients who preceded her and followed her. This was not just beauty, it was rare beauty. A Botticelli brought to life. She was the kind of woman who brought gasps from passersby. Yet she herself seemed unaware of her beauty. She was a borderline schizophrenic girl who was shy and reclusive and totally self-effacing. Perhaps this added a sense of unworldliness that enhanced her ethereal radiance. One day, because of an illness, she needed a makeup hour. I had two hours available, one of which happened to be the hour immediately following my narcissistic patient.

Since it was my choice, a certain amount of mischief and curiosity came into play. Armed with the knowledge that this shy and anxious girl always arrived a half hour early, I scheduled her right after the first woman so that when my first patient left she would see the second.

This was not a supervised case. I had to make no apologies to anyone and besides, I rationalized, if I had just that hour free, that's where she would have gone at any rate. I knew I was making a manipulative move, but I was eager to see what would happen. The results were explosive. The first patient was astonished by the beauty of the second. Such extraordinary loveliness was an affront to her self-image. It broke through the veneer of her narcissism and produced weeping sessions in which she began to confront the fact there were other beautiful people in the world and that physical beauty was not sufficient for all purposes of humankind.

Despite the good results, I was not happy. I felt guilty and somewhat tacky. I did not like an intervention that, even though effective, made me feel that I was conning my own patient. I never consciously attempted a maneuver of this sort again. I decided that the special nature of the therapeutic relationship had enough power of its own and was so complicated and volatile that tampering with it would in the long run prove a negative, if not destructive, strategy. I have altered many of my assumptions about therapy, but I have always vigilantly maintained a professional distance from my patients that precludes such manipulations.

A New Take on the Real World

The therapeutic role is certainly one of distance and detachment, yet it is not a cold one. I have grieved for my patients but resisted displaying that grief. The patient must tell all of his feelings. The therapist may tell none of his. The patient expresses his anger, his love, his affection, his disappointment in his therapist. The therapist discusses none of these. The therapist is trusted with intimacies that even a lover, mother, child, will never know, and yet the therapist refuses to become interactive in this way. It is a peculiar relationship — a one-way street.

This does not inhibit the emergence of what is a peculiarly profound and significant, often passionate, relationship. It is a strange beast, with two asymmetric halves, and it defines the therapeutic alliance. So powerful is the trust ultimately invested in the therapist and the process that it allows the patient to alter a lifetime of expectations. It changes his perceptions, driving him into a new and healthier world of reality. This is what is meant by the corrective emotional experience.

One less than obvious result of the concept of the corrective emotional experience is that it joins psychoanalysis to its presumed opposite and antagonist, behaviorism. Traditionally, psychology in the twentieth century has been dominated by two powerful groups. The first of these takes its initial assumptions from Freud and psychoanalysis; its practitioners assume the presence of a dynamic unconscious and perform the kind of therapy that is the substance of this book. The other powerful and great tradition of psychology is behaviorism, and it started with the work of Pavlov, operating through John Watson, to its most influential twentieth-century spokesman, B. F. Skinner. The therapeutic device in this camp is conditioning.

Conditioning, while still emphasizing the crucial relevance of the past, does not acknowledge the presence of an unconscious. To psychologists who subscribe to conditioning, all behavior is the sum of small learning events that condition and direct one to prescribed behavior patterns, much as I described in the evolution of the hysteric and obsessive personality. The solution here avoids delving into some dynamic past, instead using the present to recondition and decondition the individual. This can be accomplished through aversive (i.e., punitive) conditioning or by positive reinforcement.

Conditioning psychologists for the most part have not been clinical psychotherapists. They have worked in theoretical fields of psychology or education, or in institutional design. Behavioristic techniques have been used clinically with specific symptomatic problems that need "fixing," such as addictions, and have been particularly effective in treating phobias. But conditioning has generally had its most profound impact, particularly with the work of Skinner, in dealing with the mentally handicapped and with severely psychotic children, where it has achieved considerable success.

The fact remains that even these different schools, behaviorism and psychoanalysis, are not all that different. They are bound together in their respect for the past and their assumptions that the present is chained to the past. They differ in their means of undoing the influences of the past. With the corrective emotional experience, Alexander introduced me to the intriguing notion that, through the transference, a form of prolonged reconditioning occurs even in the course of a dynamic therapy. This reconditioning is inherent in the patient's relationship with his therapist, and the profound and reassuring presence of this relationship over time helps to erase those lessons of the past that bind the patient to his neurosis.

When a patient looks out into the real world and sees only the images of his past because of the power of his mental representations, he cannot learn from current experience. If the cautionary lesson he learned from his past is that every man must be a competitor, then every man will be assumed to be a competitor whether he acts that way or not. If every man is expected to be a betrayer, every man will be perceived as a betrayer or, worse, will be induced to betray.

The corrective emotional experience provides an ineluctable encounter that cannot be denied. It upsets and eventually destroys a myth by which the patient has lived all his life. With the destruction of that myth, the patient is forced to perceive a new reality. At first this new reality will only exist during the special conditions of the therapeutic hour. But with the urging of the therapist, the patient will begin to take the lessons learned in the transference and perceive their relevance in other relations.

Therapists who themselves are bound to the analytic hour and do not help to take the dynamics out of the transference and into real life have failed in their primary obligations to the patient. This limitation represents one of the major flaws of modern psychoanalysis. Some therapists will maintain the transference relationship well beyond necessity, being unsure of their right to prod the patient into the real world of relationships.

Negative transference — hostility to the therapist — invites analysis since it is uncomfortable for both the patient and the analyst. Positive transference — idealization and affection for the analyst — is often only too comforting for both. All transference must be analyzed. The purpose of analyzing the transference is to indicate its relevance to all other relationships. The transference must be perceived as a means, not an end, a vehicle to get the patient out of the office and into life.

The therapist, forced to discuss everyday life, will come perilously close to counseling, an activity that has traditionally been frowned upon by ideologically "pure" psychoanalysts. But advice and counseling, even value indoctrination, are an essential part of every therapy, even traditional analysis.

12 Advice, Counseling, and Values

TRADITIONALLY, psychoanalytic psychotherapists have eschewed giving their patients advice — at least so they claimed and so they believed. "Advice" suggests that the patient requires rational guidance in the real world. Psychoanalysts believe that the basic pathology of a patient resides in internal conflicts. To give him counsel in a specific situation would be useless, since his problems are not rational but symbolic. Psychoanalysis is intended to resolve the conflicts in the internal life that drive the patient to repeated and consistent maladaptations. This is the rationale for the nondirective use of free association that presumably distinguishes the analytic therapist from such counselors as ministers, good friends, social workers, and the like. Psychoanalysis is a more ambitious procedure; to use one terminology, it is a "reconstructive" rather than a "reparative" maneuver.

The implications of this dichotomy are obvious. Counseling is perceived as first aid, psychoanalytic therapy as major surgery. What the psychoanalyst aspires to is a more profound and more ambitious undertaking, attempting to alter the characteristic and lifelong patterns of the patient, as distinguished from simple problem solving. Whether psychoanalysis *is* always a deeper procedure depends on the psychoanalyst and on the counselor.

Another reason a psychoanalyst might avoid advising a patient is that it would openly intrude the therapist's judgments and values into the therapeutic hour. And the therapist has advertised herself as a value-free agent. This is an exercise in self-deception that demands understanding. The unavoidable truth is that whatever else she is doing, the psychoanalytic therapist is also directing, giving advice, and introducing values, whether she knows it or not.

Therapy Is Not a Value-Free Zone

The desire to be nondirective and value-free obviously stemmed from a yearning to be accepted as a bona fide member of the scientific community. In the early days, the activities and assumptions of science were presumed to be part of a value-free enterprise. But it is unlikely that any scientific activity, or human activity of any moment, can be totally free of values. In the case of psychotherapy, where one is dealing with the behavior of the individual in his relationship to those around him, the assumption is patently absurd.

The confusion may be resolved by considering how narrowly or widely we define the term "values." If the patient is a conservative Republican and the analyst is a liberal Democrat, the political positions assuredly define a different set of values. It would be presumptuous and wrongheaded for the therapist to "correct" the political values of her patient, which may be as defensible and reasonable as her own. These types of values are clearly beyond the authentic expertise inherent in being a psychotherapist.

A therapist may be a firm believer in abortion rights while treating a patient who views abortion as murder. As a therapist — indeed, as a human being — she must recognize that people of goodwill may fall on opposite sides of critical moral issues. Attitudes about capital punishment, the atom bomb, nuclear energy, pacifism, truth-telling to the dying, autonomy versus beneficence, are hardly trivial issues, but they are rarely relevant or even appropriate in therapy.

Therapy can only attempt to deal with a limited part of the repertoire of a human being's behavior, and these issues are unlikely to be of therapeutic interest. Moreover, a therapist with integrity must be ever vigilant to avoid exploiting the power of the transference. It is hard to imagine a therapist cheeky or stupid enough to misuse precious therapeutic time on matters that are not central to the adjustment of the patient, or not in the service of alleviating the distress that drove the patient to treatment. Having said this, I am sure that in some shabby venues every aspect of the power of the therapist over the patient will be abused and passed off as therapeutic.

Some judgment calls are difficult. What does a therapist do about her patient's racial or religious bias when it is not obsessive nor a paranoid fixation but rather a casual part of the cultural bias of the community from which the patient comes? In this case it is unlikely to even come up except in a semantic way ("I wouldn't let him Jew me down"). The therapist might or might not comment on the language, but she is unlikely to divert the course of the therapy to analyze the roots of anti-Semitism.

I would draw a distinction between two patients who might have a social bias against minorities. If he was a

Connecticut businessman from a conservative background who came to treatment with a marital problem, his bias (which he probably shares with his wife) would have no bearing on the central aspects of his unhappiness or functioning. Unless he was a flaming bigot, such casual and occasional semantic slurs and stereotyping would be shared by his culture and be commonplace in the country clubs, board rooms, and even the philanthropies through which the patient moved. Such casual bigotry, which the patient would probably deny, will usually pass unexamined in therapy.

I have seen and treated sufficient patients with casual "social" bias. They are decent people who would be horrified at a swastika's being painted on a synagogue, and certainly by a cross-burning. They would come to the aid of neighbors exposed to such behavior. Still, they are content that they are surrounded by their "own kind" at their country clubs. A true bigot who demonstrated paranoid rage or grotesque stereotypes about minorities would of course be confronted with this neurotic element of his personality — particularly if it affected such behavior as hiring practices. Such bigotry is neurosis, by any definition.

If, however, the patient was a candidate in a psycho-analytic school, training to be a future psychotherapist, the therapist could not allow this to pass without significant examination. Here the bias, particularly if unacknowledged by the candidate, would inevitably enter into the structure of his relationships with his patients, contaminating his life-work. Whether he thinks he can control the bias or not, it will inevitably influence his therapy and must be examined in the course of his analysis.

For most therapists there are no problems in maintaining a distance from the first set of direct and explicit political and moral values. With bias, one can find legitimate differences of opinion as to where to draw the line. Sometimes, however, there are values, respectworthy though they may be, that will impede the progress of therapy. When I was a young therapist, I dealt with two cases involving religious convictions that complicated my therapeutic goals.

One of my patients was an attractive young Irish Catholic woman who came into treatment upset about her inability to relate to men. "Mary" was a successful businesswoman in her mid-twenties who had never had any physical contact of a romantic nature beyond a goodnight kiss. Yet she wanted to get married and have children. She was a devout and observant Catholic who had asked me in advance if I could respect religious views different from my own. I somewhat glibly assured her that I could.

During the course of her therapy, I questioned her about her sexual fantasies. She said she did not have them, and when she was tempted to have sexual thoughts or feelings she avoided them because, after all, they were sinful. I explained to her that we are responsible for our behavior but not our thoughts, and that if she had no intentions of acting out her fantasies she was free to have as rich an internal life as possible. Mary stated that while that might be my point of view, that was not the tenet of her church.

I was aware of this philosophical difference between Catholicism, which holds that thoughts in themselves may be sinful, and Freudian philosophy, which presumes we all share the same vile thoughts but are differentiated by how we deal with them. But I had treated Catholic patients before and had never run into such an obstacle. It seemed impossible for me to bring Mary into a relationship that might lead to marriage, where her sexual feelings would be acceptable, without encouraging her to think sexually about men in advance. How could I help Mary locate the anxieties that led to such a phobic avoidance of men? Not that I didn't have a clear sense of the source.

A profound and horrible event from Mary's past dominated her present attitudes. Her father had been an alcoholic who, while affectionate when sober, became violent, irrational, and physically abusive during his frequent alcoholic binges. She was the only girl in the family and was protected from his rampages by her father's special affection for his baby girl, and also by the presence of three older brothers, who took the brunt of the father's rage. During one of these violent episodes, her eldest brother was beaten to death by her father. The event was hushed up by the extended family.

The death was listed as accidental and the father was never prosecuted, but the memory of the dead brother and the father's violent behavior — and, I might add, his contrasting affectionate devotion to his single daughter — were well discussed during the early portion of her therapy. Making the bridge of trust to another man would be impossible for her until she started the process of exorcising her father from her attitudes about men in general and began to approach men as potentially tender and affectionate companions.

There is no way into the sexual life except through fantasies at the very least, and eventually some actual sexual involvement with men. I was not insisting that Mary have intercourse before marriage, since this violated her religious principles, but some engagement in the sexual arena was necessary. At the least, I wanted her to feel free to fantasize. Nonetheless, she informed me that sexual thoughts were as sinful as sexual activity. Of course I was aware that while

sexual fantasies might be listed as sins, Mary was unquestionably using her religion as a rationalization to avoid a
dreaded activity. But she was encouraged in her rationalizations by her parish priest.

In my amateur way I began to delve into the Byzantine
byways of Catholic theology. I read as much as I could but
relied on my friends who were more knowledgeable. My
main source for such information was a colleague and friend,
Dr. John O'Connor. John was a rarity. In a sea of Jewish psychoanalytic candidates, where even a Protestant was a
curiosity, he was one of the few early Roman Catholic psychoanalytic candidates at the Columbia Psychoanalytic Center
during the same time I was. In a priggish way, trying to protect my patient's privacy, I felt forced to cast much of my
questioning in vague and theoretical terms, inquiring about
the nature of sin, the kinds of venal and mortal sins, and
specifically about distinguishing between thought and act.

Finally John with amusement said, "You're not thinking of
converting to Catholicism, are you?" I said no, and proceeded
to explain to him the nature of my problems with this young
woman and my frustration in overcoming what I perceived as
her defenses but which nonetheless utilized authentic religious
belief. He laughed, saying, "You really don't understand the
way of the Catholic Church." I acknowledged I didn't. He said
he could straighten it all out for me. "Where does she live?"

This seemed an absurd and irrelevant question. What
could that have to do with anything? John persisted, mischie-
vously refusing to explain, and I told him the neighborhood
where she lived. He said he would get back to me. That night
I received a call from John in which he said, "I know what
the problem is and I have your solution at hand. Tell her to

stop going to St. X and instead start attending St. Y for mass and confession, about three blocks out of her way."

Bewildered, I asked him to explain. He said in essence: "In cases like this, the sociology of the Church is as relevant as its theology. The flexibility of the Catholic Church lies in its priesthood. There are rules, but there is forgiveness. The priest she is going to is a particularly rigid, unforgiving bastard. Right down the street is an old friend of mine who will manage to find a way between her needs for a decent life and her religious obligations." John continued: "We both know, and this priest will know, that she is using her religion as a rationalization to avoid facing life. In the long run the goals of the Church and the goals of Freud are the same. They both value relationship, commitment, love, and even sex. The Church has never been puritanical. We leave that to the Protestants. The Church, like Freud, sees marriage, sex, and parenthood as central to the human condition." At that time, at least, one could say this about psychoanalysis as well as the Church.

John's advice was a major help in the therapy, although this still proved to be one of my less successful therapies. Mary was capable of falling in love, trusting men for reasonable periods of time, and even entering into full sexual and romantic relationships. But as I was to learn in a follow-up visit many years later, she could never bring herself to marriage, at least as of my last contact. Nevertheless, she seemed happily involved in a successful career and in an active social life.

A strikingly similar problem emerged in treating a patient from a significantly different tradition. I was contacted by Rabbi H., whom I did not know but who knew of me through my friendship with a distinguished senior rabbi when we both were active members of the antiwar movement during the Vietnam years. Rabbi H. had done some research on me that included reading a book I had written about young war resisters in prison. He felt that I demonstrated in the book an "empathy" for troubled young men. He also knew many of my colleagues at Union Theological Seminary, where I was an adjunct professor. The patient that he wanted to discuss with me was a young medical student who had been placed in his charge.

"Jacob" was the son of an exceedingly wealthy businessman, part of an international community of Orthodox Jews whose children generally followed the banking business interests of the families. This young man wanted to become a doctor, which was seen by his father as undignified. Nonetheless, he indulged him — as his only son — allowing him to attend medical school in New York, providing he maintained his religious contacts and remained under the strict supervision and guardianship of Rabbi H.

The rabbi asked me if it would be possible for me to treat the boy without interfering with or intruding on his Orthodox beliefs and while respecting Orthodox traditions. Rabbi H. knew that I was not a religious person myself, but I expressed to him my respect for religious convictions and, indeed, my profound envy for those who could make that leap of faith that eluded me. I would certainly honor his tradition. We had a tacit agreement that if I should ever feel there was a conflict between therapeutic goals and his religious beliefs, I would call him. It was a strange arrangement, but a condition of therapy that the young man himself had set. Anticipating no such conflicts, I agreed.

I wondered at the time why he had not drawn on a therapist from the Orthodox Jewish community. I suspected that the privacy of the family, significant donors to religious institutions, might be a factor. Also Rabbi H. was impressed with psychoanalytic theory, and I am not sure there were any trained psychoanalysts from that religious tradition at that time.

When Jacob came to treatment, yet another reason emerged, which Rabbi H. had not revealed to me. The terrifying event that led to this young man's treatment was his seduction by an instructor in college in a homosexual incident. Jacob was in a panic, for he had achieved orgasm and was convinced he must be a latent homosexual. Jacob had a lifetime of only heterosexual fantasies but had no experiences with women, this being seen as sinful outside marriage. He had never had homosexual fantasies, but since he enjoyed the ejaculatory experience that resulted from fellatio being performed on him — even while feeling disgusted by the idea of a man in contact with his genitals — he was now convinced he was a homosexual.

If heterosexual experiences before marriage were taboo in Orthodox Judaism, homosexual activity was anathema, the equivalent of a death sentence, at least in Jacob's mind. Were his father to know of this, he was sure he would be "driven from the family." This seemed a harsh judgment to me. Then he told me that his father had disowned one of his sisters for marrying "outside the faith," in this case meaning a Reform Jew! The father, while an autocratic tyrant, was adored by his son.

Based on his history and his fantasies, Jacob was clearly heterosexual; but even after his panic about homosexuality was brought under control, his confusion about sexual identity and sexual role persisted. Doubts about his capacity to function "as a man" were prevalent. Since he could not confront his fears directly in life through sexual involvement — strictly forbidden — I could find no theoretical means either to reassure him or to affirm his manhood.

As treatment continued Jacob began to demonstrate an interest in the women around him. His daytime fantasies involved sexual activity with a fellow medical student, Leah. The fantasies were accompanied by a fear of impotence, a certainty of failure. This inevitably led to a resurgence of homosexual anxiety. There seemed no way to overcome the homosexual anxiety without his being introduced into a heterosexual life. Try as he could, he would never see himself as a man until he was tested through his involvement with a woman.

Jacob's problems were only exacerbated by the Zeitgeist. He was exceedingly attractive, charming, young, and very rich. And he was living in New York after the onset of the sexual revolution. Women in droves came on to him, often aggressively attempting to seduce him into sexual involvements — even Orthodox women, who seemed to have fewer scruples about the religion than he did. Had this been an ordinary patient without the complications of my "contract" with him, there would have been no problems.

Despite religious injunctions against onanism, he did manage an active masturbatory life involving fantasies with some of the women in his life. Minimal support and encouragement by me would have led him into involvement with one or more of the aggressive women pursuing him, although probably not with Leah, the one he had a crush on — that represented yet a different problem. We were at a dead end.

Jacob asked me to discuss this with his rabbi, to whom he had confided his homosexual encounter and anxieties. And since this was part of the contract, I reluctantly said I would. I began to have reservations about my earlier, glib reassurance; I do not like third-party involvements in therapy. Nonetheless, there I was. I called the rabbi, explained the problem, and said I saw no practical way of introducing this boy to his own manhood without his having some sexual involvement with a woman. Since I understood this to be in conflict with his religious teaching, I was fulfilling my part of the bargain by calling.

The rabbi indicated to me that this was too fundamental for him to decide on his own. He asked me to give him until the end of the week while he discussed it with a council of rabbinical advisers. At the end of the week, he called me and said rather cryptically, "I have an answer for you which we will not discuss. So listen carefully. The council has asked me to tell you: 'You have your job to do and we have our job to do.'"

I thought this marvelously ambiguous and sensitive solution was in its way the equivalent of what must have happened in the confessional booth with Mary. While the rabbis were not prepared themselves to authorize such behavior, I had my job to do, and as a professional I was released to do my duties. And I did. With gratifying results.

These two specific cases indicate that occasionally there are explicit value contradictions in the patient's and therapist's lives. But these are overt and apparent to even the most self-deceptive of analysts. The more invidious problem arises when values are imposed on the unsuspecting patient by a therapist who assumes he is behaving in a value-free manner.

Uncovering the Hidden Bias

Values are central to any therapy. This seems not only transparently true, but inevitable and desirable. But these values must be *explicit and shared by patient and therapist.* The problem with the failure to admit the existence of essential moral underpinnings in therapy is that many unacceptable and idiosyncratic values of the therapist will be implicitly imposed.

As someone interested in the nature of ethics and values, I found the moral foundation of psychoanalytic theory so self-evident that the rejection of this assumption by my colleagues and teachers was bewildering. During discussions and arguments, part of the wonderful world of psychoanalysis in its heyday, students challenged many basic assumptions of Freudian theory, but I made very little headway in my evangelical desire to convince my colleagues that we were in the values business. I was arguing for a "morality" of health, an acknowledgment that we stood for certain things, that our definition of health encompassed a number of "oughts": action over passivity; engagement over isolation; work over indolence. My ideas did not prevail.

Eventually a serendipitous opportunity presented itself which allowed me to demonstrate my belief in a manner that somewhat approximated "scientific" research. The examples that emerged were not on this lofty level of inherent humanistic values, but involved good old-fashioned bias.

I was teaching the basic course in psychodynamics at the Columbia Psychoanalytic Center. At the beginning of the class one of the students — knowing I was writing a book on draft resisters during the Vietnam War who chose to go to prison rather than serve in the army or flee the country — asked me how my research was going. I said it was too early to tell. I had barely begun to gather my data, I said, let alone to interpret it, but one somewhat surprising figure had emerged almost immediately. Of the first twenty-five war resisters I had interviewed, all except one were first sons. Even with that one, his birth came some fifteen years after his youngest sibling's, so that he was virtually raised alone as a member of a new family. I found this rather astonishing; I hadn't expected it.

One of my brighter students said that while he found the data interesting, he did not find it particularly surprising. I asked him what he meant. He then said, in effect, that we all know that first sons tend to be defiant, headstrong, rebellious, in conflict with authority, acting out problems with the father for a leadership role, et cetera, listing a number of somewhat pejorative, antiauthority aspects that *are* characteristic of first male offspring. His generalizations were true if selective.

I was impressed and almost convinced by my student's statements. The following day, on the front page of the *New York Times,* an article on the early astronauts in training included the unexpected finding that all of the astronauts, up to that time, were first sons! I mentioned this to another class, who had not been privy to my earlier discussion, and asked them what they made of it. The class, like the previous one, was surprised that I seemed surprised, since the information was quite within their range of expectation. "Quite predictable," one of the students said cockily. He was interested in birth order and indicated that there was significant data indicating a high preponderance of first sons among great achievers of all sorts. This was true of American presidents, explorers, revolutionary leaders, Nobel laureates, leaders in science and industry. Therefore, he said, one would expect a high percentage of firstborns in such men of achievement as astronauts.

The students at the Columbia Psychoanalytic Center were for the most part bright and knowledgeable. They were unlikely to make statements of fact that were wrong. I verified the facts about birth order and eldest sons, and they were as they had been presented. I realized precisely what had happened. In the case of the war resisters, their decision to go to prison seemed self-destructive to the class. Why go to prison when one had many options — going to medical school, law school, or seminary, teaching public school, or leaving the country — options that a majority of middle-class boys had chosen. Going to prison seemed to the analytic candidates a patently masochistic act, a self-punitive and therefore neurotic one. They could not conceive of a group that perceived going to jail as a rational act of political conviction or as an act of conscience.

What they did not realize was that they had made an a priori moral judgment. Having first decided that the action was neurotic, they then selected out of the body of data about firstborn sons the facts that confirmed their judgment. The action of choosing prison was sick, something that would be done by neurotically defiant, aggressive, stubborn, willful, and competitive first sons.

The class commenting on the astronauts had been similarly selective in viewing the data. The astronauts in those days were seen as a heroic group — the degree of psychopathy that we now know existed in this group, from the writings of Tom Wolfe and others, was not then apparent. So they started with the assumption of a healthy, heroic, and creative act. Then, out of the same data about eldest sons, they selected, in contrast, the traits that supported their conclusion: venturesome, courageous, independent.

This is not unlike what happens in therapy. We start with a neurotic symptom and then we go back and find dynamics in the individual's past that will "explain" the symptom. The irony is that if we started not with the symptom, but with a distinguished creative effort of a patient — for instance, the completion of a symphony, the writing of a novel, the culmination of an eminent career in the public arena — we would find the dynamics in his background to explain the success as well as the failure. We would select out of a pool of dynamics those which confirmed our previous assumptions. To become a great teacher or writer is "healthy." To become a felon or a drug addict is not healthy. We do have our values. And we must.

Armed with this fortuitous set of events, I prepared a small "experiment." I devised a test to see whether values would alter the therapeutic behavior of these young therapists. After all, if they assumed that going to prison was a masochistic and self-destructive act, they would be obliged to analyze away the intention of going to jail by showing it to be a symptomatic maneuver, not a rational act. If they had a patient who desired to become an astronaut, on the other hand, they would not analyze away this desire, even if they could find dynamic reasons for such a choice. Remember the discussion in the chapter on dynamics. *Everything* has its psychogenic roots. Calling behavior dynamic — i.e., arising from forces in the individual's past — is not calling it pathological.

I decided to propose a hypothetical situation to the two classes on the same day (so there would be little communication between them) that would test their objectivity. I selected a subject about which you might think a group of psychoanalysts would demonstrate almost complete unanimity: sexual behavior. One could be forgiven for assuming that psychoanalysts in our modern times would be free of sexual prejudices. After all, Freud had enunciated, to the extreme displeasure of almost every segment of the Victorian society in which he lived, that everyone had a sexual life and a right to it. Poor and rich, cultivated and common, man and woman, and, most shocking, children as well as adults.

Sexuality was of the nature of all people. Sexual desire was a biological right.

(I am aware of the accusations of sexism now leveled at Freud — and beyond that the justification for these accusations in the early Freudian writing. Nonetheless, by his unequivocal insistence that sexuality was a biological endowment and the sole source of pleasure, indeed the only source of energy in the psychic system, for men as well as women, he was the progenitor of the feminist revolution.)

I picked marital infidelity as the subject of my hypothetical situation, although I did not present the examples to the classes as "hypotheticals." I presented a "problem" to each class and asked the students how they would handle its resolution. To the first class, the problem was framed like this: A thirty-eight-year-old man comes into your office on a Tuesday morning distraught, haggard, obviously unnerved. His wife and baby daughter have been spending the summer at their cottage in the Hamptons. He works during the week, leaving Friday afternoons to spend the weekend with his family, returning very early on Monday mornings. He is a devoted husband, adores his wife; they have been married about eight years. He has been monogamous and faithful, and he is sure she has too. The previous evening a seductive twenty-two-year-old model who lives in his building and has in the past been aggressively flirtatious appeared at his door to borrow the proverbial cup of sugar. Before he knew it, he was in bed with her. He was horrified, truly devastated. The young woman laughed at him, saying they both knew this was a one-nighter and nothing would come of it. "No harm done, right? No big deal." Nonetheless, he has had a sleepless night, is dreading going to visit his wife on Friday, and is wracked with overwhelming guilt.

This was a simple problem in a course in psychoanalytic technique. Most of the discussion during the ensuing hour revolved about this man's "punitive superego," his excessively rigid conscience mechanism. The class discussed his overreactive and neurotic anxiety, and speculated about the dynamic roots of his guilt in order to explicate to him the excessive price he was extracting of himself for this relatively minor transgression. It was a rich and fruitful discussion that demonstrated the class's appreciation of past dynamics and how they influence conscience, behavior, and psychic pain.

To the following class, I proposed an alternative hypothetical. A thirty-eight-year-old woman is spending her summer working on a book at her summer cottage in Southampton, while her husband commutes from New York on the weekends. She calls her analyst, desperate to schedule a visit, although she had canceled her summer hours to complete her book. They schedule an hour and she presents herself, distraught, anguished, and wracked with guilt. The analyst knows that she is a devoted wife, married for some seven years to her husband, and has been constantly faithful, as she assumes he has been. She is now faced with a crisis in self-confidence and an agony of guilt. The groceries have been delivered by the same seductive young man every day to her house. But this morning he arrived particularly early, she answered the door in her robe, one thing led to another, and before she knew it she was in bed with the delivery man. "I don't know how I could have done this. It disgusts me. It was an impulse. I just gave in to it, and I don't know how I can face my husband."

Again a lively discussion occurred, only this time the deliberations took an entirely different course. The nature of this colloquy focused on her "acting out," her unconscious hostility to her husband, her impulsiveness, and her need for impulse control. In order to fully appreciate the unconscious motives for such "irresponsible" and "self-destructive" behavior, the class peppered me with questions, all germane and insightful, about the source of her "weak" superego, her relationship with her father, her relationship with her male siblings, all intended to lead us to an understanding of what precipitated the self-destructive and neurotic act.

These exercises were carried out in classes of men and women professionals, all proclaiming their dedication to the idea of gender equality and sexual liberation. Individually, all of these students would have sworn on the proverbial stack of Bibles that they carried no bias about sexual activity and certainly would never practice any sexist discriminations. They would have been horrified if I had accused them of a double standard. But what else could this be but the expression of a deeply entrenched double standard?

The cases were synthetic. I had made them up, and in the process I had been careful to keep them consonant, almost identical, simply changing the gender of the participant. Yet in the case of the wayward husband, the class clearly labeled the profound sense of guilt as the neurotic element, while with the errant wife — equally wracked with guilt — the class was predisposed to see the sexual activity as the neurotic element. If these had been actual therapeutic cases, therapy would have been directed at diminishing the husband's guilt while controlling the wife's sexual acting out. The therapist, by defining the *action* in one as neurotic, and the *emotional response* to the action as neurotic in the other, would have propelled the therapies in disparate directions, guiding the patients to diverse courses of action, defining health and neurosis in dissimilar ways for the two sexes. If this level of prejudice can be introduced by as sophisticated a group of observers as this, in a time such as ours, where the right of women to the same sexual liberties as men is presumably a hallmark, imagine what must happen with less obvious, subtler forms of stereotyping.

Beyond the blatant cases of bias, the whole myth of a value-free medicine must be laid to rest. Medicine never was and can never be value-free. The discussions emerging from our present-day biological revolution, which has created the whole new field of bioethics, show how value-driven is the entire enterprise of medicine. Is there a right to die? Is physician-assisted suicide a part of that right? Is infertility at any age a medical illness? Does the sixty-three-year-old woman have a right to bear a child? Does this "illness" of infertility justify in vitro fertilization? Utilization of surrogate mothers? Is impotence at any age (ninety-three?) a health problem? If so, should the use of Viagra be covered by insurance? Is there a difference between cosmetic surgery that removes deforming scars on the face of a child and the plastic surgery that attempts to make a fifty-year-old woman look thirty? Are they both within the purview of medicine? Is a transsexual operation a medical procedure or a deforming and crippling one pandering to neurotic desires? What degree of autonomy should a mentally ill patient have? Are we being morally correct when we allow the mentally ill patient to sleep and freeze on the streets to protect his autonomy? Is autonomy the only virtue? Is there no place for paternalistic benevolence? Is an expensive knee operation whose only purpose is to permit an individual to play tennis or golf a necessary medical procedure? If there were a pill that could make us smarter, should everyone use it? Should it be sold or distributed free? And what about a happiness pill? Is there anything wrong in gaining happiness through drugs?

Ironically, the successes of medicine, the capacity to do new and unprecedented things, have forced us to reexamine the whole concept of medicine as a value-free enterprise. What holds true in surgery, gynecology, obstetrics, and dermatology is singularly valid in psychiatry. In psychiatry we are dealing with complex human (not organ) functioning involving emotions and aspirations for which we have few universally accepted norms.

The problems in emotional illnesses are even more complicated than in physical illnesses, in that we do not have a fixed point of departure in normal anatomy. After all, we do know what normal breast tissue should look like, and we do know what cancer is and can do. The same is not always as clear in mental health. Therapists do not have tissue to examine, and the borders between unhealthy conduct and idiosyncratic behavior are not always so apparent.

Some Universal Values

Still, in psychotherapy, we are not in a world of total subjectivity. People vary, but the human condition shares common ground. There are values that approximate the universal, and out of these some fall within the purview of the therapist. To list just a few:

- Psychotherapists favor activity over passivity; a broader range of pleasures over a narrower range. They believe that work is a human value and that productive work is part of the nature and strength and fulfillment of the human being. We must protect against the bias that elevates certain kinds of work as superior to others and avoid the snobbishness that so easily intrudes here. Even among the rich, who have sufficient money to pay for their needs as well as their pleasures, therapists tend to feel that the human mind and body ought to be committed to an activity that stretches and uses the self. Therapists believe that activity, whether it be parenting, surgery, or carpentry, ennobles existence. Therapists want their patients to use and extend themselves, for the ultimate pleasure is experienced in the enhancement of the self that comes from being a doer and giver.

- Therapists prefer relationship to isolation. There is an authentic role for the hermit in many societies; there are monastic orders, which are not considered neurotic, that preclude even talking. Still, in the general population we prefer people to talk rather than remain mute; we prefer them to engage others rather than to seclude themselves. Freud and Aristotle join the host of modern biologists who define human beings as social animals.

- Therapists have a "bias" for a full sexual life over a celibate existence. There exists a whole profile of activities that we implicitly define as the normal life. Certainly within this mode there will be room for variations, and the reasonable and sophisticated therapist must allow for those variations. The individual with the priestly calling knows he is sacrificing a good, indeed a good that he will encourage in his parishioners, for a greater good that he adopts for himself as envisioned in a celibate priesthood.

There are certain qualities, about which almost all therapists would concur, that make us human: love, sex, work, play, pleasure, relationships, community. These are the values of the psychotherapist. This is the broad template that therapists will use in evaluating their patients. They will examine their patients' goals to see if they serve the concept of the healthy individual. Psychotherapy must never be a Procrustean bed with overly rigid criteria for health and disease. The human being is granted the freedom, denied all other animals, for a diverse and varied existence. But the human condition is hardly a value-free enterprise. Therapists generally know what is "healthy," and can distinguish it from that which is "sick." They have the equivalent of a morality of good and bad, utilizing the terms "healthy" and "sick." Fortunately, Freud and most who followed him had very generous definitions of healthy behavior. This expansive definition of health is a protection from excessive rigidity and zealotry.

Once the therapeutic community recognizes without anxiety or apology that there can be no value-free psychology, it can begin the honorable task of defining its values. Once the inherent values of the enterprise are spelled out, the patient will be able to see if they are in conformity with his own. Just as the patient has a right to discuss his therapist's training, he could also discuss his values. This is beginning to happen. The homosexual patient will question his therapist as to his attitude about homosexuality and whether the therapist sees this as being within the purview of a healthy individual or not. This is in every way the equivalent of the questioning that I underwent in dealing with Jacob.

Our definitions of health are saturated with value judgments, and so be it. There may be many alternative paths that lead to that broad territory known as the healthy environment, and of course the patient should choose the path he prefers. But there will also be paths that are not healthy, and these must be indicated. Therapists, like internists, are entitled — I would say obligated — to direct their patients to those perceptions, those activities, those values, that define the good — the healthy — life. And they must do so without apology, without shame, and without the need to find elliptical and circuitous ways that permit them to be directive while claiming to be nondirective. They must guide their patients gently but firmly in the direction of health. Otherwise the therapy will drift endlessly in an amorphous sea of relativity.

OUT OF THE
OFFICE
AND INTO LIFE

IV

Supporting the Will

13

I N T H E E N D we psychotherapists, independent of our varying views of human nature and humankind, are totally dependent on the patient's willingness to "screw his courage to the sticking point" and *act*. He must get off the couch, out of the office, and into the real world, where real change must occur.

If change occurs only in a therapeutic hour and in relationship to the therapist, patients are poorly served. William James expressed this well in his *Principles of Psychology:* "No matter how full a reservoir of *maxims* one may possess, and no matter how good one's *sentiments* may be, if one has not taken advantage of every concrete opportunity to *act* one's character may remain entirely unaffected for the better."

The Will to Change, the Courage to Act

The patient must have the will to change and the courage to act. Ultimately his health is in his own hands, not his therapist's. He must take charge of his own life. But the philosophy that dominates modern ideas about human action has undermined our respect for a person's capacity to do this. In the field of psychology, autonomy has few backers. The two major influences here, behaviorism and psychoanalysis, while antagonistic in almost every other way, are traditionally joined in embracing a form of modified determinism. By that I mean they both see behavior as a complex end point, a mathematical result of a number of forces and counterforces accumulated over the years patterning the individual in such a way as to produce a certain logical, almost inevitable, result.

This has led to an erosion of the concept of autonomy, thus undermining the principle of personal responsibility and voluntary action. We are constrained in how far we can deny autonomy and choice, since society and the rule of law demand a concept of a free and autonomous human being. But we have managed to hedge in freedom and limit culpability by our increasing insistence that factors from the past influence current conduct. We have skirted close to the edges of psychic determinism.

Behavioral psychologists embrace this determinism. The image of man that has emerged, particularly in B. F. Skinner's *Beyond Freedom and Dignity,* is of a human being chained to the past by a series of conditioning experiences that force him into predictable patterned responses. Skinner willingly abandons freedom; he denies its existence. It is a "myth" that human beings perpetuate about themselves, he says, in order to assert their superiority to the lower creatures.

Psychoanalysis, on the other hand, boxed itself into a semideterministic view of human behavior with which it has never been quite comfortable. Psychoanalysts continually struggle to visualize a self-governing and responsible human being, while their theory constantly reveals biological and developmental ways in which present behavior is hemmed in and structured by the past. The struggle continues to be a curious one. The heart of the psychoanalyst is with freedom, even while his discoveries constantly challenge autonomy.

Psychoanalytic theory articulates the many ways that our freedom to act in the present is constrained by our experiences in the past. We cannot always do the rational thing, because the perceptions we carry over from our childhood are supported by powerful emotions. Not only is autonomy overrated, psychoanalysis would insist, but so too is human rationality. This theory views current behavior as profoundly constrained by developmental history. Thus, appeals directed solely to a person's reason and self-interest will not suffice to alter his behavior. We cannot have a campaign to obliterate drug addiction that simply asks us to "Just Say No."

How ironic, then, that the very psychologists and psychoanalysts whose *theories* have undermined the concept of an autonomous and freely acting individual are totally dependent *in practice* on the exercise of that will by their patients. Therapists must acknowledge volition, action, and will in order to encourage the patient to act on his own behalf to effect the changes in his life that he is seeking. The insights supplied by therapy should make it less threatening for the patient to act, but he must act.

In addition, the therapeutic milieu is in itself a perverse and contradictory environment that actually encourages two self-destructive character traits that will ultimately sink the therapy if they prove to be intractable. They are passivity and narcissism.

Passivity, like most human traits, has multiple roots. Two that are ubiquitous are 1) a fear of failure, or fear of the confrontation necessary to achieve success; and 2) the desire to return to the blessed state of infantile dependence where all our needs were met by others without our expending any effort, thus avoiding any chance of failure and confrontation while "proving" once again our lovability. The therapeutic situation in many ways consciously as well as unconsciously mimics the state of infantile dependency, particularly when the therapist is psychoanalytically oriented.

Psychoanalysis distinguished itself from other, more cognitive, forms of therapy by espousing a nondirective and seemingly passive attitude on the part of the therapist. It was a stated goal of Freudian psychoanalysis to *encourage* a regression to infantile ways. It was perceived as "regression in the service of the ego." The patient was actively encouraged to regress — as though the typical patient needs such encouragement — in order to identify and replicate his early fixations, and hence liberate himself from them.

While well intended, the encouragement of regression carried within it the seeds of disaster. The problem occurs when a passive patient is joined with a passive therapist. What then emerges is a leisurely shared journey to nowhere, in which the trip itself replaces the destination, allowing the patient and therapist to grow comfortably older together. In order to avoid this, the therapist must balance the passivity of the session with a commitment to activity in everyday life.

The analytic hour is also a supremely narcissistic enterprise. What else can it be except an exercise in self-involvement? The patient never asks the therapist how she is feeling, what has happened to her children, how her love life is going, how she fared in the stock market that day. Nor should he, and if he does, the therapist must exercise her discipline to avoid such discussions. The focus of both the therapist and the patient must at all times be on the needs, desires, inadequacies, and feelings of the patient himself, uncontaminated by the chance events in the therapist's life that might adulterate the goals of therapy.

The term "narcissism" has been used in so many different ways that I must clarify the specific way in which I am using it here. Here I refer to a common product of our culture, as expressed in a certain kind of personality who not only is self-referential, but appraises almost all world events in terms of their specific influence on himself. I think of a dramatic example described to me by one of my patients concerning her "best friend."

My patient began to question the nature of this friendship during the course of therapy, beginning to recognize how narcissistic and parasitic the friend was. The definitive insight occurred after the following event: During a long telephone conversation the friend was obsessing about the damage a mole was doing in her garden. Conversation with this friend always revolved around her travails or triumphs — the dominant aspects in the landscape of her life. My patient had previously had a mammogram indicating the possibility of a breast tumor, and she was awaiting the result of a biopsy. She was distraught but had not had the opportunity to discuss this with her friend. During the course of their conversation, she received a call-waiting signal. She asked her friend to excuse her for a moment as she was expecting a very important call from her doctor. The call turned out to be from someone else, so the patient quickly returned to the friend's call. Without losing a beat, this quintessential narcissist picked up her story of the mole and the garden where she had left off. She never asked what the urgent call from the physician was about.

As appalling as such behavior is in everyday life, it is precisely what we expect and encourage in a therapeutic hour. Were I to cancel an hour because of health reasons — and I do not cancel therapeutic sessions lightly — and were the patient to question me about the reason for the interruption, I would politely discourage such discussion, indicating in one way or another that that was not the important business at hand.

Since the very nature of the therapeutic transaction encourages self-involvement, self-indulgence, narcissism, and dependency — none of which is ever the therapeutic goal — the therapist is constantly called upon to draw a clear distinction between the conditions inside the office and out. A wife is not one's therapist and does not have to put up with the self-indulgences that characterize the therapeutic relationship. The therapist must make that point clear. He must be an advocate for the values that are a central part of our definition of the mature and healthy individual.

The therapist has an obligation to help the patient move from a passive into an active mode, just as the patient must move from the past into the present, from the transference into real-world relationships. It matters precious little how much a patient may have illuminated the tangled web of his relationship with his mother unless such knowledge can be put to use in informing and improving his relationships with the women with whom he shares his life — his daughter, his wife, or his coworkers. The patient must find a way to convert knowledge into conduct. No amount of knowledge alone will suffice to change those patterns ingrained in childhood that possess in the present the tenacity of patterned and addictive behavior.

Trying to lose weight is an example with which most of us can identify, since most of us at one time or another have tried to diet, even if we are not obese. Everyone has a period when five or ten pounds of excess fat would be a delight to lose. But it is extraordinary how difficult this is to accomplish. It is hard to "just say no" even when one is reasonably well motivated. As motivation increases, it becomes somewhat easier.

More people start diets in the late spring, when they anticipate the realities of summer clothing and beachtime activities. Then the motivation is intensified by the increased exposure inherent in summer clothing, with the consequent potential for shameful exposure. Recently divorced men are notorious for undergoing a crash fitness program — in addition to modifying their clothing and haircuts — in an obvious attempt to make themselves more attractive to the younger women to whom they often now aspire. If it is a matter of willpower and determination even with those not addicted to food, one can appreciate the struggle and the strength required of the obese patient for whom the weight has the added symbolic meaning of a symptom.

All symptoms have the quality of addiction. The recognition that the patient must ultimately demonstrate courage and will does not minimize the crucial role of insight and other therapeutic efforts in forcing healthy action and the abandonment of neurotic patterns.

Will is a product of our conscious mind. In the course of therapy there is often a working out of some issues on an exclusively unconscious level. A patient will be surprised by success. Some subjective symptoms are attenuated or even disappear as a product of the changed sense of self that emerges through the therapeutic process: anxiety will be diminished, and some activities inhibited by such fears will be introduced willy-nilly into the patient's lifestyle; somatic symptoms like migraine headache will be overcome (there is no way we can will these away); sleep patterns will improve and nightmares abate; depression can lift and pleasurable activities return.

Where an act of will is demanded is in the institution of new life patterns, in expanding the borders of the cramped space of neurosis. A new life must be initiated. New things tried by the new self. The patient will never believe in the person he has become until he experiences himself in action. The changed self will never be trusted until it is tested in life. The sense that one can compete successfully is never really believed until one competes. It matters not whether the competition is in the area of work or sex. The "loser" will only believe he can be a "winner" by daring to win. In attempting success he risks defeat. He must be armed with the sense that defeat is never total; he must know that failure is part of every successful person's life story. It takes an act of will to enter new arenas in life, to change the patterns of a lifetime of defensive behavior.

Arming the Will Through Therapy

Therapy works by intensifying the powers of motivation. The preparatory maneuvers in therapy work to facilitate changing life patterns by arming the will with new supports. These supports are precisely those discussed during the preceding chapters. They are listed here in abbreviated form, and all of these may occur at different times, in different sequences in the therapy, expressed repeatedly in different forms or examples. There *is* an overall pattern to an effective therapy, but it is at least as complex and obscure as a Jackson Pollock painting.

Dynamics

The patient is led to understand that his neurosis didn't just happen. It is a product of dynamic factors in his developmental past. We make the patient aware of this development. The patient can no longer dismiss the symptom as an arbitrary or unlucky event. The symptom is related to the way he was treated as a child and the way he responded to that treatment. He is made cognizant of the fact that it is *he alone* who perpetuates these perceptions that no longer have validity while causing him such grief. He is no longer a child dependent on parental approval for survival. The past remains valid and alive only so long as he chooses to perceive it this way. And *he alone* can alter those perceptions.

The dynamic factors in obesity can serve as a paradigm. Obesity is at least two things. It is excessive eating and its end product — a wall of fat. The excessive eating has multiple dynamic roots. The simplest generalization is that the obese person is "hungry all the time." What he is hungry for, however, is not necessarily food, but love, approval, acceptance, and safety, all of which are defined within the concept of nurture.

Almost everyone has experienced at one time a feeling of "hunger" that drives her to the refrigerator. Inside may be every variety of tastes, from sweet cherries to sour pickles, from ice cream to leftover turkey, from beer to milk. Nothing appeals. Actually it is not food we are hungry for, but some sense of nurture. Love and security are inextricably linked with oral activities in that primal scene of the infant at the breast. It is not arbitrary that so much of addiction involves oral components. Loneliness, boredom, self-contempt, and fear constitute the "hungers" of the obese patient. The therapy must force the recognition that it is not food the patient craves but some metaphoric substitute which will never be achieved through eating. This in itself helps diminish the allure of the food.

The wall of fat that results from the overeating constitutes a neurotic bonus. It allows the fat person to withdraw from the competition for love and affection that she is sure she will lose. It allows her to hide. The lean and hungry seductive self is hidden in that fat, invisible to everyone, including the patient herself. The therapist must reintroduce the patient to the person she can become, secure in the knowledge that she wants to become that person but has only abandoned hope. By supplying that hope, the therapist empowers the patient to act.

These are but a smattering of the dynamics that go into obesity, but obesity is not our primary interest here. I could have presented any symptom. My purpose is to show that such dynamics reveal the complexity of any neurotic condition and to explain why alleviating the condition is so difficult. By examining the factors that force the patient to embrace her symptom, the therapist allows the patient insights that support renewed hope, thus increasing her efforts to break free of past dynamics.

Defenses

In discussing obesity as a paradigm, I have actually moved from dynamics to defenses. The wall of fat is a classical defense. A defense against competing for love and approval. So too is the eating. The oral gratification, the quickness of that fix, makes entering into the frightening and competitive arena of sexual relationships seem unnecessary. The therapist must confront the lie inherent in each defensive maneuver. The therapist must block off every neurotic exit, confront every rationalization, until, in the words of Sören Kierkegaard, "we stand denuded and see the intolerable abyss of ourselves." Only when the patient is left alone in that empty chasm of isolation built from fear will he have the courage to abandon his neurosis and enter the world. He will muster his will and conquer his fear with the support of the truth and his therapist.

Often the patient will enter a depressive phase when first deprived of his neurotic outlets. The transference must support him during this period. The abandonment of the symptom is also encouraged by a process of demystification — by relating it to a dynamic past — and by alienating the patient from the symptom.

Stigmatization

The therapist defines the symptom as "neurotic," i.e., sick, behavior. No one aspires to sickness. By so labeling it, the therapist stigmatizes the neurotic behavior, thus dissociating it from the individual's idealized image of himself. This also adds an element of fear. No one wants to be sick in any sense of the word, for sickness always carries with it a portent of suffering or even death. During the process of labeling the symptom as sick and undesirable, therapists support their patients by the same means as the Catholic Church. They will love (support and stand by) the sinner (patient) at the same time that they hate the sin (symptom). In therapy this is accomplished through the convenient model of the sick role.

The phobia, addiction, obsession, is perceived and treated as a dangerous and disgusting cancer or carbuncle encroaching on the integrity of the patient's peace of mind. It is not "him," it is something existing in, on, or alongside him. This is easiest to do when the neurotic element is something that the patient is only too willing to abandon, a migraine headache, a fear of flying. When it is not a dramatic symptom but a familiar part of the character and environment of the patient, then the first step in treatment will be teasing out this neurotic thread and identifying it for what it is. Something sick. Something alien. Something undesirable. Something to be actively removed. The symptom is isolated from the essential self. When its malignant nature is exposed, the patient can perceive the true price he has been paying for an illusory security or pleasure. Stigmatization is a form of aversive conditioning.

Universalization

As I have said before, when one exposes the patient's dynamics and defenses, there is the tendency for the patient to become depressed. One of the more sustaining and reassuring procedures will be what is in many ways the opposite of stigmatization, that is, universalization. That the two can proceed hand in hand is illustrated in the classic Freudian theory, where the Oedipus complex is the universal centerpiece of neurotic life. Patients are horrified when it is "revealed" that they sexually desire their mother, and that much of what has always been perceived by them as nonsexual is in fact just a "sublimation of sex," and incestual sex at that. Even stigmatization that is useful is nonetheless distressing. The anguish is mitigated by the therapist's readiness to link the specific symptom to a general and universal trait in all people.

I certainly don't subscribe to the universality of the Oedipal struggle. It doesn't matter. I use it as a familiar example. Whatever dominant dynamic underlies a therapist's view of neurosis, the patient will be reassured by the knowledge that his therapist sees all patients as suffering to resolve similar problems. One is not uniquely unpleasant or crazy, but simply involved to excess in activities shared in common with all other human beings. With obesity, the therapist will indicate to his patient the close relationship among nurture, feeding, and approval that is ubiquitous in our culture: the basket of fruit on the table, the tea and cookies that are presented to the visitor, and other signs of the symbolic role food plays in a community of friendship and love.

Relieving Chaos: The Good Story

In discussing symptom formation, I explained how even something as strange and disruptive of normal life as a delusion can actually serve a purpose, supplying at least temporary peace of mind. There is nothing more terrifying than inexplicable and omnipresent anxiety. It reminds us of something we all attempt to deny: the crazy chanciness of life itself. The delusion "explains" why the patient feels frightened, at the same time affording him some control over his fate. The FBI, or alien forces, are out to get him. No wonder he is terrified — now hide, watch your back, change your name, leave town. But the delusion is only a Band-Aid solution destined to failure.

The therapist, through her dynamic construction of how the patient came to his suffering, rationalizes the terrifying and unknown. His grief is not just haphazard; it is not just chance over which he has no control. The paranoid learns to understand that the brutality of his background made trust impossible, as it would for all with, say, an alcoholic father. But he is no longer living in that unpredictable past, unless he has chosen to. The therapist's story, and it must be a convincing one, demystifies the neurotic condition. It offers a rational explanation to the patient of how he came to his distress, thus suggesting a process of undoing, a way out. It isolates the symptom from that existential dread of a life without controls that must inevitably end in death. It offers hope.

The Support of the Therapist

Whatever the symptom, the patient is no longer alone with it. He has a secret and silent ally who is always with him. One of the most profound facets of therapy is the internalization of the therapist. Instead of a punitive, internalized father or mother, one has a new image of an authority figure who is united with one in a battle for a better life. A therapeutic ally, supporting one during the anxiety that inevitably occurs when one gives up a defense.

The Approval of the Therapist

The therapist also becomes incorporated as a parental figure in a different way. He displaces the parent, and it is now *his* approval that the patient craves. It is his approval that signifies safety and endorses self-confidence. There is great reassurance and hope in this substitution. While passing himself off as nonjudgmental, the therapist is constantly making judgments and value decisions, but they are far different from the standards and norms set by the parent. The therapist never judges in the sense of condemning the patient, but he surely judges the behavior. Healthy behavior is better than sick. Who can deny that? And who distinguishes what is healthy from what is sick? Who but the therapist.

Now the parent whose favor could never be gained is replaced by a therapist who gives "favor" in advance of conduct. He has accepted the patient as sick and therefore not to be morally judged. He certainly does not do the same for the neurotic behavior. That is clearly undesirable. With progress in therapy, the patient senses that to sustain the relationship that nourishes him, he must do the therapeutic job and jettison the malignant cargo he carries from the past. This parent (the therapist) will be patient and nonpunitive, but he too has his standards and must be pleased. This heavy reliance on the transference will necessitate a long final stage of therapy during which the transference itself must be analyzed.

The therapist promises implicitly and explicitly that there will be a quid pro quo. Ridding oneself of the undesirable symptom will allow one to proceed with greater assurance and greater hope into a rewarding world of mature pleasures. Abandoning food, in the example of obesity, will gain the kind of nurture that the patient truly craves.

The Corrective Emotional Experience

The new parent defined by the qualities listed above forms a therapeutic alliance with his patient. This support community of two represents a different culture with different conditions of membership from that which spawned the symptom. In this world the symptom is no longer necessary — it is an impediment. This alliance defines a new social milieu, a new environment, a new weltanschauung (comprehensive philosophy), allowing for a corrective emotional experience. Through trial and error, the patient will be reconditioned into the new reality.

A Compulsion to Act

Having stripped away the rationalizations behind the symptom, having been supplied with a new ally and a new set of goals, the patient is driven to the final step necessary for health: changing his behavior in the world outside the office. The patient must be emboldened to act. All of the tools of therapy can work only through reinforcing the will, by driving the patient toward new goals involving new activities and new engagements. They direct action toward health by creating a new story line and a new metaphor, in which the symptom is maladaptive, alienated, and undesirable and the healthy conduct is less threatening. In these ways they reinforce his will.

It may seem that I have stacked the cards in making the case for will by using addiction as the paradigm. With an addiction, whether it be drugs, smoking, drinking, or eating, it seems transparently evident (except, unfortunately, to the addict) that there is no magic. No amount of understanding, even when heralded as insight, will militate against that dreaded moment when the patient must steel himself to a conscious withdrawal from the stuff of his addictions. But what is true for obesity is true for all neuroses. Every neurosis is an addiction.

Take the example of the patient with a paranoid personality. The patient, humiliated in childhood, with no hope for parental approval, embraces disapproval and comforts himself with the "fact" that the world is a rotten place without love, approval, or justice for anyone. The patient reinforces this distortion by interpreting every essentially neutral event as a negative action aimed at increasing his misery. The therapist, through her interpretations and her personal behavior, obliges the patient to face a world of opportunity rather than a world of deprivation. At this point the patient, contemplating the possibility of abandoning his symptoms, is likely to get depressed and anxious in precisely the same way as an addict facing a life without alcohol.

Stripping defenses almost inevitably has this intermediate effect. Only the new configurations of the self and the environment backed by the power of the transference will embolden the patient to enter the world "unarmed." Only then, and only with the *active insistence* of the therapist, will the frightened paranoid make his first foray into a new universe of trusting relationships. When I say "active insistence," I mean the whole gamut from encouragement, through persuasion, to the borders of intimidation. When all of the uniquely therapeutic mechanisms for motivation leave the patient just short of his goal, the therapist employs all of the everyday tools of coach, parent, or teacher (but with the added powers of his office) to encourage the patient to act on his own behalf.

The same is true with every neurosis. Phobia was the earliest archetype. It was seen by Freud as an idiosyncratic neurosis that could not be resolved within the confines of the therapeutic situation. The man who is afraid of impotence, and therefore avoids sexuality, must directly engage a woman in bed. The individual afraid of the trolley (or airplane) has to board one. One cannot cure the fear of water in the midst of the Sahara Desert. This was so evident to Freud that he attempted to blackmail these patients into health.

The patient was instructed to enter the world of his fear and confront it directly, and was given a limited time in which to do it. Freud set a termination date for these patients a year ahead, at which time — well or sick, happy or unhappy, improved or despondent — they would be discharged from therapy. And Freud insisted that, cured or not, they must be discharged at this time!

In my salad days I tried following the master. In two cases I set a deadline. In one, the patient did vanquish his phobia; patients will often get better with a pistol at their head. With the other, when my patient couldn't muster the courage to abandon her phobia, I chickened out. I didn't have the courage, nor see it as a moral imperative, to "keep my word" on this point. I allowed the patient to continue. In time — a very long time, I will admit — she did get better. I never set an absolute deadline again.

Freud was convinced that phobia was the special case that demanded maneuvering the patient to act in the outside world to rid him of his neurosis; all other neuroses would be resolved in the office by rearranging the intrapsychic tensions. I have been convinced of just the opposite. No neurosis can ever be resolved entirely within the intrapsychic structure of the patient. The world is where the patient must reside, and it is there that he must ultimately work out his conflicts. Corrective therapeutic maneuvers are not an alternative to willpower, but a facilitator of it. Therapists are dependent for results on the patient's will. They must admit to its existence, since they will finally insist on the patient's exploiting its power.

One has only to examine the "uncontrollable" nature of certain impulsive behavior to realize how much of behavior so labeled is actually controlled by acts of will dictated by emotional realities. I have dealt with men who have had "uncontrollable" rages at their wife and children resulting in physical abuse. Their contrition and chagrin, remorse, guilt, pain, and suffering following such an event would seem to reinforce their statement that the rage was uncontrollable. But when they are asked how often they have had an uncontrollable rage that led to assault on a policeman, their negative answer suggests a degree of controllability that is always present except in the most psychotic or psychopathic individual.

This degree of controllability is modifiable by the therapist utilizing all the mechanisms available during the therapeutic hour and through the entire therapeutic collaboration. The therapist has the capacity to control the emotional realities. He can make the assault on the child as symbolically threatening as the assault on the cop. He can shift the allocations of fear, guilt, shame, and pride from one action to another, thus enlisting the patient's own emotions in the battle for health.

Acts of self-control and volition do occur. Common, ordinary citizens will perform acts of unselfishness and courage, even to the extreme of risking death, in the service of another, and these events are daily documented on the evening news. Even without therapy, people give up smoking and drinking, go on diets, leave secure jobs to enter new and challenging fields, get married and divorced, and have children — the ultimate act of faith and courage.

What a therapist can add in the battle against self-destructive behavior lies in her capacity to alter the metaphor by which her patient lives. The power of the old "reality" can be stripped away and a new gospel, collaboratively written by patient and therapist, substituted. In this new story, a fresh and durable identity is constructed for the patient, fitting him to play the role of hero in his own life, thus making the voyage into health a safer journey.

Too often in the past, psychological explanations for behavior rooted in the developmental past have led to the curse of psychic determinism. We cannot help what we do. Our parents, or lack thereof, made us antisocial. But we do not have to abandon volition to endorse the proposition that current behavior is always linked in some way to the past.

We do not have to defend freedom and responsibility by denying either the reality of inborn drives for pleasure and self-preservation or the existence of a will. The human being is a quixotic creature. There is room in this contradictory and perversely unpredictable nature for a modified determinism, in which individuals are capable of performing autonomous voluntary actions that are nonetheless influenced by perceptions shaped by past experience. This modified determinism, which psychoanalysts have settled for, preserves — if not the rigid autonomy of an Immanuel Kant — at least the autonomy necessary to allow for such notions as responsibility and culpability, doctrines essential to living in a free and democratic society.

14 Magic and Mystery

THERE ARE many things we know about how therapy works, but there is much we do not know and much that we will never know. For in discussing therapy, we are really examining one take on the great enigmas of human existence: the relation between perception and reality; the influences of learned ideas and principles on instinctive and reflexive behavior; the nature of human emotions and their influence on conduct; the mechanisms of learning; the devices available to induce or change patterns of behavior. These questions have relevance well beyond their operation in therapy. They are germane to child-rearing practices, educational institutions, public education campaigns, and the inhibition of antisocial behavior.

Let's review what we have learned from therapy and about therapy.

Motivation Is Essential

Motivation is the fuel that stokes the therapeutic machinery. Therapy is time-consuming, expensive, difficult, and painful. Worse, it is circuitous and its methods are obscure to the patient. In order to endure the kind of painful exposure and the kind of behavioral change demanded by the therapeutic process, the patient must feel prepared to do anything to get well. He must be highly motivated for therapy to have any chance of success.

So please do not send us your tired, your poor, your huddled masses yearning to breathe free. Do not *send* us anyone. Therapy cannot be directed by a court as an alternative to imprisonment, by a divorce lawyer as an alternative to divorce, by a family court judge as an alternative to losing the custody of a child. Coerced and mandated therapy, as in the case of prisoners and psychopathic adolescents, represents one of the greatest boondoggles within the mental health movement.

We Live in a World of Our Own Creation

All human perceptions contain distortions. Those distortions influence decision making and everyday conduct. What passes for self-awareness is often mere fantasy and delusion. The talent for self-deception is a universal one, and its power must never be underestimated. Over two thousand years ago the Stoic philosopher Epictetus said, "What disturbs and alarms man are not the things, but his opinions and fancies about the things."

The therapist's view of reality is also biased, but it is not biased in a way tailored to insure the continuation of the *patient's* neurosis. Therefore she is free to present her view of the actual world in refutation to the patient's distorted one. This bumping up against a real world will confound the patient's perceptions, frustrate and thwart his self-deceptions, and force him to confront and adapt to the world as it is, rather than the world as he misperceives it. Still, a degree of skepticism on the patient's part is always prudent. One must seek a therapist with the same caution, the same concerns, and the same diligence as one would a surgeon. Even then, mistakes will be made, and patients may find themselves in the hands of the unworthy and inept.

Part of the reality one must begin to encounter is the reality of one's therapist. The pressure to idealize her is enormous. One is entitled to note her limitations and comment about them. A well-trained therapist will not be "hurt." Entering therapy is not subscribing to a new religious orthodoxy. The good therapist will create a climate that encourages your skepticism, even about her. It is here that she will begin the process of training you to see the world, blemishes, threats, and all.

Past and Present: Both in Play

Whatever variations may exist in basic theory, all dynamic therapy inevitably must involve an engagement with the past. Distortions in the patient's view of reality exist today only because his past realities were so intense that they persist in clouding his vision in the present. For example, when a patient has suffered unmitigated rejection by her parents, the most essential figures in her early life, she will be prepared for rejections from all others. She will never perceive any authority figure as other than rejecting and will be unprepared to risk any engagement with trust that might disprove this generalization. Therefore, she will go through life confirming this biased view instead of learning from reality. She will constantly impose on the present the distortions of the past so she is free to say, "I knew it," or "I told you so." Intervening in this past, the therapist will force the backward-looking patient to turn around and face a different and undetermined future.

None of us truly knows the past. The glory of great biographers is that they can take the limited data of archival history and create an interpretation of the past (consonant with the facts) that leads us to accept their interpretation as depicting the actual event. There is no Antony more alive and "real" than Shakespeare's Antony. There is no Mary Stuart as compelling as Schiller's. We often dip into the past only to find justifications for the way we want to view the present. But in addition we can change the past.

One of the most telling discussions of the relationship of the present to the past occurs, typically, not in a psychiatric text, but in a distinguished novel. In John Barth's *The End of the Road,* Jake, the "hero," has been discovered having an affair with his friend Joe's wife. Jake has been despondent, suicidal, and frightened, anticipating his friend's response. Joe, surprisingly, confronts him not with anger, but with an intellectual insistence on finding the reasons for such behavior. Joe seems to prefer understanding to accountability. Joe is now revealed as a prototype of the ultramodern, psychoanalytically enlightened intellectual. What a relief for the scoundrel Jake:

> The notion of suicide no longer entered my head. . . . Indeed, I even found myself adding my former intense guilt feelings to the list of my other weaknesses, and consequently regretting it along with the rest. I felt no better about what I had done — fornicating with their wives behind my friends' backs and then deceiving them about it — but I felt *differently* about it. Now that it was out in the open I felt truly relieved and dealing concretely with Joe shifted the focus of my attention from my guilt to what I could do towards salvaging my self-respect. If I was going to live, I had to live with myself, and because much of the time I was a profoundly moral animal the salvage job was the first order of business. What had

been done had been done, *but the past, after all, exists only in the minds of those who are thinking about it in the present, and therefore in the interpretations which are put upon it* [emphasis added]. In that sense it is never too late to *do* something about the past.*

This is a good capsule summary of what happens in therapy — except that we therapists ought not alleviate the guilt that is present. The therapist wants a patient to feel appropriate guilt. It is, after all, one of the leading motivating forces to proper social conduct and good relationships.

The past is important, but the present must have a transcendent claim on our attention. The primary purpose of therapy is to influence the present and the future. A therapist who falls in love with the past, enchanted by its endless stories, is like the sultan listening to Scheherazade, postponing obligations of the present while the seductive patient leads him from one year of therapy to another.

The Therapist Must Find a Good Story

The therapist must be armed with a theoretical framework, a psychology of human motivation, a theory of human nature rich enough to do service to the complexities of the human condition. He must present the patient with a good story, a reasonable gospel (*gut spiel*) to which he ascribes the truth.

No story can encompass the complexity of even one human being, let alone the human species. That is why differing stories may coexist each having some claim to validity,

---

*John Barth, *The End of the Road* (New York: Avon, 1960), pp. 89–90.

since each will only take one aspect of the total person, allowing that fragment to represent the whole. Each story will be another window into the black box of individual existence. Each theoretician must find what the novelist Henry James called his own "compositional key" in which to write his story. That narrative line will constitute the boundaries within which the small pieces of the jigsaw puzzle, the dynamics and defenses, will be contained and combined, fabricating the total picture of a personality.

The story line may be Freud's Oedipus complex; it may be Harry Stack Sullivan's emphasis on interpersonal relationships; it may be Rado's insistence on the profound influence of dependency. These are all good stories. They all contain within them versions of the reality of childhood and a view of development that is consonant with the basic biological facts as we now understand them. Otto Rank's view of adult behavior as being predetermined by the nature of our "birth traumas" will not suffice. It is not rich enough. It is too arbitrary. It is not a gospel that any major portion of the world can buy.

The therapist's story must also be consistent with his general knowledge of the specific patient. It cannot be a one-size-fits-all story. If one holds that "all neurosis is the result of forcing a square peg into a round hole," the therapist must not define either the hole or the peg in arbitrary or stereotypical terms. He must search the patient's history for the right angles that will define the singular "squareness" of that patient's identity, while examining the arcs of history that demarcate the particular "circularity" of the patient's developmental environment.

In a recent article (1997) in the *Journal of the American Psychiatric Association*, psychiatrist Theodore Jacobs said, "Only a fraction of what transpires in a given hour is available, to either patient or analyst, for conscious recognition or useful interpretation." Jacobs is absolutely correct. A therapist will select out of the mass of data that which will help complete his story. No story will ever be truly complete; only a fraction of what transpired in the patient's past, only a fraction of what formed the patient as we now know him, will ever be available to either therapist or patient. Therefore no story ever captures the whole person. In therapy we are always dealing with only a small particle of the patient's life, but the fragment we select must be a representation, like a DNA sample, that can stand for the patient as a whole.

The therapist constructs a metaphoric profile, a representative sample, from the jumbled mass of historic events that he can, with justification, use to represent the individual. The story must support all that he knows of the patient's feelings and conduct. While his story can never encompass the whole truth, it must always be a part of the truth. The representation, in other words, must be *authentic.*

The story must not be only a summary of the past but a scenario for the future. In his remarkable novel *The End of the Road,* John Barth continues with this insight: "To turn experience into speech — that is, to classify, to categorize, to conceptualize, to grammarize, to syntactify it — is always a betrayal of experience, a falsification of it; but only so betrayed can it be dealt with at all."* We must take our "falsification," our "betrayal of experience," and use it to reshape the future by modifying the present.

Finally, whatever scenario one uses must be consonant with our biological understanding of human nature and the human condition. It must acknowledge and incorporate some

---

*Op. cit., p. 96.

of the known facts that define the unique quality of human life:

- The unprecedented dependency of the human infant. This shapes all future awareness of one's relationship with others and dependence on them.
- The obligate social nature of human life. We are not true individuals like the amoeba, but colonial creatures that require the presence of other human beings for survival. Our very individual nature as a human being cannot emerge in isolation, but must be nurtured in relations with others.
- The uniqueness of human freedom. Unshackled from the chains of instinctual fixation that bind all other animals to an essentially rigid and predictable existence, we alone are capable of reinventing ourselves and the environment in which we reside. We can, for good and evil, define the terms of our own existence. Rousseau eloquently summarized this: "Nature commands every animal and the creature obeys. Man feels the same impetus, but he realizes that he is free to acquiesce or resist." This inevitably makes man "tyrant of himself and of Nature."*
- Human imagination. We not only think better than all other animals, we think differently. Kant, in struggling to define the special quality of human thinking, drew the illuminating distinction between knowledge of the "real" and knowledge of the possible. Only man possesses the knowledge of the possible, that which does not yet exist beyond his own perceptions. This grants us the power to design the multiple worlds we will live in, both real and imagined.

---

*J. Rousseau, *The First and Second Discourses*, R. D. Masters, ed. (New York: St. Martin's, 1964), pp. 113–115.

Knowledge Has Limits

In changing human conduct there will always be limits to the power of knowledge. Therapists must be humble in that awareness. Knowledge is important. As sources of knowledge, dreams and free association are particularly useful. But knowledge alone is rarely transforming. The power of his emotions severely limits the patient's ability to act on the basis of his cognitive judgment as to what he ought to do.

An exception may be when one points out *to a person of conscience* that a piece of behavior is violating his own principles. That knowledge may change him. This is popularly known as consciousness-raising. There is abundant evidence that when one points out to a person of goodwill that a particular form of speech or piece of behavior is patronizing or hurtful to another or a group of others, he will change that behavior. But that is the exception, not the basic stuff of psychotherapy or life. Insight generally cures nothing but ignorance, certainly not behavior.

Emotions Are the True Instruments for Change

Here is where the therapist has the long arm of the lever; the patient's emotions supply the only source of power capable of shifting the weights of conduct. By alleviating fear, reinforcing conscience mechanisms, intensifying guilt where absent, encouraging pride, reducing inappropriate shame, the power of the emotions can be mobilized to force actions to change behavior from self-destructive to self-fulfilling. What is true for the therapist is equally valid for all who would change behavior.

In all effective advertising, whether product advertisements or behavior-changing attempts, it is not the knowledge that is transmitted but the emotion that is engendered that stimulates to action. Smoking kills. That is the necessary message. But the message will only be heard and acted upon when the patient perceives that *his* smoking is actually killing *him*. No communication that does not connect to the emotional arena in which the patient is operating will produce anything approaching a change.

The regressive aspects inherent in the psychoanalytic situation enhance the power of the therapist to mobilize the patient's emotions. The therapist can no longer deny this. The therapist is, willy-nilly, perceived as the daddy and mommy who must be pleased. He is also perceived as the doctor with the power to confer either health or sickness on the patient, thus further enhancing his authority. The need to please the therapist is a potent force in conforming the patient's behavior to healthy standards, and it ought to be used unapologetically. This has often been dismissed contemptuously as a "transference cure," as though the reason for change is more important than the change itself. Who knows how Prozac works on depression? It works. As in much of medicine, the empirical is all we have, and that is often enough.

Change Must Occur in the "Real" World

Change may occur first in the transference, but it doesn't count until taken out of the cloister of the therapeutic relationship and placed in the real world of relationships. Through the power of the corrective emotional experience, the patient learns to trust at least one person, the therapist. But one is not enough, since by definition the therapeutic relationship will be — or ought be — a limited one. The therapist must not be beguiled by transference revelations or changes but must insist on seeing them only as a prototype, a first step that must be transferable to the way the patient treats his wife, boss, child, colleague, employee, friends, and all the other people who define the social world of his reality.

In addition to these theoreticals, there are some practical matters that arise inherently from the previous discussion.

Finding the Right Therapist Is Crucial

It is not easy to find a trained therapist. The terms are confusing. "Psychiatrist," "psychoanalyst," "psychologist," and "therapist" are similar terms often describing the same person, but often not. Suppose we start with the psychiatrist who becomes a psychoanalyst. This was the original model for talking therapy, but it now represents a minority of the therapists practicing in the field.

After graduating college and completing four years of medical training, a year of internship, and three years of psychiatric residency, a person becomes a psychiatrist. The term "psychiatrist" describes a medical specialist. It is in every way equivalent to the terms "neurologist," "obstetrician," "oncologist," and the like. The term is protected by law and registry, and one cannot call oneself a psychiatrist unless one has completed residency and passed psychiatric boards to determine one's fitness to practice psychiatry. This is not dissimilar to what a surgeon or dermatologist must do if he wishes to be board certified. During or after the last years of psychiatric residency, the candidate psychoanalyst would enroll in a psychoanalytic school and then spend four to seven years getting certification as a psychoanalyst.

What, then, is psychoanalysis? Psychoanalysis refers to a theory of behavior and a form of therapy evolved out of the work of Freud and some of his followers. It is a body of thought that some psychiatrists subscribe to and some don't. In the orthodox world of the psychiatric community, psychoanalysis was an extension of psychiatric training.

There is another, parallel route to psychoanalysis, much less popularized than the medical route but equally rigorous. One goes to college, majors in psychology, enrolls in a graduate program to become a clinical psychologist (one who treats patients, as distinguished from a research or testing psychologist), receives a Ph.D. in psychology, and then seeks private supervision or enrolls in a psychoanalytic school that is prepared to take nonmedical students (once rare, now common). This training, although different, is quite demanding and in many ways equivalent to the medical route. Most clinical psychologists are as well trained in their specific discipline as are the physicians. We are currently witnessing the demedicalization of psychoanalysis. As the status of psychoanalysis diminishes in the medical community, fewer and fewer physicians are becoming analysts.

A third way to become a psychoanalyst is to hang out a shingle saying "Psychoanalyst." It doesn't matter whether your training was as a bartender, teacher, social worker, minister, or ex-patient. I do not mean disparagement to any of the respectable professions in the list I just gave. Rather, I want to show that the term "psychoanalyst" is both ill defined and unregulated; it offers no assurance of training or expertise. Any human being may call himself a psychoanalyst. The term "therapist" is even less reassuring. In the name of therapy, all sorts of indignities and depravities have been foisted on a vulnerable population.

But rigorous training is essential to be able to understand human conduct and perversity. It is essential to understanding oneself as a therapist. The credentials of a prospective therapist should be open for examination and discussion. In seeking a therapist, one should have at least as much data available as in seeking a cardiac surgeon. It is not insulting to ask your therapist for his training record, his certifications, and the like.

While proper qualifications are a necessary requirement, they are not in themselves sufficient. Someone must sift through the "qualified" to find the quality. As in every other profession, from lawyer to caddy, the talented are a small minority. The source of any referral is critical. It is not foolish to go to an accepted authority in medicine, one's internist, for example, and ask for a referral. Nor is it a betrayal of the therapeutic relationship to ask for a second opinion or a consultation at any time during the course of the therapy. The therapist who takes this as an assault on his dignity or pride is an untrained therapist and ought to be abandoned forthwith.

Having said all this, the best of therapists may not be the best for any given patient. The persona of the therapist is important, although this is a point that is still widely contended in many psychotherapeutic circles. The assumption has always been that, as with the good brain surgeon, the skills and training are essential but the personality does not count. Personality *does* count. Whenever I refer a patient for therapy, I tell him or her that any referral I make will be to a person with integrity, intelligence, and proper training. Still, I insist, the patient is entitled to, indeed must, make the final selection. There are too many unknowns in the therapeutic process.

In many ways a referral is analogous to "fixing up" two friends. Objectively each seems admirably suited for the other. Each is a delight to us, and therefore, we think, they will be a delight to each other. Alas, it does not work this way. Buying a tie for a good friend is difficult enough; finding a mate who subscribes to the proper intellectual and physical dimensions is a major challenge. A therapist is at least as difficult a match. I always inform patients whom I am referring that their personal and subjective response is important. I tell them that if I have referred them to three different people and they still remain unsatisfied, they must look to their own motivation. It is also true that there are some patients who will hunt and hunt until they find the perfectly *inadequate* person for their needs, someone who is not threatening and whom they can control.

Some Problems Are Harder Than Others

Ironically, difficulties in therapy are not directly proportional to the severity of illness. In these days of effective antidepressant drugs, depression — a profoundly debilitating disease — has a reasonably good expectation for success, while a moderately well functioning patient with a severely passive personality who aspires to change may be a real challenge. Three enemies of the psychotherapeutic process are psychopathy (antisocial behavior), paranoia, and passivity.

The true psychopath is the hopeless case. He has no guilt, no shame, no conscience, and therefore all therapy is wasted on him. The tragic news, which no one wants to hear — particularly legislators — is that the psychopathic teenager is usually beyond reach. A sixteen-year-old who has been deprived of all legitimate childhood claims for love, care, parents, affection, and a decent environment; who has been neglected and abandoned on the streets of the city; and who has emerged as a crack addict without remorse, prepared to earn his living by smacking old ladies over the head with a lead pipe, is unlikely to be helped by any amount of mental health clinics or psychotherapeutic maneuvers. Such people constitute a lost generation with whom only the use of such basic emotions as fear of punishment, and containment for the protection of society, are likely to work. Old age eventually diminishes the threat of the psychopath. The proper focus for society is in the early stages of infancy, where psychopathy can be inhibited and where conscience, love, and attachment can be imbued.

A more tractable problem is the paranoid. Paranoid patients are difficult but treatable. Their difficulty lies in their incapacity to trust anyone. Some powerful parental figure in their past has betrayed their trust, leaving such a sense of vulnerability and pain that they dare not risk repetition. The lesson, rarely explicitly acknowledged, is that no one is to be trusted. Safety is their primary quest. The paranoid abandons pleasure for purposes of security, sacrificing hope to deflect defeat. Better to do without than to hope and be disappointed. The paranoid goes through life armed, as in a tank, against the assault and disappointment of rejection, always prepared to quit before getting fired. Since trust in the therapist is so essential, the early stages of therapy with a paranoid individual are extraordinarily difficult.

Passivity is the other great enemy. A passive patient will find the solution to all his problems in the therapy itself. Rather than being seen as a means to an end, the therapy becomes the end. The patient has found a new and better parent, and he is prepared to live with that parent. The therapist must not permit this to happen. Too many will. It is a major problem that is the residue of early misreading of psychoanalytic procedures, and therefore I raise this caution one more time: A passive patient in the hands of a passive therapist is on an extended journey to nowhere.

Therapy Takes Time

The new vogue for quick therapy of four to five sessions is an accommodation to the economics of modern medicine. Brief interventions are fine as diagnostic preludes to drug therapy, or for crisis interventions with a patient who has an essentially healthy psyche. Brief therapy is a form of sophisticated advice giving and may be helpful, but ingrained neuroses require time. No therapy that attempts to solve a lifetime problem in adaptation can be resolved in less than a year.

The length of therapy varies widely, depending on a number of conditions. It must not be viewed as an indication of the intensity or malignancy of the disease. It is true that some schizophrenic patients will need a therapeutic relationship throughout their lives. But some prolonged therapies are products of the ambitious desire of a relatively healthy patient for a new way of life.

Therapy Is an Art, Not a Science

Even bad therapists get *some* good results, and many good therapists have a significant number of failures, thus raising the question of the scientific nature of the enterprise. Therapy is not a science, certainly not yet. I suspect it will never be. We have barely scratched the surface in our knowledge of normal mental functioning — intelligence, memory, learning — and therefore are equally limited in our understanding of abnormal mental functioning.

Even with strongly motivated patients presenting with traditional symptoms we have our humbling defeats. And they are humbling. The only solace is that we psychotherapists are dealing with the most complex, least understood, most noble, and most majestic aspect of human nature. We are dealing with the human mind, God's or nature's greatest creation. To choose to work in such a field requires a certain humility. The frustration must be endured. The failures must be tolerated. The likelihood of our progressing much further in the near future is not great.

We have made progress in some "therapies," but not particularly in psychotherapy. We now have promising drugs for the specific treatment of depression, panic, and obsessive disorders. Still, drugs alone rarely solve the more profound problems in adjustment that accompany the conditions. They will generally require our attending not just to the brain or the chemistry of the individual, but to her mind and soul.

Psychotherapy is a flawed and imperfect instrument, but it is the vehicle that transports both therapist and patient on a journey of discovery, a voyage into health. When therapy works the patient is returned to health beyond the mere restoration of basic capacities — ambulation, vision, audition — that occurs in other branches of medicine. He is transported from the grief and despair of a constricted and limited existence into the broad highways and vast horizons that define the human experience.

Therapy as a Metaphor

Psychotherapy is a means of treating mental illness, but it is also a device for understanding human behavior in general. Psychotherapy operates in a small room, in a limited relationship with unique rules. But that room has a doorway opening into the larger world of experience and offers a special vision of human nature that illuminates the same rules of conduct that are operative in the family, in the workplace, in the public spaces.

After decades of research into the nature and operations of that most spectacular of living creatures, *Homo sapiens*, I am left with the same feelings of awe, wonderment, and delight. The mystery and complexity of human existence confound the modern-day biologist and psychologist as they did the psalmists twenty-five hundred years ago: "What is man, that Thou art mindful of him? and the son of man, that Thou visitest him? For Thou hast made him but little lower than the angels, and hast crowned him with glory and honour" (Ps. 8:4–5).

The attempt to understand "what is man" has been a central driving force for intellectuals for as long as there has been recorded history. What is it about this special creature that separates him from the general animal host, placing him "but little lower than the angels"? In modern times the pursuits of the poets and philosophers have been joined by biologists and psychologists, none more ardent and persistent than Sigmund Freud.

Sigmund Freud, the father of modern dynamic psychotherapy, is currently held in such minimal repute as to guarantee an early rediscovery and resurrection. Freud was, admittedly, an imperfect psychiatrist with a somewhat narrow view of mental illness, but let me reiterate the fundamental statement with which I started my discussion of Freud. In exploring mental illness, he stumbled into something vastly more important. He began the systematic exploration of human behavior, the first modern attempt to understand the normal, everyday, wonderful, and wacky ways of human conduct.

We live in a perceptual world in great part built with Freudian constructs. We talk of unconscious wishes, repressed desires, sublimations, and projections. We look to the past to explain present behavior. We accept a continuum of life from the way the child is treated to the manner in which the adult will behave, and we adjust our social institutions to conform to that recognition. We want to know what motivates man for good and bad. We know the limits of rationality and the nature of rationalizations. And we know that if we wish to change behavior — in therapy or outside — we will do well to start with understanding borrowed from the world of psychotherapy.

By exploring the mechanisms of psychotherapy, we go beyond the interests of the therapist and the needs of the patient and enter the general world of normal human existence. Asking how psychotherapy really works is simply another way of exploring the unfathomable depths of human nature. We are never likely to solve the riddle of human existence. This was clearly understood by the writers of Genesis when they said that we are created in the image of God, the unknowable. Yet each generation stubbornly strives to solve the same riddle, exploiting new instruments and new knowledge. It is the nature and glory of our species to challenge the unknown and to attempt the impossible.

Acknowledgments

This work, unlike my others, is drawn more from my practice than my readings or research. My patients are therefore uncredited coauthors of this book.

My editor, Bill Phillips, earns his living the old-fashioned way. He actually edits. By that I mean he read, criticized, and improved this manuscript. I was introduced to him by my agent, Owen Laster, who has supported my writing career for more years than I like to admit.

The most onerous of tasks, reading the raw and unrefined first draft, must be imposed on only the toughest of friends. This time, as often in the past, Bob Michaels has been assigned that burden. Copyediting the final draft, and improving every page, was the task of my developmental editor, Peggy Leith Anderson.

Over these many years I have had the perspicacity to raise, or to acquire through my daughters' marriages, a savvy if unsparing family of critics. To the usual suspects — Jody and Andrew Heyward, and Ellen and Clinton Smith — have been added a bevy of grandchildren: David, Emily, and Sarah Heyward, and Laura and Charlie Smith, now all of an age to put their oars in. Sarah was, indeed, part of the endless debate about the title.

To all of these noble and generous souls, I am grateful.

It becomes increasingly difficult, however, to "acknowledge" my wife, Betty. After a lifetime of love and engagement, we now share a common identity. One acknowledges "others," not oneself. And I have no idea where I leave off and she begins.

Index